WISE WORDS

STEPHEN TROMBLEY is a writer, editor and Emmy Award-winning film-maker. He collaborated with Alan Bullock on the second edition of *The Fontana Dictionary of Modern Thought* (1988), and was editor of *The New Fontana Dictionary of Modern Thought* (1999). His books include *The Execution Protocol*; *Sir Frederick Treves: The Extraordinary Edwardian*; *The Right to Reproduce*; *All That Summer She was Mad: Virginia Woolf and Her Doctors*; *Fifty Thinkers Who Shaped the Modern World* and *A History of Western Thought*.

THE PHILOSOPHY OF EVERYDAY LIFE

WISE WORDS

STEPHEN TROMBLEY

First published in the UK in 2016 by Head of Zeus Ltd

This paperback edition first published in the UK in 2017 by Head of Zeus Ltd

1 3 5 7 9 10 8 6 4 2

A CIP catalogue record for this book is available from the British Library.

ISBN (PB) 9781784976521
(E) 9781784971304

Designed and typeset by Broadbase

Printed and bound by CPI Group (UK) Ltd, Croydon, CR0 4YY

Head of Zeus Ltd
Clerkenwell House
45–47 Clerkenwell Green
London EC1R 0HT

www.headofzeus.com

For Colleen Murphy, with love and gratitude

CONTENTS

INTRODUCTION

The aim of this little miscellany is both to amuse and to inform the reader as I have been amused and informed while writing it. I was generously given free rein to gallop across the whole spectrum of subjects covered by philosophy, and back and forth in time, to inquire what philosophers thought about those subjects in any given era. It has been a wild journey, and I've done my best here to give an account of it.

While there has been some method to my work, whimsy is the chief criterion I employed in deciding what subjects to write about and which philosophers' thoughts on them to include. I present some of the greatest minds in history reflecting on topics that might be found in an agony column: Advice, Backbiting, Day Jobs, Drugs, Extraterrestrials, Friendship, Fun, Haircuts, Laughing, Sex, Sport and Walking. I also gather their thoughts on subjects which we might more usually expect to be treated in a philosophy book: Belief, Consciousness, Duty, Freedom, Intuition, Truth, War and others like them.

If I were composing an anthology of philosophy, as opposed to a miscellany, I would have a certain duty to the reader to be inclusive. But I'm not and I don't. Because it's a miscellany, I am at liberty to include – and exclude – anything that takes my fancy. My method has been this: each treatment of a subject under discussion here usually begins with the thoughts of the ancient Greeks, then moves progressively to the present. One reason why the Greeks get first shout is that they were the first thinkers in the West to consider these topics. After the Greeks, Roman, scholastic, Renaissance, Enlightenment, idealist, naturalist, empiricist, analytic, continental and other thinkers all get a look-in. I leave it to the reader to decide, as we work our way through the ages, whether subsequent thinkers improved upon Greek ideas. In many cases valuable clarification and introduction of new subtleties has occurred. In other cases, later thinking has offered more obfuscation than explication (*see pages* 287–94).

The ancient Greeks are usually clear in their definition of a problem and the proposed solution. There was for centuries a kind of unspoken rule among subsequent philosophers that they, too, should strive for clarity in their prose, and this continued up until the late eighteenth century and the rise of German idealism. Then, philosophers like G. W. F. Hegel earned a well-deserved reputation for dense and opaque writing; for the introduction of jargon and unnecessary neologisms. The result is often – as in the case of the twentieth-century German thinkers Edmund Husserl and Martin Heidegger – writing that is nothing less than execrable. This tendency caught hold, and marks much of what is called 'continental philosophy' in the twentieth and twenty-first centuries. My aim throughout *Wise Words* has been to find passages in the works of even the most difficult philosophers that are clear and which speak directly to a non-professional audience on subjects that might concern them, but whose concern is not great enough to justify hours of wading through turgid text.

One might ask why I've bothered to do this, given that it is no small task. I could reply that I took it on in the spirit of the Roman poet Horace, who famously declared that 'Poets wish either to instruct or to delight.'* One can also combine the two, and that is my intention. In my years of reading philosophy I have always found it instructive, if sometimes a hard slog. But on many occasions I have been delighted – charmed – with the observations, arguments or conclusions of philosophers. It is those charmed moments that I wish to share here.

A final word about the modest apparatus of this book. Because I presume it is to be sampled as a 'dipping-in' book rather than read straight through, I had to find a way of indicating the relevant eras in which individual thinkers were active without repeating myself ad infinitum. The solution is simple: a directory of philosophers consulted, including their dates, nationality and a brief description, which appears at the back of the book. I have also included a bibliography of secondary works cited, a list of internet sites where classic philosophy texts can be consulted and a brief note about online philosophy encyclopaedias. Since many of the ideas discussed by philosophers under one heading have relevance to other entries in the book, I have included a system of cross-references. Each development of an idea within sections is assigned a roman numeral. This way, cross-references may be made in the style (*see* FRIENDSHIP iv).

Philosophy is an endless task; even a lifetime's reading would give us an incomplete account of it. I make no claim to inclusiveness in this present exercise. However, I do hope that anyone who has absorbed its contents might have gained at least a passing acquaintance with Western philosophers and their ideas, and be stimulated to inquire further.

---

* '*Aut prodesse volunt aut delectare poetae.*' *Ars Poetica* (c.19 BC).

SOME THINGS

TORMENT

US WHEN THEY OUGHT NOT
TO TORMENT US **AT ALL**

THE WISE MAN
CAN SAFELY CONTROL
HIMSELF
WITHOUT BECOMING
OVER-ANXIOUS

Hold every hour in your GRASP

CHAPTER ONE

ADVICE

RENOUNCE ALL STIMULANTS,
INCLUDING LIQUEURS,
WINE, COFFEE AND TOBACCO;
**EAT SIMPLE,
SUBSTANTIAL MEALS**

?

NOTHING is so damaging to
good character as the habit

of

LOUNGING AT THE GAMES

i **SOCRATES CONSULTED THE ORACLE AT DELPHI.** *
We know this from Xenophon, one of the master's lesser-known
students. Xenophon tells of it in *The Memorabilia* (*c.*371):
'"The divinity," said he, "gives me a sign." Further, he would
constantly advise his associates to do this, or beware of doing
that, upon the authority of this same divine voice; and, as a
matter of fact, those who listened to his warnings prospered,
whilst he who turned a deaf ear to them repented afterwards.'

Xenophon reports that Socrates did not advise seeking the
oracle's advice on 'the ordinary necessities of life'; to do so, he
taught, was a type of profanity. In everyday matters he urged
his students to 'Act as you believe these things may best be
done'. But, 'in the case of those darker problems, the issues of
which are incalculable, he directed his friends to consult the
oracle, whether the business should be undertaken or not'.

As an advice-giver, Socrates practised what he preached. For
instance, he counselled thrift. Xenophon again: 'a man must
work little indeed who could not earn the quantum which con-
tented Socrates'. He was frugal where food and drink were
concerned; but Xenophon noted how, in frugality, Socrates
found pleasure. 'Of food he took just enough to make eating
a pleasure – the appetite he brought to it was sauce sufficient.'
The same with drink: 'seeing that he only drank when thirsty,
any draught refreshed'. Overindulgence in food and drink, said
Socrates, is 'bad for stomachs, brains, and soul alike'. And it
is not only physical health that is promoted by moderation in
food and drink: one's wits were also preserved: 'It must have

---

* Pythia, priestess of Delphi – more commonly known as the Delphic Oracle.
The Pythia is believed to have originated in the eighth century BC, with her last
response given around AD 395. Upon the death of each priestess, a new one was
selected.

been by feasting men on so many dainty dishes that Circe produced her pigs.'*

Thoughts of Circe lead Xenophon to reflect on Socrates' advice regarding male sexual desire for women. 'His advice was to hold strongly aloof from the fascination of fair forms: once lay finger on these and it is not easy to keep a sound head and a sober mind.' He likened a woman's kiss to that of a poisonous spider bite:

do you imagine that these lovely creatures infuse nothing with their kiss, simply because you do not see the poison? Do you not know that this wild beast which men call beauty in its bloom is all the more terrible than the tarantula in that the insect must first touch its victim, but this at a mere glance of the beholder, without even contact, will inject something into him – yards away – which will make him man? And may be that is why the Loves are called 'archers', because these beauties wound so far off. But my advice to you, Xenophon, is, whenever you catch sight of one of these fair forms, to run helter-skelter for bare life without a glance behind.

...... ● ......

ii **SENECA THE YOUNGER**, a Stoic philosopher of the first century AD, is famous for having dispensed advice to the Roman emperor Nero, whose tutor he had been. While acting as Nero's counsellor between AD 54 and AD 62 he also gave advice in

---

* In Homer's *Odyssey*, Odysseus's crew/companions are turned into swine by the island-dwelling sorceress Circe, after they have gorged themselves on a stew of cheese, meal and honey laced with a magic potion. Odysseus himself resists Circe's enchantments and later spends a year in her palace.

the form of a series of letters to Lucilius Junior, procurator of Sicily. *Moral Letters to Lucilius* is an important Stoic text and was a major influence on the sixteenth-century French philosopher Michel de Montaigne whose *Essays* (1580) include 'ON DEFENCE OF SENECA AND PLUTARCH'.

Seneca wrote 124 letters to Lucilius on topics as diverse as saving time, crowds, groundless fears, travel as a cure for discontent, the relativity of fame, asthma and death, quiet and study, pleasure and joy, harmful prayers, meeting death cheerfully, good company, taking one's own life, drunkenness and self-control. Seneca advised that time is our most valuable resource. 'Whatever years be behind us', he says, 'are in death's hands.' 'Hold every hour in your grasp. Lay hold of today's task, and you will not need to depend so much upon tomorrow's. While we are postponing, life speeds by.'

Seneca did not like crowds, and advised young Lucilius to avoid them. 'To consort with the crowd is harmful; there is no person who does not make some vice attractive to us, or stamp it upon us, or taint us unconsciously therewith. Certainly, the greater the mob with which we mingle, the greater the danger.' Seneca particularly warned against attending 'the games' (Roman gladiatorial contests, in which spectators watched armed combatants fight to the death). 'Nothing is so damaging to good character as the habit of lounging at the games; for then it is that vice steals subtly upon one through the avenue of pleasure. What do you think I mean? I mean that I come home more greedy, more ambitious, more voluptuous, and even more cruel and inhuman, because I have been among human beings.'

Seneca identifies 'groundless fear' as a great troubler of souls. He offers advice that is at once tough-minded and reassuring as a mother's touch:

There are more things, Lucilius, likely to frighten us than there are to crush us; we suffer more often in imagination than in reality. I am not speaking with you in the Stoic strain but in my milder style. For it is our Stoic fashion to speak of all those things, which provoke cries and groans, as unimportant and beneath notice; but you and I must drop such great-sounding words, although, heaven knows, they are true enough. What I advise you to do is, not to be unhappy before the crisis comes; since it may be that the dangers before which you paled as if they were threatening you, will never come upon you; they certainly have not yet come. Accordingly, some things torment us more than they ought; some torment us before they ought; and some torment us when they ought not to torment us at all. We are in the habit of exaggerating, or imagining, or anticipating, sorrow.

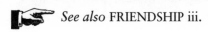 *See also* FRIENDSHIP iii.

...... ● ......

iii **ONE OF SENECA'S** more curiously titled letters is 'On asthma and death'. In it the philosopher uses his own experience as a lifelong asthma sufferer to contemplate mortality. Seneca tells Lucilius that death poses no test for him; rather, he tests death. Death is nothing but non-existence, Seneca says; 'What was before me will happen again after me.' Lest Lucilius find this view bleak, Seneca writes: 'I ask you, would you not say that one was the greatest of fools who believed that a lamp was worse off when it was extinguished than before it was lighted? We mortals also are lighted and extinguished; the period of suffering comes in between, but on either side there is a deep peace.'

Self-control is a cornerstone of Stoicism, and Seneca's letter on that subject is uncompromising in its advice. He addresses a range of emotions, including grief over the death of a friend and feeling 'down' when learning that others hold a bad opinion of one. He cautions that too much emotion of any kind is a vice. 'The wise man can safely control himself without becoming over-anxious,' says Seneca; 'he can halt his tears and his pleasures at will.' But, he cautions – and it is a radical 'but' – 'in our case, because it is not easy to retrace our steps, it is best not to push ahead at all'. Imagining his reader's reaction to what Seneca knew might appear harsh, he wrote:

I think that Panaetius* gave a very neat answer to a certain youth who asked him whether the wise man should become a lover: 'As to the wise man, we shall see later; but you and I, who are as yet far removed from wisdom, should not trust ourselves to fall into a state that is disordered, uncontrolled, enslaved to another, contemptible to itself. If our love be not spurned, we are excited by its kindness; if it be scorned, we are kindled by our pride. An easily won love hurts us as much as one which is difficult to win; we are captured by that which is compliant, and we struggle with that which is hard. Therefore, knowing our weakness, let us remain quiet. Let us not expose this unstable spirit to the temptations of drink, or beauty, or flattery, or anything that coaxes and allures.'

Seneca addresses the question of suicide in 'On taking one's own life'. He proposes the example of his friend Tullius Marcellinus who had aged prematurely from a debilitating but

---

* Panaetius of Rhodes, a Stoic of the second century BC.

not fatal disease. Today we would say that Tullius's 'quality of life' had declined – so much so that he needed assistance to carry out his plan to commit suicide. He asked his slaves to help him, but they, holding him in high regard, refused. Tullius consulted a Stoic, who advised him to parcel out his worth in gifts to his slaves. He fasted for three days. When he was near death, 'a tub was brought in; he lay in it for a long time, and, as the hot water was continually poured over him, he gradually passed away, not without a feeling of pleasure, as he himself remarked, – such a feeling as a slow dissolution is wont to give. Those of us who have ever fainted know from experience what this feeling is.' And so Tullius died. 'Though he committed suicide,' Seneca reflects, 'yet he withdrew most gently, gliding out of life.'

Seneca takes the individual example of Tullius to make a universal point. He asks what we would think of a man who wept because he was not alive a thousand years ago. A fool, of course. 'And is he not just as much of a fool who weeps because he will not be alive a thousand years from now?' And then he delivers the factual, incontrovertible judgement of Stoicism: 'It is all the same; you will not be, and you were not. Neither of these periods of time belongs to you.'

Seneca's letter about Tullius's suicide presaged his own death in AD 65. There was a plot against the life of the increasingly despotic Emperor Nero. Seneca was suspected, and Nero ordered him to commit suicide. He slit his writs and bled to death in a hot bath, surrounded by friends – a homage to Socrates.

...... ● ......

iv **THE FIFTEENTH-CENTURY** Florentine politician and philosopher Niccolò di Bernardo dei Machiavelli wrote the most enduring advice for those who would govern. *The Prince* (1532) is a handbook for rulers that reached a large and popular audience because it was written in the Italian vernacular rather than Latin. Forthright and secular in its outline of what we now call political science, *The Prince* is full of practical advice of 'the end justifies the means' variety. It spawned the eponymous noun 'Machiavellianism': 'the employment of cunning and duplicity in statecraft or in general conduct'.*

There is a great deal of common sense in Machiavelli, and his advice on how to rule is often given with an eye to just and peaceful outcomes. In his chapter 'CONCERNING THE WAY TO GOVERN CITIES OR PRINCIPALITIES WHICH LIVED UNDER THEIR OWN LAWS BEFORE THEY WERE ANNEXED' he considers the fact that prior to annexation, citizens of states had 'been accustomed to live under their own laws and in freedom'. This presents a problem of governance for the new ruler to which Machiavelli sees three solutions. 'The first is to ruin them, the next is to reside there in person, the third is to permit them to live under their own laws, drawing a tribute, and establishing within it an oligarchy which will keep it friendly to you.' An oligarchic government 'knows that it cannot stand without his [the ruler's] friendship and interest'. So, what does it do? It 'does its utmost to support him'. The result, Machiavelli forecasts, is that 'he who would keep a city accustomed to freedom will hold it more easily by the means of its own citizens than in any other way'. The worldly ethics of *The Prince* offended the Church, which placed it on the *Index*

---

* *Oxford English Dictionary.*

Librorum Prohibitorum (the papacy's list of heretical, anti-clerical or lascivious books; *see also* TRUTH vi).

...... ● ......

v **THE FRENCH THINKER** Isidore Auguste Marie François Xavier Comte – better known as Auguste Comte – presented his positivist philosophy in the six-volume *The Course in Positive Philosophy*, published between 1830 and 1842. *The Course* outlined a theory of social progress – 'The Law of Three Stages' – to explain man's evolutionary journey from a 'Theological Stage' (belief in gods or God) to an intermediate 'Metaphysical Stage' and, finally, the 'Positivist Stage'. Comte's thinking would later inform the development of sociology as a discipline. In the 1850s he founded a secular religion, the Religion of Humanity, whose followers built churches in France and Brazil.*

In 1854 Comte received a letter from Henry Edger, an American disciple of his work. Edger was a seeker who sought utopian happiness in the anarchist community called Modern Times (1851–64), founded in Brentwood, Long Island, New York, by Josiah Warren and Stephen Pearl Andrews. Rather than high-minded liberation from social rules, however, what Edger found at Modern Times was free love. He overindulged sexually to the point where he was spiritually and physically ill. He wrote to Comte, whose positivist philosophy appealed to him, for advice. He told Comte that he suffered from 'a

---

* The words in Portuguese *Ordem e Progresso* ('Order and Progress') in the flag of Brazil are inspired by Comte's positivist motto: *L'amour pour principe et l'ordre pour base; le progrès pour but* ('Love as a principle and order as the basis; Progress as the goal').

dull aching pain at the very extremity of the spinal column' and 'nervous paroxysms' which were first noticed 'after sexual orgasm', but then often and at random. He also suffered from 'a dull, heavy pain in the testicles'.

Edger now styled himself as the disciple of a 'Reverent Authority' (i.e. Comte). He sought liberation from the 'baseness' and 'degrading venality of the metaphysical Ringleaders' of the Modern Times community. He wanted to be liberated from 'slavery to corporeal necessities'. He had learned that indulging sexual desire was 'degrading' and it led to a 'brutal despotism which... defaces Human Society'. He further learned from Comte that positivism would be his salvation from free love, spiritualism and democracy. Edger signs off telling Comte he feels better already for his 'confession'.

Comte generously shared this advice with Edger. He began with a confession of his own, relating that 'From puberty to thirty, I was myself extremely troubled by the sexual instinct, which I finally surmounted in a complete manner, despite its pronounced energy in my natural constitution.' And then he told him to avoid sex for the rest of his life and to 'renounce all stimulants, including liqueurs, wine, coffee, and tobacco; to drink water; and to eat simple, substantial meals'. Edger ignored Comte's advice and carried on smoking, drinking and fornicating.

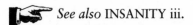 *See also* INSANITY iii.

It is not by
MUSCLE, SPEED,
OR PHYSICAL DEXTERITY
———————— *that* ————————
GREAT THINGS ARE ACHIEVED,
but by REFLECTION

CHAPTER TWO

AGEING

OLD MEN SUFFER FROM
DIZZINESS, PRURITUS OF THE
WHOLE BODY, **SLEEPLESSNESS**,
WATERY DISCHARGES
FROM THE BOWELS

It is DESIRABLE *for a man to be*
BLOTTED OUT
AT HIS PROPER TIME

i   **THE LIFE EXPECTANCY** of a man in ancient Greece was
around twenty-four years; unless you were a top philosopher,
in which case it was around seventy. Why?

Simone de Beauvoir provides a clue in *The Coming of Age*
(1970):

> Both today and throughout history, the class-struggle gov-
> erns the manner in which old age takes hold of a man: there is
> a great gulf between the aged slave and the aged patrician,
> between the wretchedly pensioned ex-worker and an Onas-
> sis... we have two classes of old people, the one extremely
> numerous, the other reduced to a small minority; and these
> two classes are brought into being by the conflict between
> the exploiters and the exploited.

The ratio of slaves to free native Greeks in the ancient world
was three to one. Of course, philosophers were free men and
that is the significant factor in their longevity. Wealth and
health have always been related (*see also* FREEDOM ii).

...... ● ......

ii **FOR PLATO,** the ideal republic was a gerontocracy, rule by the
elderly. In *The Republic* (*c.*380 BC), the guardian class under-
goes a lengthy education to emerge as wise, fit rulers around
the age of fifty (twice the life expectancy of the average person
living in Greece at the time, *see* GOVERNING i). Plato believed
that as the body declined the soul and its concerns came to the
fore. In *The Republic* he has Cephalus say, 'As age blunts one's
enjoyment of physical pleasures, one's desire for the things of
the intelligence and one's delight in them increase accordingly.'

Aristotle took a different view. As a monist, he regarded body and soul as an indivisible unit. With the decline of the body, the soul's powers did not increase in a compensatory way as for Plato. Aristotle regarded the age of fifty as the peak of a man's powers. Since they declined after that, he was opposed to Plato's gerontocracy.

His view was that younger, fitter men should rule. In his *Rhetoric* (*c*.350 BC) Aristotle writes scathingly of 'the character of Elderly Men': 'men who are past their prime... have lived many years; they have often been taken in* and often made mistakes; and life on the whole is a bad business. The result is that they are sure about nothing and underdo everything. They 'think', but they never 'know'; and because of their hesitation they always add a 'possibly' or a 'perhaps', putting everything this way and nothing positively'. So much for the wisdom of old age. Not only are old men uncertain, in Aristotle's view, they are also 'cynical; that is, they tend to put the worse construction on everything'. They are also 'distrustful and therefore suspicious of evil'. What else? He goes on: 'They are small-minded, because they have been humbled by life: their desires are set upon nothing more exalted or unusual than what will help them to keep alive... They are not generous, because money is one of the things they must have, and at the same time their experience has taught them how hard it is to get and how easy to lose.' Aristotle was not done with his case against the elderly. 'They are cowardly, and are always anticipating danger.' Old men are mean: 'If they wrong others, they mean to injure them, not to insult them.' And he has a final brickbat to hurl at the Athenian senior citizen: they are

---

* Other translations use 'deceived' here.

selfish: 'Old men may feel pity, as well as young men, but not for the same reason. Young men feel it out of kindness; old men out of weakness, imagining that anything that befalls any one else might easily happen to them.'

Hippocrates, the fifth-century BC founder of Western medicine (*see also* FOOD iii and MELANCHOLY i), characterized the 'old man'* as a collection of symptoms: 'Old men suffer from difficulty of breathing, catarrh accompanied by coughing, strangury,[†] pains at the joints, kidney disease, dizziness, apoplexy, cachexia,[‡] pruritus[§] of the whole body, sleeplessness, watery discharges from the bowels, eyes and nostrils, dullness of sight, cataract, hardness of hearing.'

...... ● ......

iii **SENECA THE YOUNGER**, the Roman Stoic philosopher, had a much brighter perspective on ageing. He declared: 'Let us cherish and love old age; for it is full of pleasure if one knows how to use it. Fruits are most welcome when almost over.' He believed that 'Life is most delightful when it is on the downward slope, but has not yet reached the abrupt decline... How comforting it is to have tired out one's appetites, and to have done with them!' Unlike Plato and Aristotle, who judged the feebleness of age in different ways (but both negatively), Seneca proclaimed:

---

* The Greeks talk about 'old men' in their observations on ageing. There is little talk of 'old women'.

† Frequent and painful passing of small amounts of urine.

‡ Wasting, muscle atrophy.

§ Itching.

I feel that age has done no damage to my mind, though I feel its effects on my constitution. Only my vices, and the outward aids to these vices, have reached senility; my mind is strong and rejoices that it has but slight connexion with the body. It has laid aside the greater part of its load. It is alert; it takes issue with me on the subject of old age; it declares that old age is its time of bloom.

25 ANCIENT GREEK PHILOSOPHERS WHO LIVED PAST SEVENTY

PYTHAGORUS	Mathematician	c.570 BC	+/- 80
ANAXIMENES	Material monist	c.550	+/- 70
PARMENIDES	Founded Eleatic school	c.544	+/- 95
ANAGAXORES	Naturalist	c.500	+/- 72
GORGIAS	Sophist	c.483	105 or 109
SOCRATES	Socratic method	469	71
HIPPOCRATES	Physician	460	90 or 100
DEMOCRITUS	Atomist	c.460	90 or 100
ANTISTHENES	A founder of Cynicism	c.445	+/- 80
ISOCRATES	Logician	436	98
XENOPHONES	Disciple of Socrates	c.430	75
PLATO	Philosopher/mathematician	429	81
DIOGENES	A founder of Cynicism	c.410	77 or 91
XENOCRATES	Platonist	c.400	+/- 86
THEOPHRASTES	Aristotelian	371	84

PYRRHO	Founder of Scepticism	365	90
EPICURUS	Founder of Epicureanism	341	71
ZENO	Founder of Stoicism	c.344	+/- 72
CLEANTHES	Stoic	331	99
TIMON	Disciple of Pyrrho	320	90
ARCESILAUS	Platonist	c.315	+/- 75
ARISTARCHUS	Astronomer/mathematician	310	+/- 80
ARCHIMEDES	Physicist/mathematician	c.287	+/- 75
CHRYSIPPUS	Stoic	c.280	+/- 73
CARNEADES	Platonist	c.214	+/- 86

This table is based on one prepared by The Gerontology Research Group.

iv **THE ROMAN ORATOR** and politician Cicero, writing a century before Seneca, was a champion of old men. He uses the analogy of a ship's captain to praise the experience of age, saying that those

> who allege that old age is devoid of useful activity adduce nothing to the purpose, and are like those who would say that the pilot does nothing in the sailing of his ship, because, while others are climbing the masts, or running about the gangways, or working at the pumps, he sits quietly in the stern and simply holds the tiller. He may not be doing what younger members of the crew are doing, but what he does is better and much more important.

What the old man does is better because 'It is not by muscle, speed, or physical dexterity that great things are achieved, but by reflection, force of character, and judgement; in these qualities old age is usually not only not poorer, but is even richer.' While not a fully paid-up member of the Stoic school of philosophy, Cicero expresses the same easy-going nonchalance in the face of death as Seneca. He writes of the inevitability of death: 'it is desirable for a man to be blotted out at his proper time. For as Nature has marked the bounds of everything else, so she has marked the bounds of life. Moreover, old age is the final scene, as it were, in life's drama, from which we ought to escape when it grows wearisome and, certainly, when we have had our fill.'

...... • ......

v **THE SEVENTEENTH-CENTURY** English polymath Robert Burton (he was a vicar, an astrologer and had encyclopaedic learning) described old age as 'trouble and sorrow'. He regarded it as an aspect of melancholy, described in his most famous work which may just take the prize for best title ever: *The Anatomy of Melancholy, What it is: With all the Kinds, Causes, Symptomes, Prognostickes, and Several Cures of it. In Three Maine Partitions with their several Sections, Members, and Subsections. Philosophically, Medicinally, Historically, Opened and Cut Up* (1621).

After seventy years (as the Psalmist sayeth) 'all is trouble and sorrow'; and common experience confirms the truth of it in weak and old persons, especially such as have lived in action all their lives, had great employment, much business, much command and many servants to oversee, and leave off *ex abrupto*, as Charles the Fifth did to King Philip, resign up all on a sudden; they are overcome with melancholy in an instant: or if they do continue in such courses, they dote at last (*senex bis puer**) and are not able to manage their estates through common infirmities incident in their age; full of ache, sorrow and grief, children again, dizzards, they carpe many times as they sit, and talk to themselves, they are angry, waspish, displeased with everything... This natural infirmity is most eminent in old women, and such as are poor, solitary, live in most base esteem and beggary, or such as are witches...

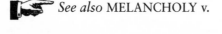 *See also* MELANCHOLY v.

...... ● ......

vi IN *THE COMING OF AGE* Simone de Beauvoir offers a scathing attack on Western societies' dehumanization of the elderly. She argues that society expects them to be 'a standing example of all the virtues. Above all they are called upon to display serenity.' This in the face of marginalization, ostracism and ridicule. De Beauvoir finds old age alienating in an existential sense: 'Since it is the Other within us who is old, it is natural that the revelation of our age should come to us from outside – from others. We do not accept it willingly.' She offers not only an analysis of what it is like to grow old, but also advice for the elderly. 'There is only one solution if old age is not to be an absurd parody of our former life,' she says; 'and that is to go on pursuing ends that give our existence a meaning.'

---

* 'An old man is in his second boyhood.'

De Beauvoir observes that 'People are often advised to "pre-pare" for old age. But if this merely applies to setting aside money, choosing the place for retirement and laying on hob-bies, we shall not be much the better for it when the day comes.' She is a realist about ageing. Despite her spirited advice to 'go on pursuing ends that give our existence a meaning', she also acknowledges that ageing is accompanied by a diminution of one's energies. 'It is far better not to think about it too much, but to live a fairly committed, fairly justified life so that one may go on in the same path even when all illusions have van-ished and one's zeal for life has died away.'

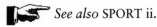 *See also* SPORT ii.

It has never yet been **OBSERVED** that any brute animal reached the stage of using *REAL SPEECH*

WHY AM I SO CONFIDENT THAT MY DOG, **LUDWIG WITTGENSTEIN,** *IS CONSCIOUS?*

CHAPTER THREE
ANIMALS

WHEN I PLAY WITH MY — **CAT** — WHO KNOWS WHETHER I DO NOT MAKE HER MORE SPORT THAN SHE MAKES ME?

Is there a POLITY *better ordered* THAN THAT OF **BEES?**

i   **AND GOD SAID, Let us make man in our image, after our
     likeness: and let them have dominion over the fish of the sea,
     and over the fowl of the air, and over the cattle, and over
     all the earth, and over every creeping thing that creepeth
     upon the earth.**

This biblical text, crafted between 540 and 330 BC, is often used
as a justification for man using animals as beasts of burden,
killing them for sport or food and domesticating them. They
are subordinate because God says they are.

Contemporaneous with Genesis were two schools of thought
that opposed its licence to kill: Jainism and Pythagorism. The
Indian philosopher Pārśva developed the founding doctrines
of Jainism, a religion that believes in the spiritual interde-
pendence and equality of all forms of life, and that all living
beings must be respected. Meanwhile, in the West, another
'pro-animal' philosophy was constructed by the fifth-century
Greek philosopher and mathematician Pythagoras. His animist
school of thought held that humans and animals possessed
identical, indestructible souls composed of fire and air. Upon
death, human and animal souls were subject to reincarnation,
from human to animal, animal to human. Pythagoras was a
vegetarian.

...... ● ......

ii   **ARISTOTLE GAVE NO CREDENCE** to Pythagoras's argu-
     ments. As the first taxonomist he shared the Old Testament
     view that man is master over animals. The Aristotelian doc-
     trine held sway among wealthy Romans, who tended to be
     carnivores. Meat on the table – pigs were roasted alive on hot

spits – was a sign of high social position. By contrast, recent research on the bones of gladiators – who were slaves or foreigners – has revealed that most of them were vegetarians. But several prominent Roman philosophers were vegetarians also, and their practice was based on metaphysical arguments. In his essay 'Abstinence from Animal Food' (written *c.*268–70) the Tyrian Neoplatonist Porphyry says: 'it does not follow, if we have more intelligence than other animals, that on this account they are to be deprived of intelligence… the soul is co-passive with the body, and that the former suffers something from the latter, when the latter is well or ill affected… It must be demonstrated, therefore, that there is a rational power in animals.'

Porphyry used the principle of monism (the view that mind and body are a single, indivisible substance) in claiming kinship with animals. He argues that they possess intelligence, and differ from us – and other animals – in degree rather than kind. By contrast, the dominant thinkers of ancient Greece, Plato and Aristotle, were dualists.

...... • ......

iii **IN 1649 THE FRENCH REDUCTIONIST** René Descartes published *Passions of the Soul*, which includes an essay titled 'Animals are Machines'. He says: 'It is much more wonderful that a mind should be found in every human body than that one should be lacking in every animal.' Do animals have minds? No, says Descartes.

After making arguments to support his view that animals are *automata* – that they lack consciousness – Descartes arrives at his final and absolute proof of the fundamental difference between humans and animals:

although all animals easily communicate to us, by voice or bodily movement, their natural impulses of anger, fear, hunger and so on, it has never yet been observed that any brute animal reached the stage of using real speech, that is to say, of indicating by word or sign something pertaining to pure thought and not to natural impulse. Such speech is the only certain sign of thought hidden in a body. All men use it, however stupid and insane they may be, and though they may lack tongue and organs of voice: but no animals do. Consequently it can be taken as a real specific difference between men and dumb animals.

For Descartes, speech was the product of mind that animals lack; it is exclusive to humans, the ultimate proof of their human-ness. He also believed that animals do not feel pain. He would publicly nail dogs' paws to a board and proceed to vivisect and dismember them. Descartes surely believed that his actions were those of a scientist, and as such were justified; not everyone would agree.

Michel de Montaigne disagreed with Descartes on the subject of mind, feelings and language in animals. In his essay 'APOLOGY FOR RAIMOND SEBOND' (1580) Montaigne asks: 'When I play with my cat who knows whether I do not make her more sport than she makes me?' He finds this feline moment to be marked by its mutuality: 'We mutually divert one another with our play.' He also finds intention, and choice – both in himself, and in his cat: 'If I have my hour to begin or to refuse, she also has hers.'

Addressing the language problem, Montaigne proposes that if there is a lack of communication between human and animal, perhaps the fault lies with the human who is unable to understand the animal. He asks, 'what is there in us that we do not see in the operations of animals? Is there a polity better ordered, the offices better distributed, and more inviolably observed and maintained, than that of bees? Can we imagine that such, and so regular, a distribution of employments can be carried on without reasoning and deliberation?' He inspects the nature of humans' communication with one another and concludes that many important transactions are carried out through gesture, not language: the look, the glance, the touch of lovers do not require the spoken word, which is not adequate to the task. Descartes gave Montaigne's views short shrift: 'I cannot share the opinion of Montaigne and others who attribute understanding or thought to animals.'

But Montaigne's ideas have stood the test of time. In his essay 'Animal Minds' (1994) the contemporary American philosopher of language John Searle elaborates:

I have said that many species of animals have consciousness, intentionality, and thought processes. Now why am I so confident about that? Why, for example, am I so confident that my dog, Ludwig Wittgenstein, is conscious? Well, why is he so confident I am conscious? I think part of the correct answer, in the case of both Ludwig and me, is that any other possibility is out of the question. We have, for example, known each other now for quite a while so there is not really any possibility of doubt.

...... ● ......

iv IN THEIR DISCUSSIONS of animal minds and animal rights, present-day philosophers are developing new ideas built on older ones. Two contemporary philosophers – the American Tom Regan and the Australian Peter Singer – have reached very large audiences and fuelled a renewed debate on the status of animals. In *The Case for Animal Rights* (1983) Regan claims animals have moral rights. Influenced by the German Enlightenment philosopher Immanuel Kant (who steadfastly denied that animals have consciousness), Regan would extend Kantian concepts of rights and freedom to non-rational lives (infants, the mentally impaired). Non-rational persons have the right to respect, and to be protected from harm. By extension, Regan argues, respect and protection should be extended to animals because they are the 'subject-of-a-life' – an existent with a unique history and experiences – as are we humans. As a moral consequence, Regan argues, we should no longer breed and kill animals for food, experiment on them, or hunt them commercially.

Peter Singer's animal rights advocacy has made him one of the best-known living philosophers. Singer is an ethicist whose *Animal Liberation* (1975) has inspired activist movements like the Animal Liberation Front and provoked a renewed interest in the utilitarianism of John Stuart Mill (the argument that what is right is what gives the greatest benefit to the greatest number of people). Singer's position is that utilitarianism is the only yardstick of ethical behaviour and that it should be extended to our treatment of animals. He believes the human-animal divide to be arbitrary, and that it leads to the prejudice of speciesism.*

---

* Term coined by the British psychologist Richard D. Ryder in a pamphlet of the same name published in 1970.

Singer caused a controversy with his 2001 essay 'Heavy Petting', a review of the English edition of Dutch biologist Midas Dekker's book *Dearest Pet: On Bestiality* (2000). Dekker explores an aspect of human–animal relations that is not much discussed, but more common than one might think. He cites the research of American biologist and sexologist Alfred Kinsley, author of *Sexual Behavior in the Human Male* (1948) and *Sexual Behavior in the Human Female* (1953), which revealed that 8 per cent of men and 3.5 per cent of women had experienced sexual contact with animals. In rural areas, the study found, more than 40 per cent of men admitted to acts of bestiality. What does Singer think about humans having sex with animals (or vice versa)? He is against *any* activity that involves cruelty to animals. 'But,' he writes in 'Heavy Petting', 'sex with animals does not always involve cruelty. Who has not been at a social occasion disrupted by the household dog gripping the legs of a visitor and vigorously rubbing its penis against them? The host usually discourages such activities, but in private not everyone objects to being used by her or his dog in this way, and occasionally mutually satisfying activities may develop.' In his memoir *My Father and Myself* (1968) the British writer and editor J. R. Ackerley described how he would relieve his Alsatian bitch Queenie when she was on heat: 'The most I ever did for her was to press my hand against the hot swollen vulva she was always pushing at me at these times, taking her liquids upon my palm.'

 See also FOOD i *and* ii; HAPPINESS ii.

A FLAT-HEADED insipid, nauseating, **ILLITERATE CHARLATAN**

AN EXERCISE in the art of misusing ___ **THE VERB** ___ **'TO BE'**

He has no talent for DISENTANGLING things

CHAPTER FOUR

BACKBITING

EMPTY VERBIAGE PUT TOGETHER IN STATEMENTS ___ *which are* ___ **ABSOLUTELY EMPTY**

A MASS of often very subtle, but desperately wrongheaded • *RATIOCINATION* •

i **THE AUSTRIAN PHILOSOPHER** Ludwig Wittgenstein
(who would later gain British citizenship) remarked to a mutual
acquaintance of G. E. Moore (who held the philosophy chair
at Cambridge and was instrumental in getting Wittgenstein his
job): 'he shows you how far a man can go who has absolutely
no intelligence whatever'.

In his *Summa Theologica* (1265–74) Thomas Aquinas, the
thirteenth-century scholastic theologian, defined backbiting
as 'denigration of a neighbour's reputation by means of secret
words'. He said the only offence more grievous than murder
and adultery is backbiting.

Aquinas argued that we might wound a person by words in
one of two ways: 'openly and to his face (that is, by insulting
him); and secretly, when he is absent – and that is backbiting'.
For Aquinas, backbiting is a mortal sin. It is worse than theft
of physical property, because it is the theft of a person's reputation. Maimonides, the rabbi, philosopher and physician who
codified Jewish law in his *Mishneh Torah* (1170–80), prohibited backbiting ('bad tongue'), 'which is, when one relates anything disgraceful of his fellow, though even he speak the truth'.

Philosophers are among the greatest backbiters in history.
They are constantly denigrating each other's work and reputation, not directly but in gossip and in published works
(the book review may well be the most effective medium of
backbiting ever devised). Few philosophers have been on the
receiving end of abuse as vitriolic as that directed at the nineteenth-century German thinker G. W. F. Hegel. Hegel's writing
may be the most difficult to understand of any philosopher's.
His champions would argue that this is because his thoughts
are so profound and richly complex that they must necessarily
find their expression in complicated language. His detractors

argue that it's impenetrable rubbish (*see also* OBFUSCATION i *and* iii).

...... ● ......

ii *THE SCIENCE OF LOGIC* (1812–13) is a cornerstone of the Hegelian edifice. After reading it, the Danish existentialist Søren Kierkegaard (*see* WALKING iv) wrote in his journal for 1844, 'If Hegel had written the whole of his logic and then said, in the preface or some other place, that it was merely an experiment in thought in which he had even begged the question in many places, then he would certainly have been the greatest thinker who had ever lived. As it is, he is merely comic.'

Kierkegaard's criticism was mild compared to Hegel's fellow German Arthur Schopenhauer, who dismissed Hegel as a puppet of the Prussian government, 'installed from above, by the powers that be, as the certified Great Philosopher'. He goes on to call him 'a flat-headed, insipid, nauseating, illiterate charlatan who reached the pinnacle of audacity in scribbling together and dishing up the craziest mystifying nonsense'. As a consequence, Schopenhauer says, 'The extensive field of spiritual influence with which Hegel was furnished by those in power has enabled him to achieve the intellectual corruption of a whole generation.' But what is it that Schopenhauer so dislikes about Hegel's thinking? In his major contribution to ethics, *On the Basis of Morality* (1839), he complains that Hegel's œuvre is 'a colossal piece of mystification which will yet provide posterity with an inexhaustible theme for laughter at our times'. Why? Because 'it is a pseudo-philosophy para-lysing all mental powers, stifling all real thinking, and, by the most outrageous misuse of language, putting in its place the hollowest, most senseless, thoughtless, and, as is confirmed by its success, most stupefying verbiage'.

...... ● ......

iii **BERTRAND RUSSELL** is one of the great backbiters of the twentieth century. In the unlikely company of Kierkegaard and Schopenhauer (whose work he discounted as typical of the 'growth of unreason' in the nineteenth century) Russell also directed scorn at Hegel. In *Unpopular Essays* (1950) he wrote, 'Hegel's philosophy is so odd that one would not have expected him to be able to get sane men to accept it, but he did. He set it out with so much obscurity that people thought it must be profound. It can quite easily be expounded lucidly in words of one syllable, but then its absurdity becomes obvious.'

Russell was the leading British philosopher of the early twentieth century. His *Principia Mathematica* (with A. N. Whitehead, 1910–13) attempted to set out rules of symbolic logic from which all mathematical truths could be proven. The German logician and mathematician Gottlob Frege persuaded the young Ludwig Wittgenstein to pursue philosophy under the direction of Russell at Cambridge University. There Wittgenstein became friends with G. E. Moore (*see also* NICK-NAMES xi), co-founder with Russell of what we now call analytic philosophy – the dominant school of thought in the anglophone world. Wittgenstein is considered by many fellow analytics to be the greatest philosopher of the twentieth century. He published only one book in his lifetime, the slim, aphoristic *Tractatus Logico-Philosophicus* (1921). The *Tractatus* is based on the idea that all philosophical problems arise from misunderstandings of the logic of language; it tries to show what this logic is, and how legitimate questions may be posed, and nonsensical (read 'metaphysical') ones dismissed.

In 1914 Wittgenstein had no academic job – he didn't even have a degree. He summoned Moore to Norway, where he was staying, to help him prepare a text later published as *Notes on Logic* (1979) in lieu of work for a bachelor's degree. Wittgenstein treated the celebrated Cambridge professor like a secretary, dictating to him and flying into a rage when Moore misunderstood what he intended. In May 1914 Moore tried to persuade university officials to accept Wittgenstein's *Logic*, but failed. Wittgenstein responded in a letter: 'If I am not worth your making an exception for me even in some STUPID details then I may as well go to Hell directly; and if I am worth it and you don't do it then – by God – you might go there.'

After serving in the Austro-Hungarian army on the Russian and Italian fronts in the First World War (*see* WAR iv), Wittgenstein returned to Cambridge in 1929. He mounted a sustained campaign of backbiting against Moore: 'he's barren'; 'he has no talent for disentangling things'. Nor did Wittgenstein hold his tongue where his mentor Russell was concerned. While he had enormous admiration for *Principia Mathematica*, he dismissed Russell's work in other areas of philosophy and his opinion on social issues: 'Russell's books should be bound in two colours, those dealing with mathematical logic in red – and all students of philosophy should read them; those dealing with ethics and politics in blue – and no one should be allowed to read them.'

In spite of Wittgenstein's tongue, Russell – who didn't suffer fools gladly – published this recollection of an encounter between them:

Quite at first I was in doubt as to whether he was a man of genius or a crank, but I very soon decided in favour of the former alternative. Some of his early views made the decision difficult. He maintained, for example, at one time that all existential propositions are meaningless. This was in a lecture room, and I invited him to consider the proposition: 'There is no hippopotamus in this room at present.' When he refused to believe this, I looked under all the desks without finding one; but he remained unconvinced.

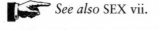 *See also* SEX vii.

...... ● ......

iv **THE OTHER PHILOSOPHER** who is often described as the greatest of the twentieth century – by continental philosophers, who differ from analytic ones mainly because they continue to pose and consider metaphysical questions – is the German existentialist and member of the Nazi Party Martin Heidegger. Heidegger's *Being and Time* (1927) is a founding text of continental philosophy and its dense language intensely annoyed most anglophone readers (*see* OBFUSCATION iv). One of the most vociferous critics of Heidegger was Karl Popper, the Austrian philosopher of science who left Germany for New Zealand in 1937 and then took up a chair at the London School of Economics. Having read the 1941 edition of *Being and Time*, from which Heidegger had removed the dedication to his teacher Edmund Husserl – a convert from Judaism – Popper told the Chinese scientist Eugene Yue-Ching Ho, 'I appeal to the philosophers of all countries to unite and never again mention Heidegger or talk to another philosopher who defends Heidegger. This man was a devil. I mean, he behaved like a devil to his beloved teacher, and he has a devilish influence on Germany.' Quite apart from Heidegger's character defects, Popper also thought he was a bad philosopher: 'One has to read Heidegger in the original to see what a swindler he was.' He called Heidegger's philosophy 'empty verbiage put together in statements which are absolutely empty'. *See also* FREEDOM ix; NICKNAMES x.

...... ● ......

v **THE BRITISH LOGICAL POSITIVIST** A. J. Ayer conducted his philosophical research using verification criteria similar to those of the empirical sciences. His mother Reine Citroën was of Dutch-Jewish descent, while his father Jules was Swiss-French. Francophone from childhood, Ayer was steeped in French philosophy and followed the development of existentialism in the mid-twentieth century. During the Second World War Ayer worked for British intelligence in MI6 and for the Special Operations Executive, which conducted espionage and sabotage operations in Europe. As a follower of Rudolf Carnap, a member of the Vienna Circle group of logical positivists and empiricists, Ayer was fervently opposed to Heidegger. In 1943 the French existentialist Jean-Paul Sartre published *Being and Nothingness*, which was heavily influenced by Heidegger's *Being and Time*. In July 1945 Ayer reviewed Sartre's book in the American arts magazine *Horizon*. He wrote: 'what is called existentialist philosophy has become very largely an exercise in the art of misusing the verb "to be"'. Ayer found the book to be nothing more than 'a mass of often very subtle, but desperately wrongheaded, ratiocination'. He described Sartre's analysis of time as 'based on 'trivial propositions', none of which 'can be regarded as contributing much towards the solution of any of the philosophical problems that are ordinarily associated with the analysis of time'.

vi **BERNARD-HENRI LÉVY** (*see also* HAIRCUTS iii) is arguably France's best-known public intellectual. Founder of the Nouveaux Philosophes movement of thinkers who broke with Marxism in the 1970s, he is famous for popularizing philosophical thought. In 2005 Philippe Cohen published a highly critical biography of Lévy. He summarized his opinion of his fellow thinker thus: 'his thinking is entirely unoriginal. There is this idea that he is a philosopher when actually he is representative of nothing other than the pauperisation of French intellectual life.'

See also DUTY iv; TRUTH ix.

KNOWLEDGE IS TRUE BELIEF

There is but one
indefectibly certain truth...
that the
PHENOMENON *of*
CONSCIOUSNESS EXISTS

CHAPTER FIVE

BELIEF

FAITH is
the GREAT
COP-OUT

Better go without
BELIEF FOREVER
than
BELIEVE A LIE!

IT IS UNDESIRABLE
*to believe a proposition when
there is no ground whatever for
supposing* IT TRUE

i **THE MEXICAS**, rulers of the Aztec Empire who settled in Tenochtitlan and Tlatelolco from around 1200, annually cut 20,000 beating hearts from the chests of live sacrificial victims in offering to Huitzilopochtli, god of the sun. They did this because they believed it was necessary to guarantee the sunrise each day, upon which their crops depended. The Mexicas *believed* the sun would rise each day if they practised human sacrifice. But they didn't *know* that it would.

One way to think of belief is that it is 'knowledge in its infancy': that is, a belief is something we believe to be true, but are currently lacking proof of. The sixteenth-century Polish astronomer Nicolaus Copernicus proved that the Earth and our solar system's other planets revolve around the sun (not vice versa, as the Greco-Egyptian mathematician Ptolemy had believed in the second century AD). Copernicus proved this using scientific method – mathematical calculation, empirical observation and experiments that could be reproduced by other investigators who could confirm the facts. This knowledge would have taken away the Mexicas' anxiety about the sun rising each day, and would have saved the lives of those 20,000 annual sacrificial victims. Copernicus's reward for proving the heliocentric model was abuse from Protestants and censorship by the Catholic Church: Martin Luther said of him in 1539: 'This fool wishes to reverse the entire science of astronomy; but sacred Scripture tells us that Joshua commanded the sun to stand still, and not the earth'; while in 1616 Copernicus's treatise *De revolutionibus orbium coelestium* ('On the Revolutions of the Celestial Spheres', 1543) would be placed on the papal index of banned books on the basis that it was incompatible with Roman Catholic faith. Reading of a 'corrected' version of the book was permitted from 1620, but in

its original, uncorrected form *De revolutionibus* would remain
on the Index until 1758. *See also* EXTRATERRESTRIALS iv;
INTUITION i.

...... ● ......

ii **IN PLATO'S *THEAETETUS*** (*c.*369 BC), the Greek mathematician after whom the dialogue is named argues with
Socrates about the nature of knowledge. During their discussion, Theaetetus proposes a definition of knowledge as 'true
belief'. Socrates warns him of false belief, and also accidental
true belief (belief without proof). Ultimately Theaetetus arrives
at the Platonic definition of knowledge: true belief supported
by an account.

In the twentieth century, the American analytic philosopher
Willard Van Orman Quine echoed Plato when he defined
knowledge as something one can believe in that is also true.
'Knowledge is true belief,' says Quine. Of belief Quine says:

> To believe something is to believe that it is true; therefore a
> reasonable person believes each of his beliefs to be true; yet
> experience has taught him to expect that some of his beliefs,
> he knows not which, will turn out to be false. A reasonable
> person believes, in short, that each of his beliefs is true and
> that some of them are false. I, for one, had expected better
> of reasonable persons.

An American predecessor of Quine's, the philosopher and
psychologist William James (brother of the novelist Henry),
would have said that Quine's comment about better expectations had to do with worry over the possibility of being

duped. In his 1896 lecture 'The Will to Believe', James wrote that 'Biologically considered, our minds are as ready to grind out falsehood as veracity, and he who says, "Better go without belief forever than believe a lie!" merely shows his own preponderant private horror of becoming a dupe.' We need to *believe*, says James, despite the fear of being wrong. The fear of being duped is one that James's hypothetical sceptic 'slavishly obeys. He cannot imagine anyone questioning its binding force.' James goes on, 'For my own part, I also have a horror of being duped.' But he also adds, 'I can believe that worse things than being duped may happen to a man in this world.'

To avoid being duped, as James would have it, we require evidence to support our beliefs. Astronomy, mathematics and observation led Copernicus to the facts that tell us the Earth revolves around the sun – something we not only believe, but know. How is objective evidence obtained? 'Objective evidence and certitude are doubtless very fine ideals to play with, but where on this moonlit and dream-visited planet are they found?' From James's perspective, they are to be found through empirical observations. 'I am, therefore, myself a complete empiricist so far as my theory of human knowledge goes. I live, to be sure, by the practical faith that we must go on experiencing and thinking over our experience, for only thus can our opinions grow more true.' However, nothing is ever set in stone for James. He says that to hold any one opinion 'as if it never could be reinterpretable or corrigible, I believe to be a tremendously mistaken attitude, and I think that the whole history of philosophy will bear me out'. So what can the seeker after knowledge rely on? 'There is but one indefectibly certain truth... the truth that the present phenomenon of consciousness exists'.

   James was sometimes wont to exaggerate for effect. He
further considers the concept of objective evidence with this
appeal to his audience: 'You believe in objective evidence, and
I do. Of some things we feel that we are certain: we know, and
we know that we do know.' How do we know? 'There is something that gives a click inside of us, a bell that strikes twelve,
when the hands of our mental clock have swept the dial and
meet over the meridian hour.'* And then, mischievously, James
inserts and twists the knife: 'The greatest empiricists among us
are only empiricists on reflection: when left to their instincts,
they dogmatize like infallible popes.'

...... ● ......

iii **IN HIS *PENSÉES*** ('Thoughts', 1670) Blaise Pascal argued
that belief in God need not be at odds with his position as a
man of science; that his belief was consistent with reason. In an
example of what we would today call game theory Pascal does
not offer a proof of God, but argues that it makes more sense to
believe than not to believe. He couches his argument in the form
of a bet – an argument which has become known as 'Pascal's
Wager' (*see also* CHANCE v). Pascal is an interesting case for
James, who acknowledges that moral questions are immediate and their solutions 'cannot wait for sensible proof'. James
defines a moral question as 'what is good, or would be good if
it did exist'. Pondering Pascal, man of science and man of God,
James remarks: 'Science can tell us what exists; but to compare
the worths, both of what exists and of what does not exist,
we must consult not science, but what Pascal calls our heart.'

---

* Actually, James is describing intuitive rather than empirical evidence.

iv **BERTRAND RUSSELL** was blunt about the contest between belief and knowledge. He said 'it is undesirable to believe a proposition when there is no ground whatever for supposing it true'. With scathing irony he wrote: 'I must, of course, admit that if such an opinion became common it would completely transform our social life and our political system; since both are at present faultless, this must weigh against it.' If such a 'common sense' opinion came to be widespread, he observed (with Pascal in mind, one thinks) 'it would tend to diminish the incomes of clairvoyants, bookmakers, bishops and others who live on the irrational hopes of those who have done nothing to deserve good fortune here or hereafter'. More recently the British evolutionary biologist Richard Dawkins remarked in a 1992 lecture at the Edinburgh Science Festival, 'Faith is the great cop-out, the great excuse to evade the need to think and evaluate evidence. Faith is belief in spite of, even perhaps because of, the lack of evidence.'

Every living thing is

* INCREDIBLY LUCKY *

simply to be alive

The universe was NOT pregnant with life
Our NUMBER came up in the Monte Carlo GAME

CHAPTER SIX

CHANCE

GOD DOES
NOT PLAY DICE
with the
UNIVERSE

CHANCE *alone is at the*
source of every

INNOVATION

i **ONE DAY** I was sitting on the banks of the Thames watching the Oxford and Cambridge Boat Race with a friend who is a businessman (he also happens to have a first in PPE from Oxford). I proposed to him a bet. 'I will wager you a pound,' I said, 'if you offer me odds of a-million-to-one that a crocodile will rise from the Thames and chop the Cambridge boat in two with its teeth.'

'I must decline,' said my friend.

'Why?' I exclaimed, pointing out that it was a sure bet.

He replied: 'You can never be sure.'

...... ● ......

ii **THE QUESTION OF CHANCE** – of random occurrences – is important for studies as diverse as physics and ethics. In fifth-century BC Greece, the pre-Socratic philosopher Leucippus (*see also* EXTRATERRESTRIALS i) – originator, with his pupil Democritus, of the theory of atomism – came up with the credo 'Nothing occurs at random (*maten*), but everything for a reason (*logos*) and by necessity.' On the other hand, Leucippus's contemporary Xenophon of Athens, a student of Socrates whose *Memorabilia* (*c*.371) are a collection of Socratic dialogues lesser known than those of Plato, gives an account of Socrates' teaching on the subject of chance in its guise as luck. He recounts how, when a student asked Socrates what he thought was the best pursuit for a man, Socrates replied, 'doing well'. The student then asks about good luck: should one pursue it? Xenophon gives Socrates' answer: 'On the contrary, I think that luck and doing are opposites. To hit on something right by luck without search I call good luck; to do something well after study and practice I call doing well; and those who pursue this

I think do well.' Xenophon's Socrates makes the moral point that doing well is properly the result of effort, not chance, the implication being that good luck is the province of the lazy; just as chance is the province of the stupid or superstitious for Leucippus.

Chrysippus, a Stoic who lived in the third century BC, believed, 'Everything that happens is followed by something else which depends on it by causal necessity. Likewise, everything that happens is preceded by something with which it is causally connected. For nothing exists or has come into being in the cosmos without a cause.' Chrysippus' view might be said to encapsulate the comfort of Stoicism which, in one of its aspects, can be characterized by the title of the 1956 popular song 'Que Sera, Sera (Whatever Will Be, Will Be)'. But, for Chrysippus and the Stoics, there is more to it than that. The consequence of not believing in causal necessity (or fate, as some would have it) is disaster. If nature is not ruled by causal necessity, then 'The universe will be disrupted and disintegrate into pieces and cease to be a unity functioning as a single system, if any uncaused movement is introduced into it.'

The physicist Isaac Newton definitively ruled out chance in favour of causal necessity in his *Mathematical Principles of Natural Philosophy* (1687). There he elaborated the concept of gravity and laid out the rules of physics that prevailed until Albert Einstein came up with his theories of relativity. Though Einstein proved that the physical operations of the universe are more complex than Newton could imagine, he also famously came down against the role of chance with his declaration, 'God does not play dice with the universe'.

...... ● ......

iii **THE PRIMACY OF DETERMINISM** in physics – the Newtonian view that depicts the physical matter of the universe as operating according to a set of fixed, knowable laws – was challenged by the nineteenth-century American philosopher Charles Sanders Peirce, who developed the theory of Tychism (after the Greek word *tyché* meaning 'chance'). His theory stated that absolute chance operates in the universe, from its inception and through its continuing evolution. In 1891 he wrote:

> The only possible way of accounting for the laws of nature and for uniformity in general is to suppose them results of evolution. This supposes them not to be absolute, not to be obeyed precisely. It makes an element of indeterminacy, spontaneity, or absolute chance in nature. Just as, when we attempt to verify any physical law, we find our observations cannot be precisely satisfied by it, and rightly attribute the discrepancy to errors of observation, so we must suppose far more minute discrepancies to exist owing to the imperfect cogency of the law itself, to a certain swerving of the facts from any definite formula.

For Peirce, Tychism was more than a way of addressing problems of physics. Rather, he believed it permeated the whole of philosophy:

> In an article published in *The Monist* for January, 1891, I endeavored to show what ideas ought to form the warp of a system of philosophy, and particularly emphasized that of absolute chance. In the number of April, 1892, I argued further in favor of that way of thinking, which it will be

**convenient to christen tychism (from *tyché*, chance). A se-
rious student of philosophy will be in no haste to accept
or reject this doctrine; but he will see in it one of the chief
attitudes which speculative thought may take, feeling that
it is not for an individual, nor for an age, to pronounce upon
a fundamental question of philosophy. That is a task for a
whole era to work out.**

Peirce's Tychism is seen by some historians as a precursor to
the ideas of the next major proponent of chance, the twentieth-
century German physicist Werner Heisenberg. Heisenberg
challenged the Newtonian view of a deterministic universe
when he developed a theory called the Heisenberg uncertainty
principle. Heisenberg's 'uncertainty principle', holds that the
more precisely we can determine the position of a particle, the
less precisely we can know its momentum (and vice versa).

...... • ......

iv **IN *CHANCE AND NECESSITY* (1971)**, the French molecular biologist Jacques Monod argues that nothing but chance
rules a universe defined by evolution. He states: 'Among all
the occurrences possible in the universe the a priori probability
of any particular one of them verges upon zero.' Yet, he continues, 'the universe exists; particular events must take place
in it, the probability of which (before the event) was infini-
tesimal. At the present time we have no legitimate grounds for
either asserting or denying that life got off to but a single start
on earth, and that, as a consequence, before it appeared its
chances of occurring were next to nil.'

Monod challenges two millennia of scientific thinking on

chance by declaring: 'Destiny is written concurrently with the event, not prior to it.' For him 'The universe was not pregnant with life nor the biosphere with man. Our number came up in the Monte Carlo game.' For scientific determinists, this view is the most unsettling of all; for the religious, it is the ultimate heresy: no creation, no purpose, no hand of God. As a consequence, Monod asks, 'Is it surprising that, like the person who has just made a million at the casino, we should feel strange and a little unreal?' One result of the rule of chance is that 'The ancient covenant is in pieces; man knows at last that he is alone in the universe's unfeeling immensity, out of which he emerged only by chance. His destiny is nowhere spelled out, nor is his duty. The kingdom above or the darkness below: it is for him to choose.'

While determinists and theologians may be dismayed by this state of affairs, Monod is celebratory – even in awe – of the workings of chance: 'chance alone is at the source of every innovation, and of all creation in the biosphere'.

Monod complains that 'Even today a good many distinguished minds seem unable to accept or even to understand that from a source of noise natural selection alone and unaided could have drawn all the music of the biosphere.' If all is chance, how does order happen? The answer is natural selection, which 'operates upon the products of chance... in a domain of very demanding conditions, and from this domain chance is barred'. The conditions of evolution impose an order upon the randomness the universe throws up. Evolution gives the impression of 'a smooth and steady unfolding'. Monod marvels at the 'prodigious wealth of structures' natural selection 'has engendered, and the extraordinarily effective teleonomic performances of living beings from bacteria to man'. Looking back on the road science has travelled, from determinism to uncertainty to blind chance, Monod reflects, 'one may well find oneself beginning to doubt again whether all this could conceivably be the product of an enormous lottery presided over by natural selection, blindly picking the rare winners from among numbers drawn at random'. Nevertheless, he argues, a review of the evidence shows that 'this conception alone is compatible with the facts'.

Ultimately, Monod comes to the conclusion – depressing to some, refreshing to others – that man has finally realized 'he is alone in the indifferent immensity of the universe, whence he has emerged by chance. His duty, like his fate, is written nowhere.' On a more cheerful note, Monod concludes: 'A totally blind process can by definition lead to anything; it can even lead to vision itself.'

...... ● ......

v **WE REMEMBER** that Xenophon's Socrates had little use for luck, characterizing it as the opposite of effort. There is a sense in which chance is different from luck in that it can involve a calculated narrowing of the odds that begins to suggest a quantifiable possibility. Seen in this light, chance is a kind of free-floating, exogenous force for good or ill (for if there is good luck, surely there is also bad) that simply *affects* one, like finding a fiver in the street, or catching a cold on the bus. Professional gamblers and stockbrokers don't count on luck: they count on the statistical probability that certain decisions will pay off. Perhaps the supreme gambler in Western thought is the mathematician, physicist, philosopher and inventor Blaise Pascal. While his fertile mind was responsible for many achievements in those four areas (including designing the first mechanical adding machine), Pascal is best known for lending his name to Pascal's Wager. As a Christian and a scientist, Pascal attempted to persuade some of his friends who were given to drinking, gambling and licentiousness that choosing to believe in God was a reasonable thing to do; that, in fact, reason demanded it. Pascal argued that it makes more sense to believe in God than not to. The context of Pascal's argument can be outlined as follows. If one bets on the existence of God, and it turns out He does exist, then one is a winner (of the ultimate prize of salvation and eternal life in Christ). If God turns out not to exist, what has been lost? Nothing. On the other hand, if one wagers that God does not exist, and He turns out to exist, then the consequence is eternal damnation. So, a reasonable person, using probability and logic as his guide, chooses to believe in God (*see also* BELIEF iii).

The scholastic philosopher Thomas Aquinas pointed out that luck was an essential element of our free will, and therefore of human freedom. If things were pre-ordained, the future foretold, man's story already written, there would be no such thing as luck because nothing could happen that was not already determined. So, to be human is to be lucky. Which is not to say that one will enjoy good luck; for the capricious nature of luck is such that it can be good or ill. In spite of our best efforts to 'angle' ourselves to increase our luck – educating ourselves, making ourselves attractive to others, cultivating skills – we are, all of us, subject to the freakish, fickle, inconstant, whimsical and unpredictable possibility of chance.

...... ● ......

vi **THE AMERICAN PHILOSOPHER** and cognitive scientist Daniel Dennett goes further than asserting we are all subject to luck; in his view we are the *products* of luck. In *Freedom Evolves* (2003) he wrote:

> Every living thing is, from the cosmic perspective, incredibly lucky simply to be alive. Most, 90 percent and more, of all the organisms that have ever lived have died without viable offspring, but not a single one of your ancestors, going back to the dawn of life on Earth, suffered that normal misfortune. You spring from an unbroken line of winners going back millions of generations, and those winners were, in every generation, the luckiest of the lucky, one out of a thousand or even a million. So however unlucky you may be on some occasion today, your presence on the planet testifies to the role luck has played in your past.

I am
THINKING
about
myself
THINKING

—— WHEN WE ——
SEE, HEAR,
SMELL, TASTE,
FEEL, MEDITATE,
WE KNOW THAT
WE DO SO

CHAPTER SEVEN

CONSCIOUSNESS

THE VERY NOTION of what is called
MATTER involves a **CONTRADICTION**

~
COGITO
ERGO SUM
~

i   'CONSCIOUSNESS is a fascinating but elusive phenomenon: it is impossible to specify what it is, what it does, or why it has evolved. Nothing worth reading has been written on it.' That's the view of British psychologist Stuart Sutherland.

Sutherland calls it 'The having of perceptions, thoughts, and feelings; awareness', but goes on to say that 'The term is impossible to define except in terms that are unintelligible without a grasp of what consciousness means. Many fall into the trap of equating consciousness with self-consciousness – to be conscious it is only necessary to be aware of the external world.'

In some ways, the question of consciousness is a simple one. We know we are conscious (or, at least, self-conscious) right now because I am writing this book and you are reading it. We're both conscious of ourselves doing that. And we are conscious of the outside world: I consciously perceive the smell of onions frying in the kitchen next door; you are conscious of the fact it is cold in your house and you must turn up the central heating.

Where's the problem?

The problem is that it's fiendishly difficult to pin down. It never has been with any certainty.

...... ● ......

ii ANCIENT GREEK PHILOSOPHERS did not devote much attention to the problem of consciousness in itself. Instead, the second-century Greek physician and philosopher Galen argued, memory, estimation and imagination had their seat in the three ventricles of the brain, so positing a physical basis for what we might call consciousness. A fully focused discussion of the problem in the modern period begins with Descartes.

Descartes' famous dictum *cogito ergo sum* ('I am thinking, therefore I am') is the starting point of his reflections in *Meditations on First Philosophy* (1641) in which he says consciousness 'is inseparable from thinking, and, as it seems to me, essential to it: it being impossible for anyone to perceive without perceiving that he does perceive. When we see, hear, smell, taste, feel, meditate, or will anything, we know that we do so.' Consciousness is the self: we are our consciousness.

Descartes describes self-consciousness; but what about the outside world? What is the status of external objects? Do they exist independently of the perceiving consciousness? He considers four possibilities: 1) they are no more than an idea I have; 2) God caused them; 3) a deceiving demon (*dieu trompeur*) caused them; 4) they exist independently of my mind. He proves the existence of external objects in the following way (having already argued for the existence of God): God is not a deceiver; God created me as a being possessed of reason and I can see that my ideas come from external objects; if my ideas do not come from external objects then God is a deceiver, which is absurd; therefore, external (material) objects exist.

...... ● ......

iii **DESCARTES BELIEVED** that our consciousness contained innate ideas; the seventeenth-century English philosopher John Locke disagreed. He argued that we are born with minds whose character is that of a *tabula rasa* – a blank slate. We have no innate ideas. Everything that is known to us comes from sensory impressions of the world outside of our consciousness. In *An Essay Concerning Human Understanding* (1690) he wrote: 'Self is that conscious thinking thing, – whatever substance

made up of, (whether spiritual or material, simple or com-
pounded, it matters not) – which is sensible or conscious of
pleasure and pain, capable of happiness or misery, and so is
concerned for itself, as far as that consciousness extends.'

Locke's Anglo-Irish contemporary George Berkeley, Bishop
of Cloyne, took an opposite view of consciousness and its
objects. He believed that the material world does not exist.
All that exists is our ideas of things. The chair you are sitting on, the book in your hand, the drink at your side – all of
them ideas, not 'real' objects. In *A Treatise Concerning the
Principles of Human Knowledge* (1710) Berkeley offered this
refutation of the existence of matter:

> By Matter, therefore, we are to understand an inert, sense-
> less substance, in which extension, figure, and motion do ac-
> tually subsist. But it is evident from what we have already
> shown, that extension (space), figure (shape), and motion
> are only ideas existing in the mind, and that an idea can be
> like nothing but another idea, and that consequently neither
> they nor their archetypes can exist in an unperceiving sub-
> stance. Hence, it is plain that the very notion of what is called
> Matter or corporeal substance, involves a contradiction in it.

Many people found Berkeley's claims absurd. One of them
was the eighteenth-century writer and lexicographer Samuel
Johnson. One day after attending church with his friend and
biographer James Boswell, the two were discussing Berkeley's
theory. Boswell remarked to Johnson, 'though we are satisfied
his doctrine is not true, it is impossible to refute it'. And then
'Johnson answered, striking his foot with mighty force against
a large stone, till he rebounded from it – "I refute it thus."'

iv **THE EIGHTEENTH-CENTURY** German philosopher Immanuel Kant was also an idealist, but his variety of idealism was much different from Berkeley's. Kant's theory of transcendental idealism, as outlined in his *Critique of Pure Reason* (1781), holds that, while matter exists,

> all our intuition is nothing but the representation of appearance; that the things that we intuit are not in themselves what we intuit them to be, nor are their relations so constituted in themselves as they appear to us; and that if we remove our own subject or even only the subjective constitution of the senses in general, then all constitution, all relations of objects in space and time, indeed space and time themselves would disappear, and as appearances they cannot exist in themselves, but only in us.

Kant's theory is intriguing. It is as if the world outside us is a 'stock cube', and our consciousness is the water that activates it.

But, we might ask, what happens to the world of material objects when they are not subjected to the consciousness which, Kant argues, constitutes them? The answer is surprising: it 'remains entirely unknown to us', he says. The world of external objects, sans us, is like the furthest reaches of outer space for Kant. Our condition as conscious persons is this: 'We are acquainted with nothing except our way of perceiving them, which is peculiar to us, and which therefore does not necessarily pertain to every being, though to be sure it pertains to every human being. We are concerned solely with this.'

...... ● ......

v **THE GERMAN THINKER** Edmund Husserl made consciousness the primary study of philosophy. He is the father of phenomenology, the study of the structure of consciousness as it directs itself towards objects ('constituting' them through the act of 'intentionality'). In *Cartesian Meditations: An Introduction to Phenomenology* (1931), Husserl returns to Descartes' *cogito* and affirms that

Anything belonging to the world, any spatiotemporal being, exists for me – that is to say, is accepted by me – in that I experience it, perceive it, remember it, think of it somehow, judge about it, value it, desire it, or the like. Descartes, as we know, indicated all that by the name cogito. The world is for me absolutely nothing else but the world existing for and accepted by men in such a conscious cogito.

Husserl combines elements of Kant's transcendental idealism with Descartes' reduction when he states that the world 'gets its whole sense, universal and specific, and its acceptance as existing, exclusively from such *cogitationes*. In these my whole life-world goes on, including my scientifically inquiring and grounding life. By my living, by my experiencing, thinking, valuing and acting, I can enter no other world than the one that gets its sense and acceptance or status in and from me, myself.' Human consciousness is the supreme granter of significance in the world.

And then Husserl makes a move known as the 'phenomenological turn'. He takes the *cogito* and makes it the object of reflection: 'If I direct my regard exclusively to this life itself, as consciousness *of* "the world" – I thereby acquire myself as the pure ego, with the pure stream of my *cogitationes*.' 'I am thinking, therefore I am' was Descartes' starting point. The starting point of a phenomenological analysis of consciousness (or anything else) is 'I am thinking about myself thinking. The Cartesian reduction is to the *cogito*. The phenomenological reduction is experiencing the experienced.

...... ● ......

vi **THE AMERICAN** philosopher-psychologist William James had nothing but scorn for the entire concept of consciousness, declaring – in a 1904 lecture entitled 'Does Consciousness Exist?': 'It is the name of a nonentity, and has no right to a place among first principles. Those who still cling to it are clinging to a mere echo, the faint rumor left behind by the disappearing "soul" upon the air of philosophy.' Author of *The Principles of Psychology* (1890), a massively influential text, James confessed in his 1904 lecture: 'For twenty years past I have mistrusted "consciousness" as an entity; for seven or eight years past I have suggested its non-existence to my students, and tried to give them its pragmatic equivalent in realities of experience. It seems to me that the hour is ripe for it to be openly and universally discarded.'

In the twentieth century consciousness gets a further kicking from the Algerian-born French deconstructionist and obscurantist Jacques Derrida, whose writings challenge those of Hegel for opacity (*see also* OBFUSCATION vii). Derrida rejects the tradition of subjectivity that runs from Kant through Husserl and the phenomenologists. Derrida asks: 'What does "consciousness" mean?' He answers indirectly: 'Most often, in the very form of meaning, in all its modifications, consciousness offers itself to thought only as self-presence, as the perception of self in presence.' So, not much. Then Derrida adds: 'And what holds for consciousness holds here for so-called subjective existence in general.' Derrida cheerfully rubbishes two millennia of thought about the human subject when he says 'Just as the category of the subject cannot be, and has never been, thought without the reference to presence as *hupokeimenon* [the underlying thing] or as *ousia* [essence], etc., so the subject as consciousness has never manifested itself except as self-presence.'

...... ● ......

vii **BY NOW MANY READERS MAY AGREE** with Stuart Sutherland that consciousness is 'a fascinating but elusive phenomenon' of which it is 'impossible to specify what it is, what it does, or why it has evolved' and that 'nothing worth reading has been written on it'. A fascinating and – many would say, sacrilegious – approach to consciousness is proposed by the Zagreb-born Imperial College London Emeritus Professor of Neural Engineering Igor Aleksander. He argues that 'The personal sensations that lead to the consciousness of an organism are due to the firing patterns of some neurons, such neurons being part of a larger number which form the state variables of a neural state machine, the firing patterns having been learned through a transfer of activity between sensory input neurons and the state neurons.'

Aleksander is not stepping outside the philosophical tradition very much as his location of consciousness in a physical seat is nothing new: remember that Galen located it in the ventricles of the brain. Aleksander introduces what had not been discovered in Galen's day, neurons and neural pathways. His machine analogy is also nothing new, as the Western medical model, with rare exceptions, treats the person as a machine. What is new is that Aleksander proposes a specific kind of machine model for understanding consciousness: 'The brain of a conscious organism is a state machine whose state variables are the outputs of neurons. This implies that a definition of consciousness be developed in terms of the elements of state machine theory.' This understanding raises the question, is it possible to reverse-engineer a machine that is conscious? Aleksander thinks so. In 2001 he published *How to Build a Mind: Toward Machines with Imagination*.

MIDWIFE *of* MARXISM

COASTAL SURVEYOR

LENS-GRINDER

MILL OWNER *and* RABBLE-ROUSER

CHAPTER EIGHT

DAY JOBS

EMPEROR *of* **ROME**

Every MOMENT think steadily as a

ROMAN *and a* MAN

i **THE STOIC PHILOSOPHER** Marcus Aurelius' day job was
emperor of Rome from AD 161 to 180 (*see also* GOVERNING
i). He was the first Western ruler to embody the ideal of the
Philosopher King, set out by Plato in *The Republic* (*c.*380
BC). Plato has Socrates speak of a 'union of qualities' that the
'guardian of the state' must have: equanimity, patriotism and
a love of wisdom (Plato's definition of a philosopher): 'such a
union of qualities is possible, and that... those in whom they
are united, and those only, should be rulers in the State'.

Stoics are followers of the early third-century BC Greek
philosopher Zeno of Citium who taught that moral and
intellectual perfection lay in taming the emotions. He advocated cultivation of human will in accord with nature. It is a
school of thought that argues we are to be judged by deeds,
not words. Marcus Aurelius' *Meditations* (*c.*170–80) is one
of the most important texts in Stoic philosophy. He had been
emperor of Rome for nine years when he began the work. He
had to deal with natural disasters like floods, earthquakes and
the Antonine Plague of 165–180.*

Meditations was composed in the field while Marcus was
leading his troops against invading Germanic tribes along the
northern border of the empire. In Book 2 of the *Meditations*,
Marcus makes an eloquent statement of the Stoic philosophy
in action, when faced with overwhelming adversity:

**Every moment think steadily as a Roman and a man to do
what thou hast in hand with perfect and simple dignity, and
feeling of affection, and freedom, and justice; and to give
thyself relief from all other thoughts. And thou wilt give**

---

*A plague that was disseminated across the Roman Empire by infected troops
returning from wars in the Near East. Scholars suspect it was measles or smallpox.

thyself relief, if thou doest every act of thy life as if it were the last, laying aside all carelessness and passionate aversion from the commands of reason, and all hypocrisy, and self-love, and discontent with the portion which has been given to thee. Thou seest how few the things are, the which if a man lays hold of, he is able to live a life which flows in quiet, and is like the existence of the gods; for the gods on their part will require nothing more from him who observes these things.

...... ● ......

ii **THOUGH A ROMAN**, Marcus Aurelius wrote in Greek. Three of the tutors most responsible for his education were Greek: Aninus Macer, Caninius Celer and the Sophist Herodes Atticus. In the *Meditations*, the first thing Marcus does is to honour those who taught him. 'From Apollonius [of Chalcedon, Stoic philosopher] I learned freedom of will and undeviating steadiness of purpose'; 'from Sextus [of Chaeronea], a benevolent disposition, and the example of a family governed in a fatherly manner, and the idea of living conformably to nature'; 'from [Marcus Cornelius] Fronto I learned to observe what envy, and duplicity, and hypocrisy are in a tyrant, and that generally those among us who are called Patricians are rather deficient in paternal affection'.

Perhaps the highest quality Marcus acquired was 'from Alexander [of Cotiaeum] the grammarian, to refrain from fault finding'. Nowhere is this aspect of Marcus's stoical disposition better illustrated than in his treatment of his wife Faustina the Younger after she encouraged Avidius Cassius to claim himself emperor after spreading a false report of Marcus's death on the northern frontier. When the plot was revealed, Avidius was murdered by a centurion. His head was sent to Marcus, who declined to look at it, and ordered it buried. For his notoriously unfaithful wife, however, Marcus never had anything but the highest praise.

...... ● ......

iii **EDWARD GIBBON WROTE** in his *Decline and Fall of the Roman Empire* (1776–89) that Rome had five good emperors – Nerva, Trajan, Hadrian, Antoninus Pius and Marcus Aurelius – whose reigns were marked by governance based on wisdom and virtue. The only area in which Marcus's wisdom seemed to falter is on the matter of the 'Christian problem'. Early Christians were persecuted, and so conducted their worship in secret. It was this secrecy that caused the majority non-Christian population to view them with suspicion. Rumours circulated that the celebration of the Eucharist involved actual blood sacrifice of humans. Marcus believed that Christians were a divisive presence, and acted brutally against them. Punishments for Roman citizens ranged from exile to beheading; slaves, immigrants and the proletariat were often devoured by wild animals in public displays.

...... ● ......

iv **THE SEVENTEENTH-CENTURY** Dutch Republic was a centre of the optical industry, and Baruch Spinoza, an Amsterdam-born Jew of Sephardi Portuguese origin, was an expert lens grinder. But behind his apparently humble trade lay a rich hinterland devoted to the study of philosophy, and specifically to the writings of René Descartes, the French thinker who coincidentally spent much of his life in the Netherlands. Enlightenment philosophers owe an enormous debt to Spinoza for helping to make rationalism a dominant force in Western thought. Spinoza rejected the mind–body dualism of Descartes, while his robust determinism is evident in the following words from his magnum opus, the *Ethics* (1677):

> the infant believes that it is by free will that it seeks the breast; the angry boy believes that by free will he wishes vengeance; the timid man thinks it is with free will he seeks flight; the drunkard believes that by a free command of his mind he speaks the things which when sober he wishes he had left unsaid... All believe that they speak by a free command of the mind, whilst, in truth, they have no power to restrain the impulse which they have to speak.

Like Marcus Aurelius, he could also be described as a Stoic. As a monist Spinoza argued that all of nature was one indivisible unity. By regarding God and nature as one, Spinoza fell foul of the religious authorities. By the age of twenty-three Spinoza's thought had made such an impact in Amsterdam that the Talmud Torah congregation issued a *cherem* against him on 27 July 1656. A *cherem* is a kind of excommunication, or expulsion, from the Jewish community. Spinoza's was especially harsh in that it also called down multiple curses upon him:

> The Lords of the ma'amad, having long known of the evil opinions and acts of Baruch de Espinoza, have endeavoured by various means and promises, to turn him from his evil ways. But having failed to make him mend his wicked ways...

they have decided, with their consent, that the said Espinoza should be excommunicated and expelled from the people of Israel. By the decree of the angels, and by the command of the holy men, we excommunicate, expel, curse and damn Baruch de Espinoza, with the consent of God, Blessed be He, and with the consent of all the Holy Congregation, in front of these holy Scrolls with the six-hundred-and-thirteen precepts which are written therein, with the excommunication with which Joshua banned Jericho, with the curse with which Elisha cursed the boys, and with all the curses which are written in the Book of the Law. Cursed be he by day and cursed be he by night; cursed be he when he lies down, and cursed be he when he rises up; cursed be he when he goes out, and cursed be he when he comes in... We order that no one should communicate with him orally or in writing, or show him any favour, or stay with him under the same roof, or within four ells of him, or read anything composed or written by him.

Spinoza lenses were prized for their brightness and clarity. While his daily grind included the manufacture of spectacles, he also created lenses for microscopes and telescopes. He would sit at a lens-grinding lathe driven by foot. He would hold the glass in his left hand, pressing it against a metal plate that was concave or convex, depending upon the lens. For polishing, the plate was covered with paper to which Spinoza applied finely ground rottenstone (limestone, or tripoli as it was sometimes called).

By night he wrote philosophy. In 1674 he completed his greatest work, *Ethics, Demonstrated in Geometrical Order*, which was published shortly after his death in 1677. Spinoza most probably died from what was called grinder's asthma (silicosis, a type of pneumoconiosis): over many years the fine glass dust that he inhaled during every working hour caused inflammation of the lungs. He died aged forty-four, in the single room he rented from the painter Henryk Von Der Spijk in The Hague. *See also* GOD v.

...... • ......

v **FRIEDRICH ENGELS,** social scientist, philosopher and mid-wife of Marxism, was a partner in the Salford, Lancashire, cotton thread firm of Ermen and Engels. Deeply ironic is the fact that one of the creators of communism also profited from capital, drawing an annual income worth more than £150,000 in today's money from the firm that was part-owned by his father.

Engels most famously co-authored *The Communist Manifesto* (1848) with Karl Marx. It can be argued that, in the West, only Christianity has had a bigger impact on thought, economics, social organization, wars and international relations in the modern period than did communism. In *The Condition of the Working Class in England* (1845, English translation 1885), one of the key analyses on which socialism and communism was built, Engels compared the increased mortality rate of the new industrial class of workers with that of agricultural labourers. In Manchester, life expectancy fell to twenty-eight years, Engels reported – half that of country dwellers.

Engels used much of his salary to support Marx and his family, a fact that has generally been seen as reason enough to justify the contradiction of being a mill owner and rabble-rouser calling for the end of capitalism. In his personal life, the contradictions went much deeper. He chose as his love interest a working-class Irishwoman, Mary Burns. Engels led a double life, keeping a bourgeois residence in Manchester while living with Mary and her sister Lizzie at numerous working-class addresses around Manchester. After Mary's death Engels developed a relationship with Lizzie, and agreed to marry her as she lay dying. In his other life, Engels rode to hounds with the Cheshire hunt, loved fine wines and conducted numerous affairs – all the while fulfilling his duties at the mill while publishing more work than many a full-time author ever did. He wrote to Marx, 'If I had an income of 5,000 francs I would do nothing but work and amuse myself with women until I went to pieces.' *See also* FREEDOM viii *and* ix; GOVERNING iv.

...... ● ......

vi **CHARLES SANDERS PEIRCE** is arguably America's greatest philosopher. Russell said of him in 1959: 'he was one of the most original minds of the later nineteenth century, and certainly the greatest American thinker ever'. He is chiefly remembered as the father of pragmatism, that school of thought which holds that propositions are true if they work, and that unpractical ideas should be rejected. For much of his life, however, Peirce's day job was a coastal surveyor for the United States Coast Survey (later the United States Coast and Geodetic Survey).

Peirce worked at the Survey from 1859 to 1891. He devised numerous instruments and perfected the use of pendula to identify local variations in the Earth's gravity. Over time, however, Peirce's attention to his paid work suffered as he wrote extensively on logic. When his reports became years overdue, there was an investigation of the department. Heads rolled, and Peirce was invited to resign.

While working at the Survey Peirce held a second job, from 1879 to 1884, teaching mathematics at Johns Hopkins University in Maryland. During this time he cohabited with Juliette Annette Froissy while still married to his first wife, Zina. The university overlooked Peirce's drug addiction (*see also* DRUGS iv), irritability and adultery – until it was learned that Froissy (whom Peirce married two days after divorcing Zina) was a gypsy. This was too much for the university authorities, and Peirce was summarily dismissed. After his resignation from the survey, Peirce never held a job again.

Peirce continued writing philosophy until his death. William James, who took Peirce's pragmatic philosophy and turned it into an enduring American school of thought, acknowledged Peirce's role in his success. He occasionally sent money to his fellow thinker, but Peirce lived in abject poverty and died destitute.

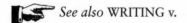 *See also* WRITING v.

THE **KING** LAY DOWN NOT TO SLEEP,
HE LAY DOWN TO **DREAM**

When the body is at
REST *the soul*
ADMINISTERS
her own
HOUSEHOLD

DAYDREAM
TRANSPORTS THE
DREAMER TO A WORLD
THAT BEARS THE
MARK OF
INFINITY

CHAPTER NINE

DREAMS

IN DREAMS
we all
RESEMBLE
THE SAVAGE

LIFE AND DREAMS
ARE LEAVES
OF THE
SAME BOOK

i   'DREAM' IS BOTH A NOUN and a double-edged verb. We *have* dreams – those fantastical night-time flights in which the impossible isn't. And we *dream*: not only the aforementioned flights, but we also dream *of* – falling in love, becoming a ballerina, being a rock star, making loads of money, world peace.

    Before philosophers applied reason to their study, dreams were confined to the realm of the supernatural. One of the earliest written references to dreams is the twenty-first-century BC Sumerian clay tablet *Lugalbanda in the Mountain Cave* which tells how 'The king lay down not to sleep, he lay down to dream – not turning back at the door of the dream, not turning back at the door-pivot. To the liar it talks in lies, to the truthful it speaks truth. It can make one man happy, it can make another man sing, but it is the closed tablet-basket of the gods.' This three-sentence text tells us much about how dreams were thought of in ancient times. Ancient rulers looked for signs in dreams as to how they should govern. The Egyptians regarded those with vivid dreams as having a special connection to the gods. Egyptians in search of help from the gods would go to sanctuaries that contained special dream beds. Many Native Americans continue to hang 'dream-catchers' made of a decorated willow hoop over their beds.

...... ● ......

ii   ARISTOTLE is among the ancient Greeks who brought the problem of dreams into the realm of scientific scrutiny. His essay 'On Dreams' (*c*.350 BC) concluded: 'It is plain therefore that this affection, which we name "dreaming", is no mere exercise of opinion or intelligence, but yet is not an affection of the faculty of perception in the simple sense. If it were the latter it would be possible [when asleep] to hear and see in the simple sense.' One of Aristotle's explanations of dreams is that they are symptoms of a physiological disorder or disease, and may aid the physician in diagnosis. The physician Hippocrates, the father of modern medicine after whom the Hippocratic Oath is named, further expounded on Aristotle's conclusion:

> when the body is awake the soul is its servant, and is never her own mistress, but divides her attention among many things, assigning a part of it to each faculty of the body... But when the body is at rest, the soul, being set in motion and awake, administers her own household, and of herself performs all the acts of the body. For the body when asleep has no perception; but the soul when awake has cognizance of all things – sees what is visible, hears what is audible, walks, touches, feels pain, ponders. In a word, all the functions of body and of soul are performed by the soul during sleep.

...... ● ......

iii **THE PROBLEM OF DREAMING** was at the heart of René Descartes' reasoning about how we know things with any certainty. Part of his attack on empiricism was to ask 'how do I know I'm not dreaming?' Following the systematic process of questioning his beliefs that has come to be called 'Cartesian doubt' Descartes proceeds from that doubt, raising other doubts, to arrive at the famous cogito (*cogito ergo sum*, 'I am thinking, therefore I am').

Descartes compared dreams to the waking thoughts of the lunatic: 'I am accustomed to sleep and in my dreams to

imagine the same things that lunatics imagine when awake.' In
Human, All Too Human (1878) Friedrich Nietzsche similarly
'dismissed' dreaming:

> in dreams we all resemble the savage; bad recognition and
> erroneous comparisons are the reasons of the bad conclu-
> sions, of which we are guilty in dreams: so that, when we
> clearly recollect what we have dreamt, we are alarmed at
> ourselves at harbouring so much foolishness within us. The
> perfect distinctness of all dream representations, which pre-
> suppose absolute faith in their reality, recall the conditions
> that appertain to primitive man, in whom hallucination was
> extraordinarily frequent, and sometimes simultaneously
> seized entire communities, entire nations.

...... ● ......

iv **THE AUSTRIAN NEUROLOGIST** Sigmund Freud (*see also*
SEX i) developed the worldview and clinical method of psychoanalysis. Dreams and their interpretation are key to his revolutionary approach to psychology in which he described the
psyche as having three parts: the id, ego and superego. The id
is the unconscious, a mental territory of unbridled possibilities;
the superego puts the breaks on the wild id, with its mixture
of rationality and understanding of moral and social strictures;
the ego is the public self that attempts to control the id and the
superego. For Freud dreams were a key to the unconscious,
and their interpretation a way of discovering repressed experiences which, in psychoanalysis, are the cause of neurosis.

Like Nietzsche, Freud found in dreams a certain connection
with the 'savage' mind. He described in *Totem and Taboo*

(1913) how the neurotic patients he treated actually lived their lives according to beliefs about themselves which resemble those of the savage.

if we subject [the neurotic] to psychoanalytic treatment, which makes his unconscious thoughts conscious to him, he refuses to believe that thoughts are free and is always afraid to express evil wishes lest they be fulfilled in consequence of his utterance. But through this attitude as well as through the superstition which plays an active part in his life he reveals to us how close he stands to the savage who believes he can change the outer world by a mere thought of his.

In *The Interpretation of Dreams*, first published in 1913 and frequently revised over eight editions, Freud engages in a rigorous clinical study of dreams and their meanings. He set out to 'demonstrate that there is a psychological technique which makes it possible to interpret dreams, and that on the application of this technique every dream will reveal itself as a psychological structure, full of significance, and one which may be assigned to a specific place in the psychic activities of the waking state'. While critics have cast a suspicious eye on Freud's claim to scientific rigour in psychoanalysis, it has nevertheless proved a successful therapeutic model for many. It has also informed philosophy and critical theory. Two French intellectual giants of the twentieth century – Jacques Lacan (*see* OBFUSCATION vi) and Julia Kristeva – are celebrated for using Freud's ideas in their philosophical writing as well as in their day-to-day work as practising psychoanalysts. In his conclusion to *The Interpretation of Dreams*, Freud comes full circle to pay homage to the ancients' view: 'the great respect with which the ancient peoples regarded dreams is based on a just piece of psychological divination. It is a homage paid to the unsubdued and indestructible elements in the human soul, to the demonic power which furnishes the dream-wish, and which we have found again in our unconscious.' *See also* DRUGS iii.

...... • ......

v **IN 1959** the American analytic philosopher Norman Malcolm, a student of Wittgenstein, published a book called *Dreaming*. His goal was to demolish the idea that dreams held the status ascribed by Freud and others (Wittgenstein himself was intrigued by Freud, but found him unscientific). Malcolm argues against the verifiability of dreams. The dreamer who writes an account of his dream in the morning has created a text which is not the dream itself, Malcolm contends; therefore the account after the fact does not support any claim that 'dreams are consciously experienced during sleep'. At bottom he argues that making judgements in sleep is impossible – against 'the received view's premise that in sleep we can judge, reason, and so forth'.

Another American analytical philosopher, Daniel Dennett, countered the received theory of dreams with his 'cassette theory'. In his article 'Are Dreams Experiences?' (1976) Dennett proposes that our brains may hold a 'library' of 'undreamed [i.e. never experienced] dreams with various indexed endings, and the bang or bump or buzz* has the effect of retrieving an appropriate dream and inserting it, cassette-like, in the memory

---

* Of, for instance, an alarm clock or other cause of waking.

mechanism'. A philosopher of mind with an interest in biology and physiological causes of mind-related phenomena, Dennett believes that 'on waking this "cassette" is played back and the person mistakenly believes that he or she had a dream experience. Dennett doesn't tell us where the "library" of undreamed dreams comes from'.

...... ● ......

vi **GASTON BACHELARD,** a philosopher of science and poetics, restores dreams and dreaming to their role as fundamental to human existence and creativity. He says that our dreams of (and daydreams about) places are part of how we locate ourselves in space and time. In *The Poetics of Space* (1958) Bachelard writes about spaces that are special to us, that contain our childhood dreams, and of which we dream as adults. Dreaming, daydreaming, reverie – all of these combine to make our reality. 'Daydream transports the dreamer outside the immediate world to a world that bears the mark of infinity,' Bachelard tells us. He believes that 'the places in which we have experienced daydreaming reconstitute themselves in a new daydream, and it is because our memories of former dwelling-places are relived as daydreams that these dwelling-places of the past remain in us for all time'.

And all the spaces of our past moments of solitude, the spaces in which we have suffered from solitude, enjoyed, desired, and compromised solitude, remain indelible within us and precisely because the human being wants them to remain so... And when we reach the very end of the labyrinths of sleep, when we attain to the regions of deep slumber, we may perhaps experience a type of repose that is pre-human; pre-human, in this case, approaching the immemorial.

vii IN *THE WORLD AS WILL AND REPRESENTATION* (1818) Arthur Schopenhauer argues that 'Life and dreams are leaves of the same book. The systematic reading of this book is real life, but when the reading hours (that is, the day) are over, we often continue idly to turn over the leaves, and read a page here and there without method or connection: often one we have read before, sometimes one that is new to us, but always in the same book.'

After I took
MESCALINE,
I STARTED SEEING
CRABS AROUND ME
all the time

PHILOSOPHERS
HAVE BEEN STRANGELY
SILENT
ABOUT THE TOPIC
of
ILLICIT DRUGS

CHAPTER TEN

DRUGS

TOXIC SHORT CUTS
to
self-transcendence

Divine
MADNESS

THAT **HEIGHTENING**
of the MENTAL POWERS
WHICH **ALCOHOL, TEA,**
or **COFFEE** INDUCE

i **PLATO** and other ancient Greeks were regular users of psycho-tropic drugs. The occasion for their use was the symposium.* Today we think of a symposium as a rather dull and studi-ous affair sponsored by a university at which invited speakers grapple with an academic issue. The original meaning of the term is 'a drinking party or convivial discussion, especially as held in ancient Greece after a banquet'.† The drinking part refers to wine which 'did not contain alcohol as its sole inebri-ant but was ordinarily a variable infusion of herbal toxins in a vinous liquid. Unguents, spices, and herbs, all with recognized psychotropic properties, could be added to the wine.'

The drug-fuelled symposium began with entertainment and a meal, after which the 'wine' was mixed specifically for the group gathered. The *symposiarch* – a sort of ancient mixolo-gist who was more pharmacist than bartender – prepared the 'wine' to a strength ordered by the host. The contemporary historian of ancient Greece David Hillman describes how 'The Greeks and Romans used opium, anticholinergics (from the nightshade‡ family), and numerous botanical toxins to induce states of mental euphoria, create hallucinations, and alter their own consciousness.'

ii **THE ANCIENT GREEKS** argued that their drug-taking was in the service of art, poetry and thought. Plato called the drug-induced inebriation of the symposia 'divine madness'. In the

---

* Plato's *Symposium* (385–370 BC) is a text in which the nature and purpose of love is explored in a sequence of speeches by individuals attending such a gathering.

† *Oxford English Dictionary.*

‡ *Atropa belladonna* (aka deadly nightshade) induces vivid hallucinations and delirium. Ingestion of just a small number of berries – or a single leaf – of the plant is generally fatal.

Phaedra, he invokes this defence of drugs: 'he who without divine madness comes to the doors of the Muses, confident that he will be a good poet by art, meets with no success, and the poetry of the sane man vanishes into nothingness before that of the inspired madmen'. The contemporary historian of ancient Greece David Hillman argues that because the Greeks used the catch-all term 'wine', 'this has allowed history teachers to present ancient revellers as merely drinkers – not "illegal drug" users'.

While Plato tolerated drug use among the class to which he belonged, he also believed that the state must be preserved at all costs, and that unchecked inebriation among the population at large was a threat to it. It was important that the city-state (*polis*) maintain a level of order (*stasis*) for it to function properly and to defend itself against enemies. The first-century Stoic Seneca the Younger wrote:

> **Think of the calamities caused by drunkenness in a nation! This evil has betrayed to their enemies the most spirited and warlike races; this evil has made breaches in walls defended by the stubborn warfare of many years; this evil has forced under alien sway peoples who were utterly unyielding and defiant of the yoke; this evil has conquered by the wine-cup those who in the field were invincible.**

He cites the example of Alexander the Great, conqueror of the Persians, who expired from the effects of a prolonged debauch in the Babylonian palace of Nebuchadnezzar II: 'it was intemperance in drinking that laid him low'.*

---

* Beyond alcoholic liver disease, other mooted causes of Alexander's decease include pancreatitis, malaria, schistosomiasis, West Nile fever, endocarditis and arsenic poisoning.

iii **SIGMUND FREUD** became so fond of cocaine that, for twelve years, he was addicted to it. In an 1884 article Freud reported: 'The psychic effect of *cocaïnum muriaticum* in doses of 0.05–0.10g consists of exhilaration and lasting euphoria, which does not differ in any way from the normal euphoria of a healthy person.' Freud's susceptibility to cocaine addiction is apparent in this reporting of its euphoric effects as 'normal'. There is no mention of any deleterious effect. He minimizes the effect of cocaine by comparing it to a more readily available drug, alcohol: 'The feeling of excitement which accompanies stimulus by alcohol is completely lacking; the characteristic urge for immediate activity which alcohol produces is also absent.' By comparison, 'One senses an increase of self-control and feels more vigorous and more capable of work; on the other hand, if one works, one misses that heightening of the mental powers which alcohol, tea, or coffee induce. One is simply normal, and soon finds it difficult to believe that one is under the influence of any drug at all' (all of which rather begs the question, why bother to take it?).

Freud noted the addictive properties of cocaine (but not in the context of his own addiction, solely as a phenomenological description of its effect) when he wrote: 'The effect of a moderate dose of coca fades away so gradually that, in normal circumstances, it is difficult to define its duration.' As its effect fades, more is required, he observes: 'If one works intensively while under the influence of coca, after from three to five hours there is a decline in the feeling of wellbeing, and a further dose of coca is necessary in order to ward off fatigue.' It must be noted that, of all Western thinkers, Freud was one of the most prolific.

Freud's conclusion after a year of cocaine use is: 'it seems probable... that coca, if used protractedly but in moderation, is not detrimental to the body'. In his view, 'Coca is a far more potent and far less harmful stimulant than alcohol, and its widespread utilization is hindered at present only by its high cost.'

...... ● ......

iv **CHARLES SANDERS PEIRCE** suffered from trigeminal neuralgia, a neuropathic disorder of the facial nerves that is one of the most painful medical conditions known. In order to relieve his pain, Peirce began self-prescribing narcotics from an early age. His first drug of choice was ether. Apart from its use as an anaesthetic in surgery, ether became a popular recreational drug in nineteenth-century Poland and Ireland (where its popularity continues to this day).*

Peirce progressed to decoctions of opium (popularly known as 'poppy tea'), which he took with his father, Benjamin Peirce, who was Professor of Mathematics at Harvard University, director of the US Coast and Geodetic Survey and a founder of the Smithsonian Institution. A decoction of opium is made by crushing poppy pods to release their seeds, which are in turn crushed and made into a tea. As his condition became more painful, Peirce moved on to cocaine. Despite his medical condition, and his drug use, he published an enormous amount in his lifetime, and his unpublished manuscripts total more than 80,000 pages. *See also* DAY JOBS.

...... ● ......

---

* Instead of breathing it in, as per administration prior to an operation, recreational users prefer to mix it with water or fruit juice.

v **IN 1937 ALDOUS HUXLEY,** former semi-detached member of the Bloomsbury Group, public intellectual and author of the dystopian novel *Brave New World* (which describes a totalitarian world in which the population is controlled by drugs), emigrated to California. Here he worked as a screenwriter, pursued his interests in spirituality and mysticism and learned of the Native American ceremonial use of the hallucinogenic cactus peyote (mescaline). In his novel *The Devils of Loudon* (1952), the subject of which was the demonic possession of an entire French town in the seventeenth century, Huxley dismissed drugs as 'toxic short cuts to self-transcendence'. However, his view changed when he read reports by the British psychiatrist Humphry Osmond describing his use of mescaline in the treatment of schizophrenics, and suggesting that mescaline might allow a normal person to see the world through the eyes of a schizophrenic. After reading Osmond's conclusion that mescaline was not addictive, Huxley approached the psychiatrist and offered himself as a guinea pig. On 3 May 1953, under Osmond's supervision, Huxley took mescaline at his house in West Hollywood. During an eight-hour trip, he and his friends visited a drugstore, listened to music, walked in his garden and drove to the hills overlooking the city. Under the influence of mescaline, Huxley discovered a new reality that transcended 'systematic reasoning', and which he described in his book *The Doors of Perception** (1954):

...spatial relationships had ceased to matter very much and that my mind was perceiving the world in terms of other than spatial categories. At ordinary times the eye concerns itself

---

* The book's title is taken from a line in William Blake's *The Marriage of Heaven and Hell* (1793).

with such problems as Where? – How far? – How situated in
relation to what? In the mescalin [sic] experience the implied
questions to which the eye responds are of another order.
Place and distance cease to be of much interest. The mind
does its Perceiving in terms of intensity of existence, pro-
fundity of significance, relationships within a pattern... Not,
of course, that the category of space had been abolished...
Space was still there; but it had lost its predominance. The
mind was primarily concerned, not with measures and loca-
tions, but with being and meaning.

...... ● ......

vi **FRENCH EXISTENTIALIST JEAN-PAUL SARTRE** was
a heavy user of amphetamines, barbiturates, alcohol and
tobacco throughout his life. This bruising daily regime was
supplemented by frequent cups of coffee and restaurant meals.
How many drugs did he take? What dosage? We know the
answers to these questions because Annie Solal-Cohen chroni-
cled his consumption in her biography *Sartre: A Life* (1987).
'Sleeping pills would assure his sleep, Corydrane would wake
him up, coffee and whisky would take care of the rest, so he
could keep working the way a drowning man swims, franti-
cally, desperately, knowing time is at his heels, ready to swal-
low him up.' Corydrane was a compound of amphetamine and
aspirin, widely available over the counter in postwar France.*
Sartre regularly took ten times the prescribed dose, a total of
200mg plus a stomach-damaging fifteen grams of aspirin.

Sartre's lifelong companion, the French philosopher and

---

* Corydrane was withdrawn from the market in France in 1971.

feminist Simone de Beauvoir, includes in her memoir, *Adieux: A Farewell to Sartre* (1984), conversations she recorded with him about his drug use.

> DE BEAUVOIR: I saw you working on the *Critique of Dialectical Reason*. It was quite terrifying. You scarcely reread at all.
> SARTRE: I reread the next morning. I used to write about ten pages. That was all I could do in a day.
> DE BEAUVOIR: It was like watching an athletic feat, seeing you write the *Critique of Dialectical Reason*. And you wrote under the effect of Corydrane.
> SARTRE: All the time.

Beauvoir talks to Sartre about the risk of self-destruction. 'I went very far,' he told her. 'I used to take not one tablet of Corydrane but ten each time.'

> DE BEAUVOIR: I know that you even reached the point of having no skin left on your tongue, and that at one point you became half deaf.
> SARTRE: A whole tube of Orthedrine* only lasted me a day... to put it briefly, in philosophy writing consisted of analysing my ideas; and a tube of Corydrane meant 'these ideas will be analysed in the next two days'.

Sartre began taking amphetamines at eight or nine in the morning. After the age of thirty, he took 'four or five' doses of Belladenal (Phenobarbitone) to sleep.

Late in life Sartre recounted an experiment with mescaline

---

* Another amphetamine compound that Sartre used.

in 1929, a bad trip that inspired a scene in his novel *Nausea* (1938) in which the main character, Roquentin, who embodies the author's theories of existential angst, is pursued by giant crayfish and lobsters. He told the author John Gerassi,

> I ended up having a nervous breakdown... after I took mescaline, I started seeing crabs around me all the time. They followed me in the streets, into class. I got used to them. I would wake up in the morning and say, 'Good morning, my little ones, how did you sleep?' I would talk to them all the time. I would say, 'O.K., guys, we're going into class now, so we have to be still and quiet,' and they would be there, around my desk, absolutely still, until the bell rang.

Gerassi asked if there were a lot of crabs. 'Actually, no, just three or four,' Sartre responded. *See also* NICKNAMES xi; OBFUSCATION v.

...... ● ......

vii **THE HUNGARIAN MATHEMATICIAN** Paul Erdős was a regular user of amphetamines. In 1979 a colleague of Erdős' (Ronald Graham) bet him $500 that he could not quit amphetamines for a month:

> Erdős accepted the challenge, and went cold turkey for thirty days. After Graham paid up – and wrote the $500 off as a business expense – Erdős said, 'You've showed me that I'm not an addict. But I didn't get any work done. I'd get up in the morning and stare at a blank piece of paper. I'd have no ideas, just like an ordinary person. You've set mathematics

back a month.' He promptly resumed taking pills, and mathematics has been the better for it.

...... ● ......

viii FIFTY YEARS AGO, many of the drugs we have been discussing were legal and could be purchased over the counter. Now they are controlled by governments. Their consumption is prohibited and possession of them is often punished by harsh prison sentences. Plato, who enjoyed the euphoria-inducing 'wine' served at philosophical symposia, cautioned that public order was of paramount importance. In the United States, a persistent strand of Puritanism combined with an increasing emphasis on law and order has filled the nation's prisons with persons whose only crime has been to do what philosophers have done.* In New York State, draconian drug laws introduced by Governor Nelson Rockefeller in 1973 filled prisons with low-level drug dealers and users, with penalties as stiff as twenty-five years to life in prison. One result was the creation of more prisons in poorer rural communities and new prison jobs for correction officers. The relaxation of these laws in 2009 brought about prison closures and unemployment. In 2015 New York approved 'medical marijuana' and went into the business of growing and selling the previously illegal drug, creating a new and rich source of taxation. Clearly, the prohibition of drugs is based on issues larger than 'moral' ones. Control of drugs by the state is always concerned with money.

The contemporary American philosopher and professor of law Douglas Husak argues that all drugs should be legalized.

---

* I am excluding here violent felons who are members of gangs, cartels and other murderous groups.

Husak says, 'philosophers have been strangely silent about the topic of illicit drugs, even though it is a goldmine of philosophical questions'. 'If there is a good reason to criminalize illicit drug use,' says Husak, 'we have yet to find it.'

While philosophers have not often been specific about drug use, we may extrapolate a view on the subject by interpreting their ethical positions. One of Hippocrates' most famous dicta is 'physician, heal thyself', which may be construed as licence to self-prescribe. But he also says 'do no harm', and there can be no doubt that overuse of drugs can be harmful. From a Christian point of view, the Bible may be said to contain passages which support an anti-drug position. Corinthians 6:15–20 of the King James Version states: 'know ye not that your body is the temple of the Holy Ghost which is in you, which ye have of God, and ye are not your own? For ye are bought with a price: therefore glorify God in your body, and in your spirit, which are God's.' If the body is the 'temple of the Holy Ghost', it follows that the temple must not be defiled. This passage is usually used to argue against fornication, but could equally be applied to drugs in the instance where one's abilities and wellbeing are compromised by their use.

In his *Inquiry Concerning Moral Good and Evil* (1725) the Scottish Enlightenment philosopher Francis Hutcheson argued that ethical choices should be made with a consideration for 'the greatest good for the greatest number'. The English utilitarian Jeremy Bentham would later adopt the phrase and the position, which was also a cornerstone of John Stuart Mill's thinking. Critics accuse the utilitarians of hedonism, since their dictate can be regarded as a pleasure-driven one that could conceivably condone drug use. On the other hand, if large numbers of a society are so affected by drug use that they cannot fully participate (work, civic duty, etc.) then drug use could be regarded as harmful since it might interfere with the greatest good dictum.

Kant, we can assume, would be against drug use since it violates his concept of our duty to ourselves to respect our rationality, which drug use can impair. One therefore has a duty not to use drugs. Contrary to the Kantian position is the libertarian one, which argues in favour of drug use. The Libertarian Party Platform (1914) states: 'We favour the repeal of all laws creating "crimes" without victims, such as the use of drugs for medicinal or recreational purposes, since only actions that infringe on the rights of others can properly be termed crimes. Individuals retain the right to voluntarily assume risk of harm to themselves.'*

Husak argues that one strand of reasoning behind criminalization of drugs – 'predictions about how its frequency would increase if punishments were not imposed' – is dubious on normative and empirical grounds. He contends that while we may not be able to predict with any confidence what effect decriminalization would have on the numbers of persons using drugs, one thing we can be absolutely confident about is that 'after decriminalization, those who use illicit drugs will not face arrest and prosecution. The lives of drug users would not be devastated by a state that is committed to waging war against them.'

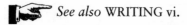   See also WRITING vi.

---

* https://www.lp.org/platform.

TO
SECURE
ONE'S OWN
HAPPINESS
IS A
DUTY

*Everyone benefits
from living in a* SOCIETY
where the duty of
MUTUAL RESPECT
is HONOURED

CHAPTER ELEVEN

DUTY

**THE PRUDENT
TRADESMAN DOES NOT
OVERCHARGE
BUT KEEPS A FIXED PRICE
FOR
EVERYONE**

*

*In duty the
individual
finds*
LIBERATION

We are not BORN *for*
OURSELVES **ALONE**

i   'WHAT IS THE TASK of all higher education?' To turn men
       into machines. 'What are the means?' Man must learn to be
       bored. 'How is that accomplished?' By means of the concept
       of duty.

Friedrich Nietzsche's view of duty in *Twilight of the Idols*
(1889) is a reaction to his profound disgust at man's conform-
ity to rules acquired by rote learning, imitation and intimida-
tion. What is this concept that so perturbed Nietzsche, and
how did it develop over two millennia?

The first-century BC Roman philosopher and political theorist Marcus Tullius Cicero wrote in *On Duties* (44 BC): 'we
ought to follow Nature as our guide, to contribute to the general good by an interchange of acts of kindness, by giving and
receiving, and thus by our skill, our industry, and our talents
to cement human society more closely together, man to man'.
Cicero was not only a philosopher and political theorist. He
was a real politician, serving as a consul under Julius Caesar,
during which time he advocated a return from dictatorship to
republican government. After the death of Caesar, he was executed as an enemy of the state on the orders of Mark Antony.

As 'Plato has admirably expressed it', says Cicero, 'we are
not born for ourselves alone, but our country claims a share
of our being, and our friends a share; and since, as the Stoics
hold, everything that the earth produces is created for man's
use; and as men, too, are born for the sake of men, that they
may be able mutually to help one another'. Cicero believed
duty and justice to go hand in hand. We are bound by a duty
not to harm one another (and also to prevent others from
doing harm to one another): 'For he who, under the influence
of anger or some other passion, wrongfully assaults another

seems, as it were, to be laying violent hands upon a comrade; but he who does not prevent or oppose wrong, if he can, is just as guilty of wrong as if he deserted his parents or his friends or his country.' Despite his strong belief in the individual's duty to the state, Cicero is sceptical of 'duty' where war is concerned:

Most people think that the achievements of war are more important than those of peace; but this opinion needs to be corrected. For many men have sought occasions for war from the mere ambition for fame. This is notably the case with men of great spirit and natural ability, and it is the more likely to happen, if they are adapted to a soldier's life and fond of warfare. But if we will face the facts, we shall find that there have been many instances of achievement in peace more important and no less renowned than in war.

...... ● ......

ii **THE ENGLISH ENLIGHTENMENT** philosopher John Locke recognizes the traditional objects of duty – God, state, self, others – but he pays particular attention to the duty of parents to their children. One reason for this may be his empiricist's view that we are born without any pre-existing knowledge of things, and that our minds are a blank slate (*tabula rasa*) on which experience is writ. Since our first experience is of our parents, our relationship with them is of particular importance to our development as people who will become citizens, friends and, most of us, parents in turn. According to Locke's *Second Treatise of Government* (1689), parents' duty towards their children is rooted in the power they have over them. The 'duty which is incumbent on them' is 'to take care of their off-spring, during the imperfect state of childhood. To inform the mind, and govern the actions of their yet ignorant nonage,* till reason shall take its place, and ease them of that trouble.' It is, says Locke, 'what the children want, and the parents are bound to do'. In return, children have a duty to their parents: 'honour and support, all that which gratitude requires to return for the benefits received by and from them, is the indispensable duty of the child, and the proper privilege of the parents'.

On a wider scale, Locke sets out the duties and obligations of the state and its citizens. He says that the state power should be 'only for the good of the society'. It must not be 'arbitrary' or 'at pleasure': 'it ought to be exercised by established and promulgated laws'. This is essential so that 'both the people may know their duty, and be safe and secure within the limits of the law; and the rulers too kept within their bounds, and not be tempted, by the power they have in their hands, to employ it to such purposes, and by such measures, as they would not have known, and own not willingly'. *See also* GOVERNING iii.

...... • ......

iii **IMMANUEL KANT,** perhaps more than any other thinker, made duty a primary focus of his thought. For Kant, freedom is the main philosophical issue, and the concept of duty is key to it. In his *Fundamental Principles of the Metaphysics of Morals* (1785) he declares: 'As my concern here is with moral philosophy, I limit the question suggested to this: Whether it is not of the utmost necessity to construct a pure thing which is only

---

* The period during which a child is considered legally underage.

empirical and which belongs to anthropology? for that such a philosophy must be possible is evident from the common idea of duty and of the moral laws.'

The first task in constructing this 'pure thing' is 'to develop the notion of a will which deserves to be highly esteemed for itself and is good without a view to anything further, a notion which exists already in the sound natural understanding'. This notion of Kantian will doesn't need be taught; it requires, rather, 'to be cleared up'. We conduct this 'clearing up' by 'estimating the value of our actions'. 'In order to do this,' says Kant, 'we will take the notion of duty, which includes that of a good will.'

In judging actions, says Kant, 'we can readily distinguish whether the action which agrees with duty is done from duty, or from a selfish view'. He gives the example of a merchant who has a duty not to overcharge an inexperienced shopper. Kant notes that 'wherever there is much commerce the prudent tradesman does not overcharge, but keeps a fixed price for everyone, so that a child buys of him as well as any other. Men are thus honestly served.' But, Kant continues, 'this is not enough to make us believe that the tradesman has so acted from duty and from principles of honesty: his own advantage required it'. Therefore, he is acting out of self-interest by performing the dutiful action. Not generally noted for his humour, Kant now offers this aside: 'it is out of the question in this case to suppose that he might besides have a direct inclination in favour of the buyers, so that, as it were, from love he should give no advantage to one over another'.

The concept of duty to oneself raises fascinating moral issues for Kant. He says we have a *duty* to maintain our lives, but notes that we also have a direct *inclination* to do it. This direct inclination nullifies the moral acts of persons if 'They preserve their life as duty requires, no doubt, but not because duty requires.' As a result, 'their maxim has no moral import'. Kant provides an example of self-preservation that *does* have moral import. He imagines the case of a person for whom 'adversity and hopeless sorrow have completely taken away the relish for life'. If this person is 'strong in mind' and – 'indignant at his fate' – elects not to be despondent, and not to wish for death – perhaps by his own hand – and instead 'preserves his life without loving it – not from inclination or fear, but from duty – then his maxim has a moral worth'.

Kant is rigorous in denying moral worth to the actions of those who 'without any other motive of vanity or self-interest... find a pleasure in spreading joy around them and... take delight in the satisfaction of others so far as it is their own work'. He argues that 'To be beneficent when we can is a duty.' The action of a spreader of joy,

> however proper, however amiable it may be, has neverthe-less no true moral worth, but is on a level with other inclina-tions, e.g., the inclination to honour, which, if it is happily directed to that which is in fact of public utility and accord-ant with duty and consequently honourable, deserves praise and encouragement, but not esteem.

Kant's maxim: actions should 'be done from duty, not from inclination'.

So: how, to meet Kant's criterion, can we achieve moral worth? First, we must secure our own happiness. Why? Because 'To secure one's own happiness is a duty.' But why is the securing of self-worth a duty? Because 'discontent with one's condition, under a pressure of many anxieties and amidst unsatisfied wants, might easily become a great temptation to transgression of duty'. Kant is led to reflect on the chief commandment of Jesus Christ: love one another (even if the other is our enemy). He is highly critical of this commandment because 'love, as an affection, cannot be commanded'. On the other hand, 'beneficence for duty's sake may; even though we are not impelled to it by any inclination – nay, are even repelled by a natural and unconquerable aversion'. Kant calls this beneficence for duty's sake 'practical love and not pathological – a love which is seated in the will, and not in the propensions [sic] of sense – in principles of action and not of tender sympathy; and it is this love alone which can be commanded'.

After discussing personal instances of duty, Kant tells us that there is nothing really personal about duty at all: 'Duty is the necessity of acting from respect for the law.' Why is this so? Kant explains, 'I may have inclination for an object as the effect of my proposed action, but I cannot have respect for it, just for this reason, that it is an effect and not an energy of will. Similarly I cannot have respect for inclination, whether my own or another's; I can at most, if my own, approve it.' What is 'connected with my will as a principle... what does not subserve my inclination, but overpowers it, or at least in case of choice excludes it from its calculation' is, quite simply, 'the law of itself, which can be an object of respect, and hence a command'. So,

an action done from duty must wholly exclude the influence of inclination and with it every object of the will, so that nothing remains which can determine the will except objectively the law, and subjectively pure respect for this

practical law, and consequently the maxim that I should
follow this law even to the thwarting of all my inclinations.

He gives this example of how the 'personal' is actually 'the law':

Since we also look on the improvement of our talents as a
duty, we consider that we see in a person of talents, as it
were, the example of a law (viz., to become like him in this
by exercise), and this constitutes our respect. All so-called
moral interest consists simply in respect for the law.

Thus we arrive at Kant's famous *kategorischer Imperativ* ('categorical imperative') which states: 'Act only according to that
maxim whereby you can at the same time will that it should
become a universal law.'

...... ● ......

iv **JUST WHEN WE THINK** that Kant is as good a thinker on
duty as any, and that he is able to translate the highest level of
philosophical thinking into rules we can live by, along comes
Friedrich Nietzsche who concludes that, as a moralist, Kant is
an idiot. He writes in *The Antichrist* (1895):

A word now against Kant as a moralist. A virtue must be
our invention; it must spring out of our personal need and
defence. In every other case it is a source of danger. That
which does not belong to our life menaces it; a virtue which
has its roots in mere respect for the concept of 'virtue,' as
Kant would have it, is pernicious. 'Virtue,' 'duty,' 'good for
its own sake,' goodness grounded upon impersonality or a

notion of universal validity – these are all chimeras, and in them one finds only an expression of the decay, the last collapse of life, the Chinese spirit of Koenigsberg.* Quite the contrary is demanded by the most profound laws of self-preservation and of growth: to wit, that every man find his own virtue, his own categorical imperative. A nation goes to pieces when it confounds its duty with the general concept of duty. Nothing works a more complete and penetrating disaster than every 'impersonal' duty, every sacrifice before the Moloch of abstraction. – To think that no one has thought of Kant's categorical imperative as dangerous to life! ... The theological instinct alone took it under protection! – An action prompted by the life-instinct proves that it is a right action by the amount of pleasure that goes with it: and yet that Nihilist, with his bowels of Christian dogmatism, regarded pleasure as an objection... What destroys a man more quickly than to work, think and feel without inner necessity, without any deep personal desire, without pleasure – as a mere automaton of duty? That is the recipe for decadence, and no less for idiocy... Kant became an idiot.

...... ● ......

v **G. W. F. HEGEL EXPLORES** the role of the subject in relation to his duties to the state as one of a freedom born of necessity. In his *Elements of the Philosophy of Right* (1820) Hegel argues for a 'doctrine of duties' founded on a 'philosophical science'. Any doctrine which is not a philosophical science 'takes its material from existing relationships and shows its

---

* In his remark 'the Chinese spirit of Koenigsberg' he is poking fun at Kant. Nietzsche viewed oriental culture as mediocre.

connection with the moralist's personal notions or with principles and thoughts, purposes, impulses, feelings, &c., that are
forthcoming everywhere; and as reasons for accepting each
duty in turn, it may tack on its further consequences in their
bearing on the other ethical relationships or on welfare and
opinion'. That doctrine is therefore inferior. He concludes that
'an immanent and logical "doctrine of duties" can be nothing except the serial exposition of the relationships which are
necessitated by the Idea of freedom and are therefore actual in
their entirety, to within the state'.

Hegel acknowledges that 'The bond of duty can appear as a
restriction only on indeterminate subjectivity or abstract freedom, and on the impulses either of the natural will or of the
moral will which determines its indeterminate good arbitrarily.' He argues that an understanding of necessity is the key to
freedom:

> in duty the individual finds his liberation; first, liberation
> from dependence on mere natural impulse and from the
> depression which as a particular subject he cannot escape
> in his moral reflections on what ought to be and what might
> be; secondly, liberation from the indeterminate subjectivity
> which, never reaching reality or the objective determinacy of
> action, remains self-enclosed and devoid of actuality. In duty
> the individual acquires his substantive freedom.

For Hegel, duty is the key to freedom:

> Duty is a restriction only on the self-will of subjectivity. It
> stands in the way only of that abstract good to which sub-
> jectivity adheres. When we say: 'We want to be free', the

primary meaning of the words is simply: 'We want abstract freedom', and every institution and every organ of the state passes as a restriction on freedom of that kind. Thus duty is not a restriction on freedom, but only on freedom in the abstract, i.e. on unfreedom. Duty is the attainment of our essence, the winning of positive freedom.

When the universal will identifies with the individual will, 'right and duty coalesce, and by being in the ethical order a man has rights in so far as he has duties, and duties in so far as he has rights'. As the atomists (*see* CHANCE ii) argued that indeterminacy or chance in the universe would cause it to unravel, Hegel believes that if rights and duties were separated, 'the whole would be dissolved, since their identity alone is the fundamental thing, and it is to this that we have here to hold fast'.

...... ● ......

vi **THE ENGLISH PHILOSOPHER** T. H. Green was a follower of Hegel (as were many of his countrymen at the time). He was also a temperance campaigner and one of the founders of social liberalism, which sought to balance individual freedom with social justice. He referred to duty as 'obedience to law', but was ever wary of any sign of coercion or compulsion on the part of the state. In *The Principles of Political Obligation* (1895) he wrote:

The relation of constraint, in the one case between the man and the externally imposed law, in the other between some particular desire of the man and his consciousness of some-

thing absolutely desirable, we naturally represent in English, when we reflect on it, by the common term 'must'. 'I must connect with the main-drainage,' says the householder to himself, reflecting on an edict of the Local Board. 'I must try to get A.B. to leave off drinking,' he says to himself, reflecting on a troublesome moral duty of benevolence to his neighbour. And if the 'must' in the former case represents in part the knowledge that compulsion may be put on the man who neglects to do what he 'must,' which is no part of its meaning in the second, on the other hand the consciousness that the constraint is for a common good, which wholly constitutes the power over inclination in the second case, must always be an element in that obedience which is properly called obedience to law, or civil or political obedience. Simple fear can never constitute such obedience.

...... ● ......

vii **THE TWENTIETH-CENTURY** American philosopher John Rawls believed that 'fairness' should be the basis of a liberal democracy. For Rawls, fairness meant justice. He argued that justice depended upon the inviolability of individual rights. But he also recognized that, in practical terms, a successful and (financially) thriving society necessarily involved social equality. In a world of 'haves' and 'have-nots', many people – minorities and the poor among them – are pushed to the margins. Rawls believed that the rights and needs of 'have-nots' should be the focus of any conversation about justice. In *A Theory of Justice* (1971, revised 1999), Rawls considered the principles of 'natural duty' and elaborated his principle of fairness. While recognizing the individual's duty to the state, he explored the concepts of civil disobedience and 'conscientious refusal' of duty.

Natural duties include 'the duty of helping another when he is in need or jeopardy, provided that one can do so without excessive risk or loss to oneself; the duty not to harm or injure another; and the duty not to cause unnecessary suffering'. In contrast to Hegel, Rawls says that natural duties 'have no necessary connection with institutions or social practices; their content is not, in general, defined by the rules of these arrangements'. The state is also bound by natural duties: 'From the standpoint of justice as fairness, a fundamental natural duty is the duty of justice.' A just society demands a duty of the individual; 'this duty requires us to support and to comply with just institutions that exist and apply to us. It also constrains us to further just arrangements not yet established, at least when this can be done without too much cost to ourselves... everyone has a natural duty to do his part in the existing scheme.'

The duty of government is not to obstruct the rights of the individual and the duty of the individual is to comply with the duties demanded by the state. But 'the real question', says Rawls, 'is under which circumstances and to what extent we are bound to comply with unjust arrangements?':

For one thing, it is evident that our duty or obligation to accept existing arrangements may sometimes be overridden. These requirements depend upon the principles of right, which may justify noncompliance in certain situations, all things considered. Whether noncompliance is justified depends on the extent to which laws and institutions are unjust.

Even though laws may be unjust, 'our natural duty to uphold just institutions binds us to comply with unjust laws and policies, or at least not to oppose them by illegal means as long as they do not exceed certain limits of injustice'. What are those limits? They 'are exceeded in two cases: first, where basic liberties are not upheld, and second, where citizens do not share equitably in the inevitable injustices'. Rawls allows for civil disobedience as a last remedy where 'substantial' and 'clear' violations of justice have occurred. He also recognizes 'conscientious refusal' – the individual's moral decision not to comply based on a deeply held ethical view. This refusal is an individual, rather than a shared, act.

Individual laws may be unjust, but if they are underwritten by a just constitution, then we have a duty to uphold that constitution. So, 'Being required to support a just constitution, we must go along with one of its essential principles, that of majority rule. In a state of near justice, then, we normally have a duty to comply with unjust laws in virtue of our duty to support a just constitution.'

A note on John Rawls and the practical application of his philosophy. He was born into a prominent Maryland family and, upon graduating from Princeton University in 1943, he enlisted as an infantryman in the US Army. He served for two years in the Pacific theatre and participated in bloody trench warfare. He was awarded the Bronze Star and, when offered promotion as an officer, he declined it. After the death of an academic colleague, he took on financial responsibility for the upbringing of his children. He did social work with the poor of Boston. 'Everyone benefits then from living in a society where the duty of mutual respect is honoured,' Rawls wrote. 'The cost to self-interest is minor in comparison with the support for the sense of one's own worth.' *See also* JUSTICE viii.

There is an
INFINITE
NUMBER
of **WORLDS,**
some like this world,
OTHERS UNLIKE IT

I HAVE IN SOME
MEASURE, PROVED
WHAT AT THE FIRST
I PROMISED,
A WORLD
IN THE **MOONE**

CHAPTER TWELVE

EXTRATERRESTRIALS

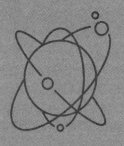

IT FOLLOWS *NOT*
THEY HAVE THE SAME

SHAPE

AS US

These ANIMALS *emit nothing*
EXCREMENTITIOUS

i There is an infinite number of worlds, some like this world, others unlike it. For the atoms being infinite in number, as has just been proved, are borne ever further in their course. For the atoms out of which a world might arise, or by which a world might be formed, have not all been expended on one world or a finite number of worlds, whether like or unlike this one. Hence there will be nothing to hinder an infinity of worlds.

These words were written in the fourth century BC by Epicurus in his 'Letter to Herodotus'. Around the same time, Aristotle argued that we are the only creatures in the universe. But many ancient Greek stargazers, mathematicians and philosophers disagreed with Aristotle and shared Epicurus' view that we are not alone. In his *Lives and Opinions of Eminent Philosophers* Diogenes Laertius tells us that, a century before Aristotle, Democritus conjectured that 'In some worlds there is no Sun and Moon, in others they are larger than in our world, and in others more numerous. In some parts there are more worlds, in others fewer... in some parts they are arising, in others failing. There are some worlds devoid of living creatures or plants or any moisture.' From Diogenes we learn that Leucippus not only believed in other worlds, but had a theory as to how they arise: 'The worlds come into being as follows: many bodies of all sorts and shapes move by abscission* from the infinite into a great void; they come together there and produce a single whirl, in which, colliding with one another and revolving in all manner of ways, they begin to separate like to like.'

---

* Leucippus uses the term 'abscission' as a metaphor borrowed from botany. It is 'the natural detachment of parts of a plant, typically dead leaves and ripe fruit'. *Oxford English Dictionary.*

ii **DE RERUM NATURA** ('On the Nature of Things') is the only surviving work of Lucretius, a Roman poet and philosopher of the first century BC. For centuries after the decline of Rome, *De rerum natura* more or less disappeared from view, until, in 1417, a copy was discovered in the library of a Benedictine monastery by the Italian humanist Poggio Bracciolini. In *De rerum natura*, Lucretius reflects that 'empty space extends without limit in every direction... seeds innumerable are rushing on countless courses through an unfathomable universe'. These observations lead him to conclude that 'it is in the highest degree unlikely that this earth and sky is the only one to have been created and that all those particles are accomplishing nothing'. Writing in the first century AD, the Greek historian and essayist Plutarch wrote in *Concerning Nature*: 'The Pythagoreans say that the moon appears to us terraneous, by reason it is inhabited as our earth is.' He was one of the first in a long line of speculators to imagine other worlds with life forms more beautiful than those of our own planet: 'there are animals of a larger size and plants of a rarer beauty than our globe affords... animals in their virtue and energy are fifteen degrees superior to ours'. These animals are unique in that 'they emit nothing excrementitious'. In addition, lunar days are fifteen times longer than ours.

...... • ......

iii **THE THIRTEENTH-CENTURY** scholastic philosopher and Church father Thomas Aquinas (*see* GOD iv) did not believe in other worlds or extraterrestrials (apart from angels). Medieval Christian teaching precluded extraterrestrials by this logic: God sent his only son, Jesus Christ, to save us from sin. Christ was crucified and died so that we could find forgiveness from sin and eternal life with God in heaven. Since God is a supreme and munificent being, there could not be other life forms on other planets because, after sacrificing his *only* son, God would not be able to offer salvation to those beings: it would be inconsistent with his mercy, to create beings doomed to hell because they have no chance of salvation through Jesus Christ.

In *Summa Theologica* (1265–74) Thomas Aquinas wrote:

> no agent intends a material plurality as an end; because a material multitude does not have a fixed term, but of itself tends to infinity; infinity, however, is contrary to the notion of 'end'. When it is said, however, that many worlds are better than one, this is said according the material multitude. This sort of better, however, does not belong to the intention of God as agent, because for the same reason it could be said that if he made two, it would be better that there were three; and thus ad infinitum.

······ ● ······

iv **NICOLAUS COPERNICUS,** a polymathic scholar who lived and worked in what is now northern Poland in the late fifteenth and early sixteenth centuries, proposed a model of the universe in which the Earth revolves around the sun (rather than vice versa), rather as our moon – and those of the other planets – revolves around the Earth. In the early part of the next century, the German Johannes Kepler advanced Copernicus's work to elaborate laws of planetary motion. His study of the planets and their moons led him to a belief in life on Jupiter: 'Our Moon exists for us on Earth, not the other globes. Those four little moons exist for Jupiter, not for us. Each planet in turn, together with its occupants, is served by its own satellites. From this line of reasoning we deduce with the highest degree of probability that Jupiter is inhabited.'* *See also* BELIEF i.

...... ● ......

v **JOHN WILKINS** was an Anglican clergyman and a founding member of the Royal Society (1660), who took a keen interest in mathematical and experimental philosophy, popularizing the discoveries of Copernicus, Kepler and Galileo. In *The Discovery of a World in the Moone* (1638) he speculated that the moon had a landscape much like ours and was habitable. He predicted that man would fly to the moon 'as soone as the art of flying is found out':

> **As wee now wonder at the blindnesse of our Ancestors, who were not able to discerne such things as seeme plaine and obvious unto us. So will our posterity admire our ignorance in as perspicuous matters. Keplar doubts not, but that as soone as the art of flying is found out, some of their Nation will make one of the first colonies that shall inhabite that other world. But I leave this and the like conjectures to the fancie of the reader; Desiring now to finish this Discourse, wherein I have in some measure proved what at the first I promised, a world in the Moone.**

...... ● ......

---

* Astronomers have now identified as many as sixty-seven satellites orbiting Jupiter. The four largest moons referred to by Kepler – Io, Europa, Ganymede and Callisto – were discovered by Galileo in January 1610.

vi CHRISTIAAN HUYGENS, scion of a wealthy Dutch family, was an intensely practical – as well as intellectually inquisitive – polymath of his country's Golden Age: he invented the pendulum clock, studied the rings of Saturn through his telescope, derived what became the standard mathematical description of the centripal force, and wrote the first work on probability theory (*On Reasoning in Games of Chance*, 1657). In 1698 Huygens published *Cosmotheoros*, subtitled *The Celestial Worlds Discover'd: Or, Conjectures Concerning The Inhabitants, Plants And Productions Of The Worlds In The Planets*. This title alone tells us something of Huygens' enthusiastic sense of the potential of other worlds to harbour life. He believed that other planets have animals and plants 'not be imagin'd too unlike ours', and also water 'but not just like ours'. Huygens had the following to say about the nature of extraterrestrial water:

> I can't say that they are exactly of the same nature with our Water; but that they should be liquid their use requires, as their beauty does that they should be clear. For this Water of ours, in Jupiter or Saturn, would be frozen up instantly by reason of the vast distance of the Sun. Every Planet therefore must have its Waters of such a temper, as to be proportion'd to its heat: Jupiter's and Saturn's must be of such a nature as not to be liable to Frost; and Venus's and Mercury's of such, as not to be easily evaporated by the Sun. But in all of them, for a continual supply of Moisture, whatever Water is drawn up by the Heat of the Sun into Vapors, must necessarily return back again thither.

And all planets have fire, says Huygens. Furthermore, the

extraterrestrials who live there have all the senses that we humans enjoy: they have hands and feet and stand upright (though 'it follows not therefore that they have the same shape with us'). They are also rational. Because of this, they practise astronomy 'and all its subservient Arts' including geometry, arithmetic, writing and optics. 'They have Houses to secure 'em from Weather' and 'They have Navigation, and all Arts subservient.' Huygens' extraterrestrials also enjoy 'Musick'. He speculates about the nature of this music and concludes: 'why we should look upon their Musick to be worse than ours, there's no reason can be given... Nay, to go a step farther, what if they should excel us in the Theory and practick part of Musick, and outdo us in Consorts of vocal and instrumental Musick, so artificially compos'd.'

Huygens' *Cosmotheoros* is written in a breathlessly cheerful and optimistic style that betrays the author's positive feelings about our extraterrestrial neighbours. He dreams of other worlds as places of peace, prosperity and friendship:

Perhaps in the Planets they have such plenty and affluence of all good things, as they neither need or desire to steal from one another; perhaps they may be so just and good as to be at perpetual Peace, and never to lie in wait for, or take away the Life of their Neighbour: perhaps they may not know what Anger or Hatred are; which we to our cost and misery know too too well. But still it's more likely they have such a medly as we, such a mixture of good with bad, of wise with fools, of war with peace, and want not that Schoolmistress of Arts Poverty. For these things are of no small use: and if there were no other, 'twould be reason enough that we are as good Men as themselves.

vii A MILLENNIUM and a half before Huygens, Lucian of
Samosata – a rhetorician and satirist of Assyrian origin who
wrote in Greek during the second century AD; *see also* SPORT
iii) – wrote a satire on the exaggerations of contemporary travel
writing which introduced themes that, centuries later, would
feature among the favoured tropes of modern science fiction.
True Stories (second century AD) tells of a group of explor-
ers whose boat, having sailed westward through the Pillars
of Hercules (the Strait of Gibraltar), is blown off course by
a strong wind, lifted up by a whirlwind and deposited on the
Moon. Here the adventurers encounter an alien world where
there are no women and children grow inside the calves of
men. It is also a world that, far from enjoying Huygens' 'perpetual peace', is engulfed by interplanetary warfare. Lucian's
travellers are caught up in a conflict raging between the King
of the Moon and the King of the Sun over colonization of
the planet Venus. The war is eventually won by the armies
of the Sun, which cloud over the Moon.

A journey to the moon was also the subject of Cyrano de
Bergerac's seventeenth-century satire *The Other World:
Comical History of the States and Empires of the Moon* (1657).
Here the narrator, in the course of fantastic journeys to both
moon and sun, meets the daemon* of Socrates, enjoys discussions about heliocentrism, the movements of the Earth and the
infinity of the universe. At one point he is tried by a court of
moon-dwellers for his belief that the moon is a satellite of the
Earth (the moon-dwellers, of course, believe the opposite to be
the case).

---

* In Plato's *Apology* Socrates tells how he had a *daimonion* that warned him
against mistakes but never told him what to do.

viii **REGARDING THE EXISTENCE** of extraterrestrial life Immanuel Kant declared in *The Critique of Pure Reason* (1781, 1787): 'I should not hesitate to stake all on the truth of the proposition.' In *The Universal Natural History and Theory of the Heavens* (1755) Kant set out his views on the nature of our neighbours on other planets. In a passage that includes one of the longer sentences in Western philosophy he says:

> We have established a comparison between the characteristics of the matter with which the creatures endowed with reason on the planets are essentially united; and after the introduction of this observation it can easily be seen that these relationships will have a consequence in regard to their intellectual abilities as well. If therefore these intellectual abilities have a necessary dependence on the material of the machine they inhabit, we will be able to conclude with a more than probable conjecture: that the excellence of thinking natures, the sprightliness of their ideas, the clarity and liveliness of the concepts they receive through external impressions, along with the faculty to put them together, and finally also the agility in the actual exercise, in short, the entire extent of their perfection stands under a certain rule, according to which they become more and more excellent and perfect in proportion to the distance of their domiciles from the Sun.

What is the place of our human species in the Kantian great chain of celestial being? We occupy 'the middle rung on the ladder of beings,' he says. If we are to be jealous of the 'most sublime classes of rational creatures that inhabit Jupiter or Saturn', we may also be satisfied that our neighbours on Venus and Mercury 'are lowered far below the perfection of human nature'. Kant says that he does 'not wish to extend these conjectures beyond the limits marked out for a physical treatise, we merely note again the analogy adduced above: that the perfection of the spiritual world as well as of the material world increases and progresses in the planets from Mercury on to Saturn or perhaps even beyond it (insofar as there are yet other planets) in a correct sequence of degrees in proportion to their distances from the Sun'. While the intelligence and spirituality of dwellers of more distant worlds increases, the material of which they are made decreases: 'The stuff, out of which the inhabitants of different planets as well as the animals and plants on them, are built, should in general be lighter and of finer kind, and the elasticity of the fibres together with the principal disposition of their build should be all the more perfect, the farther they stand from the sun.'

In his *Natural History* Kant also successfully predicted the mechanism by which our solar system came into being. The Kant–Laplace theory,* which we today call the nebular hypothesis, holds that a nebula (an interstellar cloud of dust, hydrogen, helium and other ionized gases) rotated, cooled and then contracted into a flat disc that bulged in the middle. This condensation of space matter formed planets, moons, asteroids, comets and the sun. It is mind-boggling to contemplate that Kant came up with his hypothesis without the aid of technical equipment. All he required was a quill pen, a pot of ink and a ream of paper.

...... ● ......

---

* Kant's idea was elaborated in the 1790s by the French mathematician Pierre-Simon Laplace.

ix **IN 1920 ALBERT EINSTEIN** told the *Daily Mail*, 'There is
every reason to believe that Mars and other planets are inhabited.' He asked,

> **Why should the earth be the only planet supporting human
> life? It is not singular in any other respect. But if intelligent
> creatures do exist, as we may assume they do elsewhere in
> the universe, I should not expect them to try to communicate
> with the earth by wireless. Light rays, the direction of which
> can be controlled much more easily, would more probably
> be the first method attempted.**

Einstein's remarks pre-date the creation of powerful telescopes, space probes and other technological advances that
may answer our questions about extraterrestrial life. British
astronomers Martin Dominik and John Zarnecki are active
researchers in this area. They claim that 'The search for life
elsewhere is nothing but a search for ourselves, where we came
from, why we are here, and where we will be going'.

> **It encompasses many, if not all, of the fundamental ques-
> tions in biology, physics, and chemistry, but also in philos-
> ophy, psychology, religion and the way in which humans
> interact with their environment and each other. The ques-
> tion of whether we are alone in the Universe still remains
> unanswered, with no scientific evidence yet supporting one
> possible outcome or the other. If, however, extra-terrestrial
> life does exist, an emerging new age of exploration may well
> allow living generations to witness its detection.**

~
EAGLE PÂTÉ

stuffed with

BAD LARD

˘

The
GOURMAND
*possesses
an enlightened
sense of*
TASTE

CHAPTER THIRTEEN

F(O)(O)D

COOKERY

is the MOST ANCIENT of ARTS

MUSTARD
is *SINGULARLY*
SALUTARY in its
EFFECTS upon the
BRAIN

Let food be thy MEDICINE *and*
MEDICINE BE THY **FOOD**

i **IN GREEK MYTHOLOGY** mortals and gods met at
Mecone* to discuss the problem of animal sacrifice. The issue
to be settled was how to divide the sacrifice between mortals
and gods. Prometheus – creator of man – slew an ox and, after
butchering it, arranged it in two piles. The first pile contained
all the meat and most of the fat. He disguised it, however, with
the stomach in an effort to make it look less appealing. In the
second pile he arranged the bones, covering them with shiny
fat, attempting to make it appear more inviting. He then asked
Zeus, king of the gods, to choose. Zeus chose the pile of bones,
leaving man with the meat. This event lives in legend as the
'trick at Mecone'.

Zeus punished Prometheus for tricking him by hiding fire
from man (no more cooked meat, enforced vegetarianism).
Prometheus took pity on mankind and stole fire for them.
As his punishment Prometheus was chained to a rock where
an eagle pecked away at his liver (eventually Heracles killed
the eagle, releasing Prometheus from his torment).

...... ● ......

ii **IN REALITY,** meat was scarce in ancient Greece. It was an
agrarian society, and beasts of burden were prized for their
toil in sowing and harvesting crops: to slaughter them for food
made no economic sense. Some wealthy Greeks indulged in
meat, mainly pork (the pig has no use in crop production).
Even the wealthy did not indulge frequently in meat eating,
with its time-consuming requirement of ritual offering to the
gods. After the trick at Mecone, the gods themselves were

* A city in ancient Greek mythology thought to have existed between Corinth and
Achaea (in the present-day region of Corinthia).

vegetarian. They had to make do with nectar (honey) and ambrosia (a dish of oranges and shredded coconut).

Scarcity aside, arguments against meat were common among Greek philosophers. In the first century AD Plutarch reflects upon his fellow vegetarian Pythagoras' aversion to meat:

> Can you really ask what reason Pythagoras had for abstaining from flesh? For my part I rather wonder both by what accident and in what state of soul or mind the first man did so, touched his mouth to gore and brought his lips to the flesh of a dead creature, he who set forth tables of dead, stale bodies and ventured to call food and nourishment the parts that had a little before bellowed and cried, moved and lived. How could his eyes endure the slaughter when throats were slit and hides flayed and limbs torn from limb? How could his nose endure the stench? How was it that the pollution did not turn away his taste, which made contact with the sores of others and sucked juices and serums from mortal wounds?

While Plato is not an advocate of vegetarianism, in his dialogues he often advocates moderation. His ideal diet consists of cereals, legumes, fruits, milk, honey and fish. Meat should be consumed occasionally. Plato's recommendations are similar to those in what we nowadays call 'the Mediterranean diet'.

...... ● ......

iii **HIPPOCRATES FAMOUSLY SAID,** 'Let food be thy medicine and medicine be thy food.' He goes further, in his work 'On Ancient Medicine' (400 BC), to say that diet is the foundation of medicine as a science:

...the art of Medicine would not have been invented at first, nor would it have been made a subject of investigation (for there would have been no need of it), if when men are indisposed, the same food and other articles of regimen which they eat and drink when in good health were proper for them, and if no others were preferable to these.

Hippocrates was an early advocate of the plant-based diet, having observed the eating habits of animals:

I hold that the diet and food which people in health now use would not have been discovered, provided it had suited with man to eat and drink in like manner as the ox, the horse, and all other animals, except man, do of the productions of the earth, such as fruits, weeds, and grass; for from such things these animals grow, live free of disease, and require no other kind of food.

Hippocrates noticed that meat consumption was a recent phenomenon in the history of man who 'suffered much and severely from strong and brutish diet, swallowing things which were raw, unmixed, and possessing great strength, they became exposed to strong pains and diseases, and to early deaths'. Recommending a proto-Mediterranean diet, he argued that 'growth, and health, would arise'. In fact, diet is medicine: 'To such a discovery and investigation what more suitable name could one give than that of Medicine?'

In his *Moralia* (AD 100) Plutarch includes a chapter titled 'Advice About Keeping Well' in which he counsels rest and drinking water to recover from the consumption of wine and meat: '...we ought to be watchful of ourselves and forestall any trouble by means of rest and quiet when fresh from the pleasures of love, or when fatigued; also by drinking water after the free use of wine and after social gaiety, and especially, after indulging in a heavy diet of meat or multifarious foods.'

Plutarch says one should eat lightly 'and leave no mass of superfluous residue in the body. For these very things are of themselves the causes of many diseases.' Overindulgence leads to 'superfluity and overcrowding'.

...... • ......

iv **DURING THE ROMAN EMPIRE,** meat continued to be an uncommon luxury, reserved for the wealthy. Butchers' meats included venison, beef, pork, veal, goat, lamb, rabbit, hare, mutton, swan, heron and poultry. Noblemen hunted deer, boar, hares and rabbits on their land. The poor could not afford butchers' meat, and suffered death if they were caught poaching.

The cereal-based diet of the poor continued in medieval Europe. Perhaps the most powerful factor in the medieval diet was Church law, which required fasting for almost a third of the year. In addition, diet was an aspect of class and one was expected to eat in accordance with the rules governing class. The rise of trade in the late Middle Ages meant that commoners possessed wealth equal to or exceeding that of the nobility. This enabled them to enjoy the same benefits as the aristocracy, including fine clothes and a sophisticated diet. This revolutionary change caused state authorities to respond with 'sumptuary laws' – 'Laws made for the purpose of restraining luxury or extravagance, particularly against inordinate expenditures in the matter of apparel, food, furniture, etc.' The poor had always consumed a largely plant-based diet de facto; now the emerging middle class was the subject of legal strictures against enjoying a more varied one.

The variety of diet – choice – is largely a French invention.* It is no accident that the word for a well-defined style of cooking – cuisine – is a French one, along with *gastronomie* (the study of food and culture), *haute cuisine* (fine cooking), *gourmet* (a person with critical taste buds) and *gourmand* (a person who enjoys fine food in quantity).

The fourteenth-century cookery book *Le Viandier de Taillevent*[†] sets out the early regime of French cuisine. There are chapters on boiled and roasted meat, freshwater fish, round and flat sea fishes, unboiled and boiled sauces and 'Concerning Wine and Other Things'.

It was the French who brought philosophy and science to bear on the subject of food. Alexandre Balthazar Laurent Grimod de La Reynière published *L'Almanach des gourmands* annually from 1803 to 1812 – these were, in effect, the first restaurant guides.[‡] 'Thanks to the progress of knowledge and philosophy gourmandise[§] has become an art,' he wrote. For Grimod,

---

* France has 350–400 cheeses, depending on which source you prefer. Charles de Gaulle, President of France, once said: 'How can you govern a country which has two hundred and forty-six varieties of cheese?' Ernest Mignon, *Les Mots du Général* (1962).

† By Guillaume Tirel, aka Taillevent. The earliest version of *Le Viandier* was written by an unknown author around 1300, nearly a decade before Tirel was born. Medieval and early modern recipe collections were often plagiarized and augmented by later writers.

‡ Restaurant is – no surprise – a French word and concept. They first appeared in Paris in the eighteenth century.

§ 'A weakness for good food', *Oxford English Dictionary*.

The Gourmand is more than just a creature whom Nature has graced with an excellent stomach and a vast appetite... he also possesses an enlightened sense of taste, the first principle of which lies in an exceptionally delicate palate, developed through extensive experience. All his senses must work in constant concert with that of taste, for he must contemplate his food even before it nears his lips. Suffice it to say that his gaze must be penetrating, his ear alert, his sense of touch keen, and his tongue able.

Grimod staged his own funeral to see who would come. He arose from a coffin to dine with guests, then retired from Parisian life.

As a critic Grimod inspired others to write gastronomic essays that nurtured the philosophy of food. He particularly influenced an Englishman who wrote under the pseudonym of Launcelot Sturgeon. Sturgeon was the author of *Essays, Moral, Philosophical, and Stomachical, on the Important Science of Good Living* (1822). One essay in particular, 'On Mustard, Philosophically Considered; And On the Use of Garlick As a Perfume', might have appealed to Hippocrates and Plutarch for its marriage of gastronomical acuity and medical insight:

Of all the stimulants which are used at table to savour meats, to excite appetite, or to hide the faults of cooks, mustard is doubtless that which – everything considered – deserves to hold the first place; both from its antiquity, which may be traced to the earliest history of the Jews, and its beneficent qualities. If we put any faith in doctors, this seasoning acts powerfully upon the organs of digestion; it augments the force and elasticity of the fibres, attracts the digestive

juices into the stomach, separates the nutritive from the inert matter, and accelerates the peristaltic motion. It is, besides, singularly salutary in its effects upon the brain: it expands the mind, exalts the imagination, and sublimates the fancy.

...... ● ......

v **PERHAPS THE MOST RENOWNED** of gastronomic essayists is Jean Anthelme Brillat-Savarin, a French lawyer who served in the National Constituents Assembly during the French Revolution. Falling foul of the authorities, he fled to the newly born United States of America, before returning to France and serving as a magistrate. In *The Physiology of Taste: or Meditations on Transcendental Gastronomy* (1825) he considers not only the flavour of cooking, but the manner in which gastronomy is at the centre of our existence and our social and economic networks:

Gastronomy is a chapter of natural history, for the fact that it makes a classification of alimentary substances.

Of physics, for it examines their properties and qualities.

Of chemistry, from the various analysis and decomposition to which it subjects them.

Of cookery, from the fact that it prepares food and makes it agreeable.

Of commerce, from the fact that it purchases at as low a rate as possible what it consumes, and displays to the greatest advantage what it offers for sale.

Lastly it is a chapter of political economy, from the resources it furnishes the taxing power, and the means of exchange it substitutes between nations.

In a chapter entitled 'Philosophical History of the Kitchen', Brillat-Savarin says:

> COOKERY is the most ancient of arts, for Adam must have been born hungry, and the cries of the infant are only soothed by the mother's breast.
>
> Of all the arts it is the one which has rendered the greatest service in civil life. The necessities of the kitchen taught us the use of fire, by which man has subdued nature.
>
> Looking carefully at things, three kinds of cuisine may be discovered.
>
> The first has preserved its primitive name.
>
> The second analyses and looks after elements: it is called chemistry.
>
> The third, is the cookery of separation and is called pharmacy.
>
> Though different objects, they are all united by the fact that they use fire, furnaces, etc., at the same time.
>
> Thus a morsel of beef, which the cook converts into potage or bouillion, the chemist uses to ascertain into how many substances it may be resolved.

Brillat-Savarin's name lives on today: there is a cheese named after him; and a baking tin called a Savarin mould, in which one bakes a Gâteau Savarin.

...... ● ......

vi **WHILE GRIMOD,** Sturgeon and Brillat-Savarin were gourmands, they were aware of the relationship between diet and health and paid attention to health issues at the same time as promoting gastronomy. Julien Offray de La Mettrie, a physician as well as a philosopher, sneered at the moderation of Hippocrates and Plutarch. Addressing the question of whether he had his life to live again, would he do anything different, he wrote:

> I would only like to live again as I have lived, in the midst of good food, good company, joyfulness, study and seduction, dividing my time between women – that charming school of the Graces – Hippocrates and the Muses, always both hostile to debauchery and favourable to sensuality, and entirely given over to that charming mixture of wisdom and folly which together, by sharpening each other, make life more enjoyable and, in a way, more spicy.

La Mettrie was a mechanistic materialist and a determinist, a virtuous atheist and a hedonist. In 1745 he published his *Natural History of the Soul* in which he argued against the existence of a substance separate from matter called 'soul'. Three years later he published *Man a Machine*, a book with a particularly self-descriptive title. His views caused a scandal in France and he fled to Holland. Unwelcome there, he went to Berlin, where he practised as a physician under the protection of Frederick the Great.

In 1751 La Mettrie was the guest of honour at a dinner held by the French ambassador to Prussia whom he had cured of an illness. La Mettrie is said to have eaten a large quantity of truffled pheasant pâté, from which he developed a gastric illness and died. Voltaire described the pâté in question as 'eagle pâté stuffed with bad lard, minced pork and ginger'.*

...... ● ......

vii **PERHAPS THE MOST FAMOUS** killer pâté in French cultural history is the one that appears in Marco Ferreri's French–Italian arthouse film *La Grande Bouffe* (Blow-Out, 1973). The film depicts the last days of four friends – an airline pilot, a TV producer, a judge and a chef – who make a pact to commit suicide by indulging in an orgy of overeating in a rambling Parisian villa. After two of the quartet die in what can only be described as disgusting bowel-related scenes, the character Ugo, a chef, prepares an enormous dish made from three different types of liver pâté in the shape of St Peter's Basilica. He serves it to his remaining friend Philippe and Andrea (a buxom schoolteacher who has joined them). When the two are sated, Ugo continues in a determined effort to eat the entire pâté. He dies recumbent on the kitchen table as Philippe helps him stuff the pâté into his mouth while Andrea provides him with manual sexual relief. Philippe dies in Andrea's arms after eating a cake she has baked for him made to look like a pair of breasts.

Upon its opening at the Cannes Film Festival Roger Ebert, the celebrated American film critic, wrote that *La Grande Bouffe* was 'attended by gleeful controversy; the critics chose up sides and attacked it as either (a) the most disgusting and decadent film in the history of France or (b) a savage, radical attack on the bourgeois establishment'. It is certainly one

* In a letter to Mme Denis (14 November 1751).

of the most powerful satires of French bourgeois culture ever conceived, and directs its barb at a subject at the heart of that culture: food. The film critic Peter Bradshaw described the film as 'jaded, authentically perverted, drenched in ennui'.*

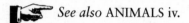 *See also* ANIMALS iv.

* 'La Grande Bouffe review, A fabulous feast of desire and disgust', in the *Guardian*, 2 July 2015.

The only **FREEDOM** which deserves the name, is that of pursuing our **OWN GOOD** in our **OWN WAY**

FREEDOM is the KEY *PHILOSOPHICAL* PROBLEM

CHAPTER FOURTEEN

FREEDOM

The essence of SPIRIT *is* FREEDOM

REPRESSIVE TOLERANCE

MAN is *BORN FREE* *but is everywhere* *in* **CHAINS**

The CHILD must be brought up FREE

i 'FREEDOM IS THE KEY philosophical problem, the crown of all the efforts of theoretical thinking, the culminating moment of any mature philosophical system,' the Russian Marxist Alexander Spirkin claims in *Dialectical Materialism* (1948). But, he reminds us, 'Hegel wrote: "Of no idea can it be stated with such complete justification that it is vague, ambiguous, and capable of generating the greatest misunderstanding, and therefore liable to be misunderstood, as the idea of freedom, and no idea is discussed with so little understanding of its nature."' What is freedom? For Spirkin it is 'the ability, based on knowledge of necessity, to choose and to act in accordance with this necessity. It consists not only in knowledge of natural and social laws but also in the practical realisation of this knowledge.' An example of 'practical realisation' would be that while I, Stephen Trombley, may desire to be a ballet dancer, the exercise of 'practical realisation' on my part would be to accept that my physique and natural ability render my desire impractical. While Spirkin's definition seems a good one, the Russo-British philosopher Isaiah Berlin reminds us in *Two Concepts of Liberty* (1958) that freedom is a protean word with more than 'two hundred senses of it recorded by historians of ideas'.

...... ● ......

ii ONE OFTEN HEARS in conversations about political freedom the view that ancient Greece was the birthplace of democracy. What must be kept in mind in that conversation is that Greek society was founded on slavery, with three slaves to every free man. The key question in any debate concerning freedom is 'freedom for whom?'. Plato, writing on freedom and democracy in *The Republic* (360 BC), identifies, in descending order of desirability, five types of regime: aristocracy, timocracy,* oligarchy, democracy and tyranny. He dismisses democracy as 'a charming form of government, full of variety and disorder; and dispensing a sort of equality to equals and unequals alike'. In a democracy 'there is freedom and plainness of speech, and every man does what is right in his own eyes, and has his own way of life'. But it is, in Plato's view, a disordered state of affairs, ultimately leading to tyranny:

> **Tyranny springs from democracy much as democracy springs from oligarchy. Both arise from excess; the one from excess of wealth, the other from excess of freedom. 'The great natural good of life,' says the democrat, 'is freedom.' And this exclusive love of freedom and regardlessness of everything else, is the cause of the change from democracy to tyranny.**

...... ● ......

iii '**METAPHYSICS** has as the proper object of its enquiries three ideas only: God, freedom, and immortality.' So wrote Immanuel Kant in *The Critique of Pure Reason* (1781; 1787). He offers a modern view of freedom as a concept realized and protected by laws created by men (not God) through the use of reason. In 'What is Enlightenment?' (1784) he answered that it is 'the freedom for man to make public use of his reason in all matters'. What is freedom? In *The Metaphysics of Ethics* (1796) he defines it thus: 'Freedom is the alone unoriginated birthright of man, and belongs to him by force of his humanity; and is

---

* A system of government in which only property owners may participate.

independence on the will and co-action of every other in so far as this consists with every other person's freedom.' So for Kant, while freedom is every person's birthright, it exists in a social context. And the nature of that birthright is that 'its appearances, which are human actions, like every other natural event are determined by universal laws'. While human actions may seem obscure, he argues in his 'Idea for a Universal History from a Cosmopolitan Point of View' (1784) that history will reveal their 'regular movement':

> However obscure their causes, history, which is concerned with narrating these appearances, permits us to hope that if we attend to the play of freedom of the human will in the large, we may be able to discern a regular movement in it, and that what seems complex and chaotic in the single individual may be seen from the standpoint of the human race as a whole to be a steady and progressive though slow evolution of its original endowment.

The individual and his freedom are always to be seen in a social context: 'The greatest problem for the human race, to the solution of which Nature drives man, is the achievement of a universal civic society which administers law among men' (*see also* JUSTICE vi). The preparation of participation in a universal civic society begins with the individual child's education:

> The child must be brought up free (that he allow others to be free). He must learn to endure the restraint to which freedom subjects itself for its own preservation (experience no subordination to his command). Thus he must be disciplined. This precedes instruction. Training must continue without

interruption. He must learn to do without things and to be cheerful about it. He must not be obliged to dissimulate, he must acquire immediate horror of lies, must learn so to respect the rights of men that they become an insurmountable wall for him. His instruction must be more negative. He must not learn religion before he knows morality. He must be refined, but not spoiled (pampered). He must learn to speak frankly, and must assume no false shame. Before adolescence he must not learn fine manners; thoroughness is the chief thing. Thus he is crude longer, but earlier useful and capable.

...... ● ......

iv 'MAN IS BORN FREE; and everywhere he is in chains.' The celebrated opening pronouncement of the Genevan philosopher Jean-Jacques Rousseau's *The Social Contract* (1762) ushered in what would be an era of revolution in the American colonies (1765–83) and in France (1789–99). Like Kant, Rousseau (*see also* WALKING iii) saw individual freedom in the context of what he called 'the social order', which he regarded as 'a sacred right which is the basis of all other rights'. Although Rousseau calls this freedom a 'sacred right', it has nothing to do with God or nature: 'this right does not come from nature, and must therefore be founded on conventions'. In other words, it must be founded on laws created by men, for men.

In *The Social Contract* he had this to say about the relationship of the governed and those who govern them: 'As long as a people is compelled to obey, and obeys, it does well; as soon as it can shake off the yoke, and shakes it off, it does still better; for, regaining its liberty by the same right as took it away, either it is justified in resuming it, or there was no justification for those who took it away.' But, he also warns:

> **Peoples once accustomed to masters are not in a condition to do without them. If they attempt to shake off the yoke, they still more estrange themselves from freedom, as, by mistaking for it an unbridled licence to which it is diametrically opposed, they nearly always manage, by their revolutions, to hand themselves over to seducers, who only make their chains heavier than before.**

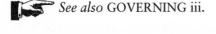 *See also* GOVERNING iii.

...... ● ......

v **IN THE SIXTEENTH CENTURY,** the French political philosopher Jean Bodin created the doctrine of the 'divine right of kings', according to which God bestowed upon monarchs the power and the right to rule as they saw fit, subject to no judgement other than that of God. In reality, the ability of rulers to rule wisely and fairly was never assured by the genetic dice game that is hereditary monarchy. Inevitably, revolution ensued.

The Dublin-born philosopher Edmund Burke, widely regarded as the father of conservatism, disapproved strongly of the French Revolution but supported the American colonists in their fight against the British crown. On 22 March 1775 he gave a speech to Parliament on 'Reconciliation with the Colonies'. He said of the colonists 'a love of freedom is the predominating feature which marks and distinguishes the whole'. He pleaded unsuccessfully with the government to settle the colonists' grievances peacefully. Burke admired the Americans' combative spirit, but had no such regard for the French. In his *Reflections on the Revolution in France* (1790) he wrote: 'we are led to a very natural question: What is that cause of liberty, and what are those exertions in its favour to which the example of France is so singularly auspicious?' Immediately, Burke voices his concern that the revolution in France might spread to Britain. The American Revolution was taking place three thousand miles away, and its outcome would not include regicide; but the prospect of that happening just a few miles across the English Channel deeply troubled Burke, who asked: 'Is our monarchy to be annihilated, with all the laws, all the tribunals, and all the ancient corporations of the kingdom? Is every landmark of the country to be done away in favour of a geometrical and arithmetical constitution? Is the House of Lords to be voted useless? Is episcopacy to be abolished?' And then the racism which frequently stokes conservative worries rears its head: 'Are the church lands to be sold to Jews and jobbers or given to bribe new-invented municipal republics into a participation in sacrilege?'

For Burke, there was no real freedom without the power of a state religion. Unlike Kant or Rousseau, Burke had no trust in the unfettered action of free men to form their own government and to create their own laws. He demanded the stern power of a combined state and Church to exert a restraining power on individual freedom:

> The consecration of the state by a state religious establishment is necessary, also, to operate with a wholesome awe upon free citizens, because, in order to secure their freedom, they must enjoy some determinate portion of power.

To them, therefore, a religion connected with the state, and with their duty toward it, becomes even more necessary than in such societies where the people, by the terms of their subjection, are confined to private sentiments and the management of their own family concerns.

...... • ......

vi **FOR G. W. F. HEGEL,** freedom is the essence of what he called Spirit (*Geist*) – by which he meant not only the mind of the individual, but a consciousness that includes a community along with its structures and laws. Contrasting matter and spirit, Hegel wrote in his *Lectures on the Philosophy of History* (1832):

As the essence of Matter is Gravity, so, on the other hand, we may affirm that the substance, the essence of Spirit is Freedom. All will readily assent to the doctrine that Spirit, among other properties, is also endowed with Freedom; but philosophy teaches that all the qualities of Spirit exist only through Freedom; that all are but means for attaining Freedom; that all seek and produce this and this alone.

For Hegel, freedom must develop beyond the state of individual, subjective freedom, to have a social reality, to become an objectified in law. 'The State is the Divine Idea as it exists on earth. We have in it, therefore, the object of history in a more definite shape than before; that in which Freedom obtains objectivity. For Law is the objectivity of the Spirit.'

...... • ......

vii AS BURKE WAS THE FOUNDING FATHER of conservatism, the philosopher and political economist John Stuart Mill is a founder of liberalism. While he opposed despotic rule, Mill also warned against what he called 'the tyranny of the majority'. In his essay *On Liberty* (1859) Mill identified three essential human freedoms: of thought and emotion (including free speech); to pursue tastes that may be judged 'immoral', provided they do not harm others; and the freedom to assemble or unite (again, without harm to others). He wrote: 'The only freedom which deserves the name, is that of pursuing our own good in our own way, so long as we do not attempt to deprive others of theirs, or impede their efforts to obtain it.' He believed that freedom of thought was essential for all persons (not just those for whom thinking is a profession) because a free society depended upon it: 'Not that it is solely, or chiefly, to form great thinkers, that freedom of thinking is required. On the contrary, it is as much, and even more indispensable, to enable average human beings to attain the mental stature which they are capable of.' *See also* WRITING v.

...... ● ......

viii THE REVOLUTIONARY socialist thinker Karl Marx said that capitalism made slaves of the proletariat. In his *Economic and Philosophic Manuscripts of 1844* he wrote that man is different from animals in that he produces things beyond his immediate needs, expresses himself in his production and that the objects of his production can be things of beauty. In producing under capitalism, man is alienated from himself and the fruits of his labour – he is not free. Ironically, the more he is paid for this alienating labour, the more unfree he becomes:

'the raising of wages gives rise to overwork among the workers. The more they wish to earn, the more must they sacrifice their time and carry out slave-labour, completely losing all their freedom, in the service of greed. Thereby they shorten their lives.' The only road to freedom in an industrial society, Marx said, was communism:

> **communism, as fully developed naturalism, equals humanism, and as fully developed humanism equals naturalism; it is the *genuine* resolution of the strife between existence and essence, between objectification and self-confirmation, between freedom and necessity, between the individual and the species. Communism is the riddle of history solved, and it knows itself to be this solution**

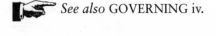 *See also* GOVERNING iv.

...... ● ......

ix **IN KARL POPPER'S VIEW,** Plato, Hegel and Marx are nothing less than enemies of the democratic state. For Popper, a celebrated twentieth-century Austro-British philosopher of science, this trio of philosophical felons stand indicted as malicious proponents of a teleological* historicism by which history unfolds according to predetermined universal laws. In *The Open Society and Its Enemies* (1945) (whose first volume – tellingly – was entitled 'The Spell of Plato') Popper brands this historicism as essentially totalitarian in nature and inimical to the open society – or liberal democracy – of which he is

---

* Teleology is the description of a phenomenon in terms of its end, purpose or goal.

in favour. He is particularly contemptuous of what he sees as Plato's intellectual bullying:

> As usual when Plato's style, to use a phrase of [James] Adam's becomes a 'full tide of lofty thoughts and images and words', it does so because he urgently needs a cloak to cover the intellectual nakedness of his arguments, or rather, the total absence of any rational thought whatever. He uses invective instead, identifying liberty with lawlessness, freedom with licence, and equality before the law with disorder. Democrats are described as profligate and niggardly, as insolent, lawless, and shameless, as fierce and as terrible beasts of prey, as gratifying every whim, as living solely for pleasure, and for unnecessary and unclean desires.

Marx's collaborator Friedrich Engels referred to Marxism as 'scientific socialism'. Popper is at pains to point out that Marxism is anything but scientific in its predictive view of history.

...... ● ......

x **THE GERMAN-AMERICAN PHILOSOPHER** Herbert Marcuse achieved notoriety as a perceived 'guru' of the student movements of the 1960s. His Neo-Marxism was seen as an influence both on the anti-capitalist counter-culture of that decade and on more radical and violent far-left groups such as the Red Army Faction – originally the Baader-Meinhof Gang – in West Germany.* Marcuse developed an original

---

* Marcuse did not condone what he called 'violence of aggression'; but he did allow for 'violence of defence'.

criticism of freedom in liberal democracies; he believed that societies like the United States offer an illusory freedom and are characterized by what he called 'repressive tolerance'. We are free, he argues, to say whatever we like, to think whatever we like – so long as we don't act on our thoughts. In *Repressive Tolerance* (1965) he writes:

> **The tolerance which enlarged the range and content of freedom was always partisan – intolerant toward the protagonists of the repressive status quo. The issue was only the degree and extent of intolerance. In the firmly established liberal society of England and the United States, freedom of speech and assembly was granted even to the radical enemies of society, provided they did not make the transition from word to deed, from speech to action.**

Tolerance, Marcuse says, is a way of pacifying the masses. A certain amount of toleration of the patently true and obviously false, of conflicting opinion, is acceptable, Marcuse says. 'But society cannot be indiscriminate where the pacification of existence, where freedom and happiness themselves are at stake: here, certain things cannot be said, certain ideas cannot be expressed, certain policies cannot be proposed, certain behaviour cannot be permitted without making tolerance an instrument for the continuation of servitude.' 'False tolerance', Marcuse argues, is the mechanism by which workers in a free society are enslaved – and by which they collaborate in their own enslavement:

> **The subversive character of the restoration of freedom appears most clearly in that dimension of society where false**

tolerance and free enterprise do perhaps the most serious and lasting damage, namely in business and publicity. Against the emphatic insistence on the part of spokesmen for labour, I maintain that practices such as planned obsolescence, collusion between union leadership and management, slanted publicity are not simply imposed from above on a powerless rank and file, but are tolerated by them and the consumer at large.

...... ● ......

xi **ISAIAH BERLIN EMIGRATED** with his family from Russia in 1920 following the Bolshevik revolutions of 1917. His inaugural lecture as Chichele Professor of Social and Political Theory in the University of Oxford was titled *Two Concepts of Liberty* (1958). In it he proclaimed: 'Everything is what it is: liberty is liberty, not equality or fairness or justice or culture, or human happiness or a quiet conscience.' The two concepts of liberty Berlin identified were 'positive' and 'negative'. *Positive* liberty means for Berlin self-mastery, including the freedom to participate in the democratic process of choosing leaders. *Negative* liberty is the freedom to act as one wishes, without interference from others. Let's simplify: I would like to have lunch at my favourite French restaurant. Since no one is holding me hostage at present, I am at liberty to do so: my negative liberty is intact. On the other hand, if I am prevented from lunching at the restaurant because I have insufficient funds, my positive liberty is affected because I lack the wherewithal to act.

Berlin was the foremost twentieth-century philosopher of liberalism. In *Two Concepts of Liberty* he is highly sceptical of 'social reformers', partly because he had witnessed an excess of social reform during the Bolshevik revolutions in Russia which caused him to reflect that 'to manipulate men, to propel them towards goals which you – the social reformer – see, but they may not, is to deny their human essence, to treat them as objects without wills of their own, and therefore to degrade them'. Berlin disliked programmatic political change (like that advocated by Marxists) because 'All forms of tampering with human beings, getting at them, shaping them against their will to your own pattern, all thought control and conditioning is... a denial of that in men which makes them men and their values ultimate.'

Berlin's concept of freedom is this:

> **I am normally said to be free to the degree to which no man or body of men interferes with my activity. Political liberty in this sense is simply the area within which a man can act unobstructed by others. If I am prevented by others from doing what I could otherwise do, I am to that degree unfree; and if this area is contracted by other men beyond a certain minimum, I can be described as being coerced, or, it may be, enslaved.**

Berlin abhorred coercion, but warned that it and other obstacles of freedom should not be confused with what one might call 'natural' restrictions on what one can do – for instance, *inability* to do something. Consequently,

> **Coercion is not... a term that covers every form of inability. If I say that I am unable to jump more than ten feet in the air, or cannot read because I am blind, or cannot understand**

the darker pages of Hegel, it would be eccentric to say that I am to that degree enslaved or coerced. Coercion implies the deliberate interference of other human beings within the area in which I could otherwise act.

Most of all, Berlin regarded freedom as an end in itself, as opposed to a means to some other end. He wrote,

If, as I believe, the ends of men are many, and not all of them are in principle compatible with each other, then the possibility of conflict – and of tragedy – can never wholly be eliminated from human life, either personal or social. The necessity of choosing between absolute claims is then an inescapable characteristic of the human condition. This gives its value to freedom as Acton conceived of it – as an end in itself, and not as a temporary need, arising out of our confused notions and irrational and disordered lives, a pre-dicament which a panacea could one day put right.

 See also FUN iv.

~ YOU MUST TRUST ~

WE ARE EACH OF US **ANGELS** WITH ONLY ONE WING, AND WE CAN ONLY FLY **EMBRACING** ONE ANOTHER

CHAPTER FIFTEEN

FRIENDSHIP

A **FRIEND** is a sort of paradox in **NATURE**

What we commonly call FRIENDS and FRIENDSHIPS, are nothing but ACQUAINTANCE and FAMILIARITIES

FRIENDSHIP that possesses the **WHOLE SOUL** CANNOT POSSIBLY ADMIT OF A *RIVAL*

i **ARISTOTLE WAS FOND** of taxonomies, and in his *Nichomachean Ethics* he organized friendship under three categories: utility, pleasure and goodness. A friendship based on utility is one where each side derives some kind of benefit for themselves. 'Those who love each other for their utility do not love each other for themselves but in virtue of some good which they get from each other,' says Aristotle. Friendships based on mutual pleasure are, like those formed of utility, inferior: 'So too with those who love for the sake of pleasure':

> Therefore those who love for the sake of utility love for the sake of what is good for themselves, and those who love for the sake of pleasure do so for the sake of what is pleasant to themselves, and not in so far as the other is the person loved but in so far as he is useful or pleasant. And thus these friendships are only incidental; for it is not as being the man he is that the loved person is loved, but as providing some good or pleasure. Such friendships, then, are easily dissolved, if the parties do not remain like themselves; for if the one party is no longer pleasant or useful the other ceases to love him.

Aristotle's third, and highest, form of friendship is that based on goodness. 'Those involved in friendship of the good must be able to value loving over being loved and as such, their relationship will be based more around loving the other person and wanting what is good for them. Goodness is an enduring quality, so friendships based on goodness tend to be long lasting.'

Friendship for Aristotle is not just a personal phenomenon, it is the glue that holds communities together. In its civic form, friendship is also an aspect of justice. 'Between friends there is no need for justice, but people who are just still need the quality of friendship; and indeed friendliness is considered to be justice in the fullest sense. It is not only a necessary thing but a splendid one.' *See also* JUSTICE i.

...... ● ......

ii **ARISTOTLE DESCRIBES CATEGORIES** of friends; but what *is* a friend? Pythagoras said, 'Friends are as companions on a journey, who ought to aid each other to persevere in the road to a happier life.' Zeno of Elea said simply, 'A friend is our alter ego.' His contemporary Euripides noted that 'friends show their love in times of trouble'. Epicurus said, 'It is not so much our friends' help that helps us, as the confidence of their help.' In the first century BC Lucretius said, 'We are each of us angels with only one wing, and we can only fly embracing one another.'

...... ● ......

iii **SENECA THE YOUNGER** wrote a letter to Lucilius 'On True and False Friendship'. He was replying to a letter from his young correspondent who mentions that it was delivered by a friend of a friend. Seneca writes, 'You have sent a letter to me through the hand of a "friend" of yours, as you call him. And in your very next sentence you warn me not to discuss with him all the matters that concern you, saying that even you yourself are not accustomed to do this; in other words, you have in the same letter affirmed and denied that he is your friend.' He admonishes Lucilius: 'if you consider any man a friend whom you do not trust as you trust yourself, you are

mightily mistaken and you do not sufficiently understand what
true friendship means'.

For Seneca, friendship means being able to share anything
and everything. Once a friendship is formed, he says, 'you
must trust'. But before trust comes judgement. He admonishes
Lucilius to 'Ponder for a long time whether you shall admit a
given person to your friendship; but when you have decided to
admit him, welcome him with all your heart and soul. Speak as
boldly with him as with yourself... Why need I keep back any
words in the presence of my friend? Why should I not regard
myself as alone when in his company?' *See also* ADVICE ii.

...... ● ......

iv **MICHEL DE MONTAIGNE**, writing in the sixteenth century, said, 'what we commonly call friends and friendships, are
nothing but acquaintance and familiarities, either occasionally
contracted, or upon some design, by means of which there happens some little intercourse betwixt our souls'. Montaigne's
purpose is not to denigrate friendship, but, rather, to try and
identify what real, enduring friendship means. Real friends,
says Montaigne, 'mix and work themselves into one piece,
with so universal a mixture, that there is no more sign of the
seam by which they were first conjoined'. It is an admirable
description of a state of affairs; but if we inquire of Montaigne
how such a friendship develops, he says: 'If a man should
importune me to give a reason why I loved him, I find it could
no otherwise be expressed, than by making answer: because it
was he, because it was I.' If we question him further as to the
mechanism of friendship, Montaigne replies: 'There is, beyond
all that I am able to say, I know not what inexplicable and

fated power that brought on this union.' He ascribes to true friendship a mystical aspect, of two souls destined to form a bond:

> We sought one another long before we met, and by the characters we heard of one another, which wrought upon our affections more than, in reason, mere reports should do; I think 'twas by some secret appointment of heaven.

How many good friends can one person have? Does one's 'best friend' take up all of one's friendship potential? Can one have many friends? Montaigne says, 'Common friendships will admit of division; one may love the beauty of this person, the good-humour of that, the liberality of a third, the paternal affection of a fourth, the fraternal love of a fifth, and so of the rest.' But the perfect 'friendship that possesses the whole soul, and there rules and sways with an absolute sovereignty, cannot possibly admit of a rival'. On the subject of multiple friends, Montaigne asks:

> If two at the same time should call to you for succour, to which of them would you run? Should they require of you contrary offices, how could you serve them both? Should one commit a thing to your silence that it were of importance to the other to know, how would you disengage yourself?

His answer is:

> A unique and particular friendship dissolves all other obligations whatsoever: the secret I have sworn not to reveal to any other, I may without perjury communicate to him who is

not another, but myself. ' 'Tis miracle enough certainly, for a man to double himself, and those that talk of tripling, talk they know not of what.'

...... • ......

v 'I AWOKE THIS MORNING with devout thanksgiving for my friends, the old and the new.' The American transcendentalist Ralph Waldo Emerson ranked friendship among the highest human attributes. In his essay 'Friendship' (1841), he reflected:

> What so delicious as a just and firm encounter of two, in a thought, in a feeling? How beautiful, on their approach to this beating heart, the steps and forms of the gifted and the true! The moment we indulge our affections, the earth is metamorphosed; there is no winter, and no night; all tragedies, all ennuis, vanish, – all duties even; nothing fills the proceeding eternity but the forms all radiant of beloved persons. Let the soul be assured that somewhere in the universe it should rejoin its friend, and it would be content and cheerful alone for a thousand years.

Before enumerating the aspects of true friendship, Emerson writes of what friendship is not. Ones that are made from 'a texture of wine and dreams, instead of the tough fibre of the human heart' will always 'hurry to short and poor conclusions'. Attachments born of rude attraction never last. It is as if 'We snatch at the slowest fruit in the whole garden of God' in search of 'a swift and petty benefit, to suck a sudden sweetness'. True 'sweetness' cannot be had suddenly, because it takes 'many summers and many winters' to ripen. Friendship is a sacred state which, if sought with 'an adulterate passion which would appropriate him to ourselves', will be 'in vain'.

Against attractions formed of 'wine and dreams', Emerson defines real friendships as being made of 'not glass threads or frostwork, but the solidest thing we know'. In true friendship we find the essence of knowledge – of nature, and of ourselves. 'The sweet sincerity of joy and peace, which I draw from this alliance with my brother's soul, is the nut itself, whereof all nature and all thought is but the husk and shell.'

'Every man alone is sincere,' says Emerson; but, 'At the entrance of a second person, hypocrisy begins.' But if the second person is a friend, he is someone 'with whom I may be sincere'. By sincerity, Emerson means that state of being which arises from being 'in the presence of a man so real and equal, that I may drop even those undermost garments of dissimulation, courtesy, and second thought, which men never put off, and may deal with him with the simplicity and wholeness with which one chemical atom meets another'.

Emerson identifies three chief aspects of friendship: entertainment, tenderness and difference. 'My friend gives me entertainment without requiring any stipulation on my part,' he writes; but the nature of this entertainment is unusual. For Emerson, the friend entertains by acting as a mirror which gives birth to an image of my self 'in a foreign form'. 'A friend, therefore, is a sort of paradox in nature. I who alone am, I who see nothing in nature whose existence I can affirm with equal evidence to my own, behold now the semblance of my being, in all its height, variety, and curiosity, reiterated in a foreign form; so that a friend may well be reckoned the masterpiece of nature.'

> **The other element of friendship is tenderness. We are holden to men by every sort of tie, by blood, by pride, by fear, by hope, by lucre, by lust, by hate, by admiration, by every circumstance and badge and trifle, but we can scarce believe that so much character can subsist in another as to draw us by love. Can another be so blessed, and we so pure, that we can offer him tenderness? When a man becomes dear to me, I have touched the goal of fortune.**

An important aspect of friendship is that friends must be sufficiently like one another – but also sufficiently different from one another. Emerson identifies this difference as 'that rare mean betwixt likeness and unlikeness, that piques each with the presence of power and of consent in the other party'.

...... • ......

vi **IN 1938 THE ENGLISH NOVELIST** E. M. Forster published an essay entitled 'What I Believe'. In it he advocated so passionately for friendship that he skated very close to sedition. The timing of the essay was crucial. It was published in July 1938, just weeks shy of British prime minister Neville Chamberlain signing the Munich Pact with Adolf Hitler on 30 September. This appeasement handed Czechoslovakia over to Nazi Germany in exchange for a peace that Hitler never intended keeping. A year later, the Second World War broke out. The mood of the time was fearful. Everyone knew that conscription was just around the corner. It was a time for displaying one's loyalty and devotion to nation; a time when patriotic feeling was running high. These events form the background to Forster's encomium on friendship:

Personal relations are despised today. They are regarded as bourgeois luxuries, as products of a time of fair weather which is now past, and we are urged to get rid of them, and to dedicate ourselves to some movement or cause instead. I hate the idea of causes, and if I had to choose between betraying my country and betraying my friend I hope I should have the guts to betray my country. Such a choice may scandalize the modern reader, and he may stretch out his patriotic hand to the telephone at once and ring up the police. It would not have shocked Dante, though. Dante places Brutus and Cassius in the lowest circle of Hell because they had chosen to betray their friend Julius Caesar rather than their country Rome. Probably one will not be asked to make such an agonizing choice. Still, there lies at the back of every creed something terrible and hard for which the worshipper may one day be required to suffer, and there is even a terror and a hardness in this creed of personal relationships, urbane and mild though it sounds. Love and loyalty to an individual can run counter to the claims of the State. When they do – down with the State, say I, which means that the State would down me.

BY MY FOURTH YEAR I HAD BECOME **GAY** AND **FLIPPANT**

The chief function of

— **PLAY** —

is its POSITIVE AFFECTIVE quality

No other modern language has the exact equivalent of the English 'FUN'

CHAPTER SIXTEEN

FUN

The FUN of PLAYING

resists all

ANALYSIS

In fifteenth-century PARIS, burning cats was a form of

• _HOME ENTERTAINMENT_ •

i **UNLIKE MOST OF THE TOPICS** in this miscellany, the word 'fun' has no Greek or Latin root. Its origins are to be found in the Middle English verb *fonnen* (to 'befool') and in the use in the 1680s of the verb *fun*, meaning to 'cheat' or 'hoax' someone. By 1727 it had acquired the more contemporary meanings 'diversion, amusement, mirthful sport'. Fun is a modern concept.

In his book *Homo Ludens: A Study of the Play Element in Culture* (1938)* the Dutch cultural historian Johan Huizinga writes:

> **No other modern language known to me has the exact equivalent of the English 'fun'. The Dutch 'aardigkeit' perhaps comes nearest to it (derived from 'aard' which means the same as 'Art' and 'Wesen' in German, and thus evidence, perhaps, that the matter cannot be reduced further). We may note in passing that 'fun' in its current usage is of rather recent origin. French, oddly enough, has no corresponding term at all; German half makes up for it by 'Spass' and 'Witz' together.**

What makes fun different from sport, amusement, pleasure, recreation and a host of other concepts with which it may be commonly – perhaps, mindlessly – associated? If we were asking this question of most of the ideas in this book we could easily turn to the ancient Greeks, then the Romans, the Church fathers, and on through the Renaissance and modern period to find any number of interpretations of the concept. For once, however, our source is a near-contemporary. The phenomenon, as a focus of study, is new. So why have previous ages ignored

---

* *Homo ludens* refers to 'man the player', or 'playing man'.

this concept? It may be, Huizinga reasons, because 'The fun of playing resists all analysis, all logical interpretation. As a concept, it cannot be reduced to any other mental category.'

...... ● ......

ii **ANOTHER EXPLANATION MIGHT BE** that what we acknowledge to be 'fun' may not have elicited the same affect in our ancient and even recent forebears. The New Zealand play theorist Brian Sutton-Smith observes of amateur sport that 'most people nowadays say they are playing for "fun"' and that they 'judge their play by whether it is fun or boring, both unimaginable notions in prior history'. Fun an unimaginable notion?

We must go back to Plato and discover that, for him, games and sport were combat training (*see* SPORT i). When we look at the Romans, their notion of gladiatorial combat as sport or 'fun' was based on the cruel spectacle of watching one human being kill another (with the crowd having a say in whether or not a fallen combatant should live or die). John Morreall, an American professor of religion and founder of the International Society for Humor Studies, notes that 'The Roman emperor Trajan celebrated a military victory in AD 106 by having 5,000 pairs of gladiators fight to the death.' He reminds us that 'in fifteenth-century Paris, burning cats was a form of home entertainment'. And then there is the twentieth-century Ugandan dictator Idi Amin, who 'cut off the limbs of one of his wives and sewed them onto the opposite sides of her body, for his own amusement'.

...... ● ......

iii **FUN OFTEN INVOLVES FLIGHTS** of fancy, even among the most venerable of philosophers. In his *Autobiography* (1975) Bertrand Russell tells how he discovered the fun of philosophy during his fourth year at Cambridge:

> I remember a few months before I came into residence [at Cambridge University], going to see my tutor about rooms, and while I waited in the ante-room I turned over the pages of the *Granta* (the undergraduate newspaper). It was May Week, and I was shocked to read in the paper that during this week people's thoughts were not devoted to work. But by my fourth year I had become gay and flippant. Having been reading pantheism, I announced to my friends that I was God. They placed candles on each side of me and proceeded to acts of mock worship. Philosophy altogether seemed to me to be great fun, and I enjoyed the curious ways of conceiving the world that the great philosophers offer to the imagination.

...... ● ......

iv **WHILE HISTORIC CONCEPTS** of 'fun' often included 'making fun of' someone (*see* LAUGHING ii), Johan Huizinga observes that the chief aspect of fun as expressed in modern play is that 'it is free, is in fact freedom'. To define fun as an aspect of and an expression of freedom – which, along with truth and justice, has always been placed among the highest goods by philosophers of all eras – is a bold declaration indeed. For Huizinga, the fun of play derives from the fact that 'play is not "ordinary" or "real" life. It is rather a stepping out of "real" life into a temporary sphere of activity with a disposition all of its own.' Fun provides relief from the pressures of everyday 'real' life. So, 'the consciousness of play being "only a pretend" does not by any means prevent it from proceeding with the utmost seriousness, with an absorption, a devotion that passes into rapture and, temporarily at least, completely abolishes that troublesome "only" feeling'.

Reacting against the seriousness of Plato in the matter of play, the American child psychologist Michael Lewis argues that 'The important meaning of play, at least for humans, would appear to be in its affective function: in a word, play is fun.' He says 'the chief function of play is its positive affective quality, a combination of fun and whimsy, with distinguishes this activity from all others, even other positive experiences such as eating or sexual behaviour'.

Capriciously *malevolent* BULLY

How many
ANGELS
may fit upon the point of a
NEEDLE?

A BEING
ABSOLUTELY
INFINITE

CHAPTER SEVENTEEN

Consciousness of GOD is self-consciousness

†

GOD *is* DEAD

LORD of TIME
and
OMNISCIENT

UNMOVED MOVER

i   **ARISTOTLE DID NOT ASCRIBE** to God the human emotions of the Abrahamic gods – wrath, vengeance, anger, jealousy, love. God is the thought that precedes the material world. Aristotle came up with the idea of the 'unmoved mover' or 'first cause' to explain the existence of our physical world. He may be considered a polytheist because he argues that there can be more than one unmoved mover:

> ...though there may be countless instances of the perishing of unmoved movers, and though many things that move themselves perish and are succeeded by others that come into being, and though one thing that is unmoved moves one thing while another moves another, nevertheless there is something that comprehends them all, and that as something apart from each one of them, and this it is that is the cause of the fact that some things are and others are not and of the continuous process of change; and this causes the motion of the other movers, while they are the causes of the motion of other things. Motion, then, being eternal, the first mover, if there is but one, will be eternal also; if there are more than one, there will be a plurality of such eternal movers.

...... ● ......

ii   **PHILO OF ALEXANDRIA** was a Jewish Stoic who lived in the Roman province of Egypt in the first century AD. In his reflection *On the Unchangeableness of God* Philo is at pains to separate God from any human qualities. For him, 'God is utterly inaccessible to any passion whatever. For it is the peculiar property of human weakness to be disquieted by any such feelings, but God has neither the irrational passions of the soul, nor are the parts and limits of the body in the least belonging to him.' Philo's god is not wrathful, 'for wrath is characteristic of human weakness'. Nor is he angry. Philo explains that 'such expressions are used by the great Lawgiver [Moses], in order to lesson those who cannot otherwise be chastened'. Comparing God to man 'involves the unspeakable mythology of the impious'. The object of Moses, says Philo, 'is to benefit all his readers, and if the men of body cannot be schooled by means of truth, let them learn the falsehoods by means of which they will be benefited. They need a terrible master to threaten them.' Moses recognized 'two attitudes of God's worshippers, fear and love. To them who conceive of the Absolute without any mortal part or passion, but honour him as he is, belongs the love of God, and the fear of God to every other.'

Philo characterized God as 'lord of time and omniscient'. Lacking a physical presence, God is to be recognized through his immortality. God is the 'creator of time'. He is

the father of its father, and the father of time is the world, which made its own mother the creation of time, so that time stands towards God in the relation of a grandson; for this world is a younger son of God, inasmuch as it is perceptible by the outward sense; for the only son he speaks of as older than the world, is idea*, and this is not perceptible by the intellect; but having thought the other worthy of the rights of primogeniture, he has decided that it shall remain with him; therefore, this younger son, perceptible by the external senses being set in motion, has caused the nature of time to shine forth, and to become conspicuous, so that there is

---

* Philo believed God to be the 'idea of ideas'.

nothing future to God, who has the very boundaries of time subject to him; for their life is not time, but the beautiful model of time, eternity; and in eternity nothing is past and nothing is future, but everything is present only.

...... ● ......

iii **AUGUSTINE OF HIPPO IN *HIS CONFESSIONS*** (written 397–400) defines God in terms that defy temporality: 'God is eternal.' He explains: 'In eternity, God is before all things.' Augustine uses Aristotelian language when he describes God as 'a spirit who has no parts extended in length and breadth, whose being has no mass – for every mass is less in a part than in a whole – and if it be an infinite mass it must be less in such parts as are limited by a certain space than in its infinity. It cannot therefore be wholly everywhere as Spirit is, as God is.' But, as a Christian, Augustine must anthropomorphize God, giving him human emotions. So, 'God is good' and 'God is righteous'. God is now more than the unmoved mover of Aristotle. He is now Christ the saviour who can 'cancel the death of justified sinners'. God, as Christ,

was manifested to holy men of old, to the end that they might be saved through faith in his Passion to come, even as we through faith in his Passion which is past. As man he was Mediator, but as the Word he was not something in between the two; because he was equal to God, and God with God, and, with the Holy Spirit, one God.

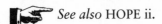 *See also* HOPE ii.

iv THE SCHOLASTIC PHILOSOPHER Thomas Aquinas grappled with the first question of any discussion of God: does he exist? In *Summa Theologica* (written 1265–74), Aquinas offers five proofs for the existence of God, the conclusions of which can be summarized as:

Argument from Motion. It is necessary to arrive at a first mover, put in motion by no other; and this everyone understands to be God.

Argument from Efficient Causes. It is necessary to admit a first efficient cause, to which everyone gives the name of God.

Argument from Possibility and Necessity (the 'reductio argument'). Some being exists of its own necessity, and does not receive its existence from another being, but rather causes them. This all men speak of as God.

Argument from Gradation of Being. There must also be something which is to all beings the cause of their being, goodness, and every other perfection; and this we call God.

Argument from Design. Some intelligent being exists by whom all natural things are directed to their end; and this being we call God.

Having proved his existence, Aquinas describes God as
- One
- Simple
- Perfect
- Good

- Infinite
- Immutable
- Eternal

Like Augustine, Aquinas relied heavily on Aristotelian logic to drive the detailed minutiae of theological arguments. One which has attracted both serious attention and ridicule over a millennium and a half is the riddle 'how many angels can dance on the head of a pin?' Aquinas didn't pose the question quite like that. In *The Reasons of the Christian Religion* (1667) the English Protestant theologian Richard Baxter paraphrased the old chestnut as 'how many Angels may fit upon the point of a Needle?' Whether the question may be asked of the head of a pin or the point of a needle is mere hair-splitting. Aquinas's answer is: 'It would seem that several angels can be at the same time in the same place. For several bodies cannot be at the same time in the same place, because they fill the place. But angels do not fill a place, because only a body fills a place, so that it be not empty, as appears from the Philosopher [Aristotle] (Phys. iv, text. 52, 58). Therefore several angels can be in one place.'

...... • ......

v **IN HIS *ETHICS*** (1677) Baruch Spinoza (*see also* DAY JOBS iv) described God as 'a being absolutely infinite, of whom no attribute that expresses the essence of substance can be denied'. For Spinoza 'God is one, that is (by Def. vi.) only one substance can be granted in the universe, and that substance is absolutely infinite.' He is 'the absolutely first cause'.

Earlier, we read that Philo said God is 'idea' – a difficult concept which Spinoza clarifies when he states that 'Thought is an attribute of God':

> The order and connection of ideas is the same as the order and connection of things. Hence God's power of thinking is equal to his realized power of action – that is, whatsoever follows from the infinite nature of God in the world of extension (*formaliter*), follows without exception in the same order and connection from the idea of God in the world of thought (objective).

His belief that 'Extension is an attribute of God, or God is an extended thing' is what causes some observers to label Spinoza a pantheist.

In *Tractatus Theologico-Politicus* (published anonymously, 1670) Spinoza challenged two deeply held views of seventeenth-century Jewish theology: that God was not 'extended' and that God spoke only to the Jews as the 'chosen people'. His first 'heresy' was to write on the matter of extension:

> ...the law of Moses... which was set up as a national standard of right, nowhere prescribed the belief that God is without body, or even without form or figure, but only ordained that the Jews should believe in His existence and worship Him alone: it forbade them to invent or fashion any likeness of the Deity... Nevertheless, the Bible clearly implies that God has a form, and that Moses when he heard God speaking was permitted to behold it, or at least its hinder parts.

Perhaps the greater 'heresy' was to suggest that God belonged to all of mankind, not just the Jews:

it is plain that God had ordained for the whole human race the law to reverence God, to keep from evil doing, or to do well, and that Job, although a Gentile, was of all men most acceptable to God, because he excelled all in piety and religion... We conclude, therefore (inasmuch as God is to all men equally gracious, and the Hebrews were only chosen by Him in respect to their social organization and government), that the individual Jew, taken apart from his social organization and government, possessed no gift of God above other men, and that there was no difference between Jew and Gentile.

Spinoza's God was for everyone. He exalted intellectual activity because 'The intellectual love of the mind towards God is that very love of God whereby God loves himself... in other words, the intellectual love of the mind towards God is part of the infinite love wherewith God loves himself.' Einstein said:

The God Spinoza revered is my God, too: I meet Him everyday in the harmonious laws which govern the universe. My religion is cosmic, and my God is too universal to concern himself with the intentions of every human being. I do not accept a religion of fear; my God will not hold me responsible for the actions that necessity imposes. My God speaks to me through laws.

...... ● ......

vi HEGEL DECLARED: 'philosophy has no other object but God and so is essentially rational theology and, as the servant of truth, a continual divine service'. Like Philo and Spinoza, Hegel viewed God as 'idea', as 'thought'. But he goes beyond his predecessors to argue that God arises in the self-consciousness of a person. He argued in *The Phenomenology of Mind* (1807) that consciousness 'does not set out from its own inner life, does not start from thought, and in itself combine the thought of God with existence; rather it sets out from immediate present existence, and recognizes God in it'.

Hegel's follower Ludwig Andreas Feuerbach completed the thought his master was heading towards – that God is in us, because we *are* God. In *The Essence of Christianity* (1841) he said: 'Consciousness of God is self-consciousness, knowledge of God is self-knowledge. By his God thou knowest the man, and by the man his God; the two are identical.'

...... ● ......

vii **AND SO WE COME** to Nietzsche, who famously declared in *The Gay Science* (1882) that 'God is dead'. Less well-remembered are the lines that follow Nietzsche's headline statement:

> **God is dead. God remains dead. And we have killed him. How shall we comfort ourselves, the murderers of all murderers? What was holiest and mightiest of all that the world has yet owned has bled to death under our knives: who will wipe this blood off us? What water is there for us to clean ourselves? What festivals of atonement, what sacred games shall we have to invent? Is not the greatness of this deed too great for us? Must we ourselves not become gods simply to appear worthy of it?**

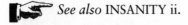 *See also* INSANITY ii.

viii **IN *PROCESS AND REALITY*** (1929) Alfred North Whitehead described a view of the world in which it is in a constant state of flux and development. Nothing remains the same through time; everything changes. He developed a theology around this idea (called process theology) in which the unmoved mover of Aristotle is replaced by a God whose nature is mutable. He further challenges received theology by denying his 'ruler' qualities: 'the Church gave unto God the attributes which belonged exclusively to Caesar'. Whitehead says God is born of a 'brief Galilean vision of humility' that

> does not emphasize the ruling Caesar, or the ruthless moralist, or the unmoved mover. It dwells upon the tender elements in the world, which slowly and in quietness operates by love; and it finds purpose in the present immediacy of a kingdom not of this world. Love neither rules, nor is it unmoved; also it is a little oblivious as to morals. It does not look to the future; for it finds its own reward in the immediate present.

...... ● ......

ix 'THE GOD OF THE OLD TESTAMENT is arguably the most unpleasant character in all fiction: jealous and proud of it; a petty, unjust, unforgiving control-freak; a vindictive, bloodthirsty ethnic cleanser; a misogynistic, homophobic, racist, infanticidal, genocidal, filicidal, pestilential, megalomaniacal, sadomasochistic, capriciously malevolent bully.' So says the British evolutionary biologist Richard Dawkins in his book *The God Delusion* (2006).

Dawkins' fellow countryman Christopher Hitchens echoes

those thoughts in his 2007 book provocatively titled *God is Not Great: The Case Against Religion* (the US subtitle is *How Religion Poisons Everything*). Hitchens says religion is 'Violent, irrational, intolerant, allied to racism and tribalism and bigotry, invested in ignorance and hostile to free inquiry, contemptuous of women and coercive toward children.' He concludes, 'organized religion ought to have a great deal on its conscience'.

Dawkins and Hitchens, along with Daniel Dennett and the American philosopher Sam Harris (*The End of Faith*, 2004) belong to a group of thinkers dubbed the New Atheists. They promote knowledge over belief. In his blog 'An Atheist Manifesto', Harris argued:

When we have reasons for what we believe, we have no need of faith; when we have no reasons, or bad ones, we have lost our connection to the world and to one another. Atheism is nothing more than a commitment to the most basic standard of intellectual honesty: One's convictions should be proportional to one's evidence. Pretending to be certain when one isn't – indeed, pretending to be certain about propositions for which no evidence is even conceivable – is both an intellectual and a moral failing. Only the atheist has realized this. The atheist is simply a person who has perceived the lies of religion and refused to make them his own.

One people, one body politic, under one

✳ SUPREME GOVERNMENT ✳

There can be no civil
government without
a **SOVERAIGNE**

CHAPTER EIGHTEEN

GOVERNING

CIVIL GOVERNMENT
*cannot be brought
about by*
FORCE

DEMOLITION
of the
BOURGEOIS
STATE MACHINE

Freedom in CAPITALIST SOCIETY
always remains
FREEDOM *for* SLAVE-OWNERS

i **SINCE GOVERNING MAY BE** the most impactful thing a person or group of people can do, it would be reasonable to wonder if philosophy ever informs it. Plato created the idea of the philosopher king, of which there have been three examples over the past 2,000 years: the Roman emperor Marcus Aurelius (*see* DAY JOBS i *and* ii); the fifteenth-century King of Hungary and Croatia Matthias Corvinus; and the political theorist, and first premier of the Soviet Union, Vladimir Ilyich Ulyanov – otherwise known as Lenin (*see* GOVERNING iv). Both Aurelius and Corvinus were influenced by Plato's writing on governing. Under the influence of Karl Marx, Lenin wrote a new handbook on leadership by whose tenets he lived and died.* Lenin was the first to rule from the position of a new ideology, communism. Before communism, governments had largely been forms of monarchy or limited democracy.

...... ● ......

ii **THOMAS HOBBES** of Malmesbury, a political thinker who lived through an era of warfare between Royalists and Parliamentarians in England, was a supporter of absolute monarchy. In *De Cive* ('On the citizen', 1642) he argued that the first governor of persons is God, whose will is enforced by an earthly king or queen. The duty of the governed is to God, whose representative on earth makes the laws of state. 'There can be no civill government without a Soveraigne; and that they who have gotten this Soveraigne command must be obey'd simply, that is to say, in all things which repugne not the Commandments of God: There is this one thing only

---

* From a series of strokes, aggravated by a bullet lodged in his neck from an assassination attempt.

wanting to the complete understanding of all civill duty, that is, to know which are the Laws and Commandments of God.' Those who do not 'know' God – atheists, or those who believe in God, but think they are not bound by his laws – are not citizens and have no rights: 'Those onely therefore are suppos'd to belong to Gods Kingdome, who acknowledge him to be the Governour of all things, and that he hath given his Commands to men, and appointed punishments for the transgressours; The rest, we must not call Subjects, but Enemies of God.' Such persons also become enemies of the state.

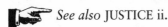 *See also* JUSTICE ii.

...... ● ......

iii **JOHN LOCKE'S** *Two Treatises of Government* (published anonymously in 1689) laid a foundation for modern liberal democracy by proposing a social contract between government and governed:

> **The state of nature and civil society are mutually opposed. In a state of nature men are their own lawmakers and their own judges; they decide the conflicts between themselves and do not look to any other earthly authority. In a civil society, men constitute one body with an agreed-upon authority that is given the responsibility of making laws and executing them. This civil government is only formed by the consent of those who decide to leave the state of nature. It cannot be brought about by force.**

Against Hobbes, he argues for separation of Church and

state, while advocating religious tolerance.* For Locke, 'political societies all began from a voluntary union, and the mutual agreement of men freely acting in the choice of their governors and forms of government'.

Locke's sense of good government is that it respects the individual's freedom, which he defines as 'liberty of acting according to his own will'. But that freedom must be tempered by reasoning which recognizes the liberty of others. Selfish liberties enjoyed in the state of nature must give way to ones leavened by reason under the social contract which can occur 'when and only when a number of men are united into one society in such a way that each of them forgoes his executive power of the law of nature, giving it over to the public. And this comes about wherever a number of men in the state of nature enter into society to make one people, one body politic, under one supreme government.'† Thus, every man makes an agreement with every other man 'to make one body politic under one government' in which he 'puts himself under an obligation to everyone in that society to submit to the decisions of the majority, and to be bound by it'. *See also* DUTY ii; FREEDOM iv; JUSTICE iii.

...... ● ......

iv **THE RUSSIAN POLITICAL THEORIST** V. I. Lenin differed from Hobbes and Locke in that he had the opportunity to put

---

* One reason for his appeal to the founding fathers of the United States when writing that country's constitution.

† Locke observes: 'This makes it evident that absolute monarchy, which some people regard as the only genuine government in the world, is actually inconsistent with civil society and so can't be a form of civil government at all!'

his theories about governing into practice. He ruled Russia for seven years – first, from 1917 until 1922 as head of the Russian Soviet Federative Socialist Republic; then as leader of the Soviet Union from 1922 until his death in 1924. Lenin was a student of the nineteenth-century socialist Karl Marx; the official political ideology of the Communist Party of the Soviet Union was Marxism-Leninism. In (1917) Lenin derives from Marx's theorizing a programme of governing: 'Marx deduced from the whole history of socialism and of the political struggle that the state was bound to disappear.' What Lenin was after was 'demolition of the bourgeois state machine'. He attacked capitalist democracy as a form of government too limited to bring about the relief he thought was needed from tsarist rule:

In capitalist society, providing it develops under the most favourable conditions, we have a more or less complete democracy in the democratic republic. But this democracy is always hemmed in by the narrow limits set by capitalist exploitation, and consequently always remains, in essence, a democracy for the minority, only for the propertied classes, only for the rich. Freedom in capitalist society always remains about the same as it was in the ancient Greek republics: freedom for the slave-owners.

This state of affairs, Lenin argues, militates against the illusory freedom of the working class. 'Owing to the conditions of capitalist exploitation the modern wage slaves are so crushed by want and poverty that... in the ordinary, peaceful course of events the majority of the population is debarred from participation in public and political life.'

Lenin looks at the 'machinery of capitalist democracy' and

finds critical cracks in it by exposing 'petty' details: residential qualifications for voting, women's exclusion from the vote, 'obstacles to the right of assembly ("public buildings are not for 'beggars'!")' and 'the purely capitalist organization of the daily press'. Lenin's communist revolution replaces the machinery of capitalist oppression by creating a dictatorship of the proletariat. It promises 'an immense expansion of democracy, which for the first time becomes democracy for the poor, democracy for the people, and not democracy for the money-bags'; more than that, 'the dictatorship of the proletariat brings about a series of restrictions on the freedom of the oppressors, the exploiters, the capitalists'.

Lenin's ideal state is brought about through violence. 'Resistance must be crushed by force; it is clear that where there is suppression, where there is violence, there is no freedom and no democracy' (Lenin finds no irony in the replacement of violence by one group with that of another). The precondition of freedom, Lenin argues, is to make the state 'disappear': 'when the capitalists have disappeared, when there are no classes (i.e., when there is no difference between the members of society as regards their relation to the social means of production), only then the state "ceases to exist", and it "becomes possible to speak of freedom"'.

So, how did Lenin's experiment fare? On the plus side, he brought about social changes that, even a hundred years later, are still being argued in the West. Lenin was the first national leader to decriminalize homosexuality and abortion (free access to birth control and abortion). He instituted no-fault divorce and established universal free health care and education. Women received equal pay with men and all enjoyed a seven-hour working day. Nearly half the members of the USSR

Academy of Sciences were women, and more than half of the country's doctors. A study conducted in 1962–64 during the height of the Cold War found that women earned 4 per cent of the chemistry PhDs given in the Soviet Union; in the same period, the figure for American women was 5 per cent.

On the minus side, Lenin was a mass murderer. He wrote in 1917 that 'only communism makes the state completely unnecessary, for there is nobody to be suppressed'. Only months after Lenin wrote these words, he created the Cheka, or secret police, to round up and deal with the opposition (party rivals, or those who disagreed with him on the detail of Marxism-Leninism). In what became known as the Red Terror of 1918, Lenin had, at the most conservative estimate, 50,000 people murdered. The Cheka also ran the gulag system of forced labour camps. Lenin was succeeded by Joseph Stalin, who is credited with the deaths of fifty million citizens between 1924 and 1953. This does not include casualties from the Second World War.

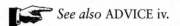 *See also* ADVICE iv.

All affliction, vexation, loss, grief, **TIME** *alone digests*

~

I HAVE LOST
THE ONE THING
THAT BOUND ME
TO LIFE

~

CHAPTER NINETEEN

GRIEF

All **PERTURBATION** is **MISERY**
GRIEF is the **RACK** itself

A FRIGHTFUL,
MISERABLE,
—— AND ——
DETESTABLE
THING

A *MODERATE*
INDULGENCE
is not to be
DISAPPROVED

i **THE GREEKS WERE MADE** of tougher stuff than we are today. It is self-evident that when one of our contemporaries dies, an aspect of our grieving is the confrontation of the fact that we, too, are going to die. Most of us don't like contemplating our own deaths (even those who believe in an afterlife). Our instinct is to preserve our lives. The deaths of loved ones call the security of our own lives into question.

Crantor, a Greek philosopher of the fourth century BC, set the tone of classical thinking on the subject with his work *On Grief*, written for his friend Hippocles upon the death of his son. Crantor's text is lost, but many other philosophers refer to it; Cicero is thought to have taken most of the third book of his *Tusculan Disputations* (*c*.45 BC) from it.*

In his book – an attempt to popularize Stoic philosophy – Cicero summarizes Crantor's position on grief:

> Do you, then, think that it can befall a wise man to be oppressed with grief, that is to say, with misery? for, as all perturbation is misery, grief is the rack itself. Lust is attended with heat, exulting joy with levity, fear with meanness, but grief with something greater than these; it consumes, torments, afflicts, and disgraces a man; it tears him, preys upon his mind, and utterly destroys him: if we do not so divest ourselves of it as to throw it completely off, we cannot be free from misery.

For Crantor/Cicero grief must be dismissed 'if we are desirous to pass this share of life that is allotted to us with ease and satisfaction'. They address the problem, should a wise man be

---

* After other philosophers followed Crantor's lead with similar reflections on grief, he was credited with having created a new genre – the 'consolation'.

subject to grief? No, they write: 'our business at present is to drive away grief if we can'. Their answer to the question 'should a wise man grieve?' is a resounding 'no', for grief is 'a frightful, miserable, and detestable thing, which we should fly from with our utmost efforts – with all our sails and oars, as I may say'.

Cicero believed that the mind is quicker at dispelling grief than time is. In *Letters to Atticus* he writes in 46 BC, 'I am very sorry to hear about [the death of Atticus's friend] Athamas. But your grief, though it is a kindly weakness, should be kept well in check. There are many roads to consolation, but this is the straightest: let reason bring about what time is sure to bring about.' Grief is an evil for Cicero, partly because he views it as a waste of time and, at bottom, self-indulgent. In 46 BC he wrote again to Atticus, upon the death of another of the latter's friends: 'I am sorry to hear about Seius. But one has to learn to put up with all human troubles. For what are we ourselves and how long will they be bothering us? Let us look to a thing that is more in our power, though not very much, – what we are to do about the Senate.'

And then Cicero's daughter Tullia dies in February of 45 BC, a month after giving birth. Cicero is stricken with deep sorrow. He writes the *Consolatio* ('Consolation', the text is lost). Suffering real grief of his own, Cicero abandons his tough love stance on the subject. On 19 March he writes to Atticus, 'I have lost the one thing that bound me to life'. Cicero visits Atticus and, while there, reads in his friend's library every Greek text on grief he can find. He writes to Atticus: 'There is nothing written by anyone that I did not read while at your place. But my grief defeats all consolation,' an affecting and un-Stoic quote. At the end of the day, Stoicism failed one of its greatest promoters.

ii **ABOUT A CENTURY AND A HALF** after Cicero's loss
of his daughter, the Greek scholar Plutarch of Chaeronea, in
a letter of condolence to his friend Apollonius, argued for
the necessity of grief. He wrote: 'The pain and pang felt at
the death of a son has in itself good cause to awaken grief,
which is only natural, and over it we have no control.' Most
modern readers will concur with Plutarch that the tough positions taken by Crantor, Cicero and Seneca on grief and their
admonishments against it are useless because, as Plutarch says
in his *Consolation to Apollonius*, it is beyond our power to
contain it. Death descends upon us with a weight that is too
great simply to shrug off.

Plutarch believes that admonishments against grief run the
risk of inhibiting finer aspects of the human character such as
sympathy or empathy: 'I, for my part, cannot concur with those
who extol that harsh and callous indifference, which is both
impossible and unprofitable. For this will rob us of the kindly
feeling which comes from mutual affection and which above all
else we must conserve.' At the same time, Plutarch warns against
excessive grief. 'To be carried beyond all bounds and to help in
exaggerating our griefs I say is contrary to nature, and results
from our depraved ideas. Therefore this also must be dismissed
as injurious and depraved and most unbecoming to right-minded
men, but a moderate indulgence is not to be disapproved.'

...... ● ......

iii **SOMETIMES GRIEF** does not express itself from a place of
abject darkness; occasionally the death of a friend inspires an
immediate eulogy – a celebration of the character, the essence
of the deceased. Such was the case with the letter written in

November 1776 by the political economist Adam Smith to the Scottish publisher William Strahan following the death of the philosopher David Hume in August of that year. After giving 'some account of the behaviour of our late excellent friend, Mr Hume, during his last illness', Smith goes on to quote the words of a Dr Black, describing the stoicism with which Hume faced death, before adding his own richly generous encomium:

'DEAR SIR, — Yesterday, about four o'clock, afternoon, Mr. Hume expired. The near approach of his death became evident in the night between Thursday and Friday, when his disease became excessive, and soon weakened him so much that he could no longer rise out of his bed. He continued to the last perfectly sensible, and free from much pain or feelings of distress. He never dropped the smallest expression of impatience; but when he had occasion to speak to the people about him, always did it with affection and tenderness. I thought it improper to write to bring you over, especially as I heard that he had dictated a letter to you desiring you not to come. When he became very weak, it cost him an effort to speak, and he died in such a happy composure of mind, that nothing could exceed it.'

Thus died our most excellent and never to be forgotten friend; concerning whose philosophical opinions men will, no doubt, judge variously, every one approving or condemning them, according as they happen to coincide or disagree with his own; but concerning whose character and conduct there can scarce be a difference of opinion. His temper, indeed, seemed to be more happily balanced, if I may be allowed such an expression, than that perhaps of any other man I have ever known. Even in the lowest state of his fortune, his great and necessary frugality never hindered him from exercising, upon proper occasions, acts both of charity and generosity... His constant pleasantry was the genuine effusion of good nature and good humour, tempered with delicacy and modesty, and without even the slightest tincture of malignity, so frequently the disagreeable source of what is called wit in other men. It never was the meaning of his raillery to mortify; and, therefore, far from offending, it seldom failed to please and delight, even those who were the objects of it... that gaiety of temper, so agreeable in society, but which is so often accompanied with frivolous and superficial qualities, was in him certainly attended with the most severe application, the most extensive learning, the greatest depth of thought, and a capacity in every respect the most comprehensive. Upon the whole, I have always considered him, both in his lifetime and since his death, as approaching as nearly to the idea of a perfectly wise and virtuous man, as perhaps the nature of human frailty will permit.

...... • ......

iv **THE DEATH** of Queen Victoria's husband Albert, Prince Consort, in 1861 thrust her into an abyss of grief that caused her to abandon her duties for three years. She expressed her grief by wearing widow's weeds for the remaining forty years of her life. Her ostensible abdication of her role and attendant duties provided an obstacle to government and fuelled republican feeling. Victoria's mourning characterized a response to death that was the opposite of classical Stoicism. It prompted a cult of mourning unique to the Victorians. It was the age of large and elaborate monuments, of extravagant public display.

Victoria was fond of explaining her love of animals by quoting Arthur Schopenhauer: 'If it were not for the honest faces of dogs, we should forget the very existence of sincerity.' She might also have read these lines from Schopenhauer: 'It is not without meaning that mythology depicts Cronus as devouring and digesting stones: for that which is otherwise quite indigestible, all affliction, vexation, loss, grief, time alone digests.'

...... ● ......

v   **ONE QUESTION** that must be faced about grieving is this: is it self-regarding? The ancient Greeks' 'buck up' or 'pull up your socks' attitude would certainly suggest this. In her essay 'Is Grief Self-Regarding?' Christiane Pohl writes, 'Seldom are we so preoccupied with ourselves as when we grieve. Taking leave of someone close to you – whether the occasion is separation or death – can consume immense spiritual energy and last many years.' Furthermore, 'grieving also acts as a catalyst, bringing to the fore an awareness of our own mortality and transience'. As a result, 'the question arises as to whether grief is an expression of egoism':

> Why do we weep for someone who has died? Because he or she can no longer participate in life? Is it that we would have wished this life to have continued for its own sake, independently of our own needs and desires? Or is it that, in grieving, we are lamenting the loss we ourselves have incurred? Do we maybe wish that the deceased person might have continued to live for our sake, for the satisfaction and enrichment of our own existence?

For Pohl, self-love is not a negative phenomenon in the grieving process; it is not (necessarily) simple selfishness. The fact is,
the death of a loved one forces us to concentrate on our own
selves; where else is the emotion to be directed in the absence
of the loved one? Pohl counsels:

**To this extent, grief is a process which must of necessity con-
centrate intensely on one's own person. Self-love, which we
have described as a form of egoism, is a necessary precondition for a person to carry through the difficult labour of grief
and finally also to overcome their loss. This kind of egoism
must be alive in a person if they are to regain a footing in
the world.**

The Anglican priest Michael Williams disagrees with Pohl's
view that self-love is a 'necessary precondition' for dealing with
grief. Pohl says that her concept of self-love should be regarded
as temperate; Williams argues for 'an understanding of grief
[that] is not a temperate one, it is, rather, something fierce
which demands our coming to terms with a total voluntary
loss of self'. He refers to Socrates speaking in Plato's *Phaedo*
on the concepts of 'purification' and 'deliverance', which
'speak of something deeper which, in the later philosophical and theological tradition, is called detachment. Contrary
to expectations, it is detachment alone which is the gateway
through which we must pass if we are truly to engage with life.
This is the aporia* of death.'

---

* A term meaning 'irresolvable contradiction'.

A WILD *and* GRIEVOUS *sight to* BEHOLD

A MAN WHO IS **BALD** HAS LEAST REASON TO FEEL **ASHAMED**

CHAPTER TWENTY

HAIRCUTS

GOD IS DEAD BUT MY HAIR IS BEAUTIFUL

HAIR is there where BRAINS have taken their DEPARTURE

i **THE WORST BAD HAIR DAY** in the history of Western philosophy was recorded by the Greek thinker and orator Dio Chrysostom around the year AD 80. In his 'Encomium on Hair' the sophist tells how he awoke one morning to find his hair 'a wild and grievous sight to behold'. He reports: 'it was proving difficult to get it loosened up, and most of it threatened to tear out and resisted my efforts'. This event caused Dio to reflect on haircuts, and to praise those 'who, being beauty-lovers and prizing their locks most of all, attend to them in no casual manner, but keep a sort of reed always in the hair itself, wherewith they comb it whenever they are at leisure'. He is disparaging of the bald.

Dio argues that well-coiffed hair makes a man both beautiful (but not effeminate) and 'terrifying'. He cites Herodotus, who tells of a Persian scout who was astonished to find Spartan troops attending to their hair just before the Battle of Thermopylae. Haircare, Dio claims, is crucial to military success. He describes the method by which fierce Spartans maintained their coifs in the field:

> while sleeping on the ground they are careful never to let their hair touch the earth, placing a small prop of wood beneath their head so as to keep it as far as possible from the earth, and they are more concerned to keep their hair clean than they are to enjoy sweet sleep. The reason, it would seem, is that hair makes them both beautiful and at the same time terrifying, while sleep, however sweet it be, makes them both sluggish and devoid of caution.

Dio combs the texts of Homer to discover that when the great poet wants to sing the praises of female beauty, hair does not figure in his acclamations. Homer refers to 'golden Aphroditê', 'great-eyed Hera' and 'Thetis of the silver feet' – no mention of golden braids anywhere. By contrast, the beauty of Zeus is defined by his 'ambrosial locks'. Dio nails down his thesis with the observation that, upon the death of Euphorbus, hero of the Trojan War, Homer singled out the great soldier for one thing only – his hair:

> His locks, so like the Graces', were wet with blood,
> His braids with gold and silver tightly claspt.

Soldiers were not the only ones who self-identified with hairstyles:

> In Athens haircuts and hairstyles had social and political im-plications. Aristocratic horsemen still wore long braids and gold hairpins. The common man (and the politicians who spoke for him) preferred a short cut, though not quite a crewcut... (At Athens any man with a long unkempt beard ran the risk of being mistaken for a philosopher.)

...... ● ......

ii **DIO'S SEEMINGLY IRREFUTABLE ARGUMENT** was challenged by the Greek Neoplatonist and cleric Synesius, whose career bridges the fourth and fifth centuries AD. In busts, Dio is portrayed sporting a fine head of curly hair; by contrast portraits show that Synesius was bald and proud of it. Against Dio, Synesius praises baldness as a mark of intelligence and equates long hair on a man with, among other things, stupid-ity, effeminacy and viciousness.

In 'A Eulogy of Baldness' Synesius writes, 'My argument, then, will lay it down that of all men a man who is bald has least reason to feel ashamed.' Baldness is associated with brains: 'just as man is the most intelligent, and at the same time the least hairy of earthly creatures, conversely it is admitted that of all domestic animals the sheep is the stupidest, and that this is why he puts forth his hair with no discrimination'. After a survey of portraits and busts of philosophers in a museum, Synesius concludes: 'If anyone is wise he is also bald, and if he is not bald, neither is he wise.' His proof? Portraits of Diogenes and Socrates. The opposite is true of the hirsute: 'hair is there where brains have taken their departure'. Synesius even goes so far as to call the bald head 'a temple of God'.

But it is not just brains and divinity that attach to baldness. Synesius, who studied astronomy under Hypatia (*see* MAR-TYRDOM ii), demonstrates that light – always associated with goodness – is reflected by the smooth, shiny surface of the bald head. By contrast, 'hairy stars [comets] are portents of evil'. Hair 'befits darkness'. Synesius calls it a 'natural parasol'. The hirsute are like dense forests that 'have no share in light, for they are excessively shaded and bearded with hair'.

Synesius has a special contempt for the sexually intemperate, particularly adulterers and male prostitutes. He is scornful of adulterers because they are destructive of the very fabric of society, and of prostitutes because they wallow in 'abominable pleasure'. Both groups, he says, are typically drawn from the ranks of the long-haired. 'The adulterers', Synesius writes, 'certainly come from the men who care for their hair. Homer depicts the seducer as one fingering his shining locks, in the sense that his hair was adorned for the ruin of women.' Of male prostitutes, 'let it be said that these effeminate wretches all make a cult of their hair'. Synesius hoped that, after reading his essay, 'the wearers of long hair are put to shame and that they adopt at least a rather moderate and restrained cropping of their hair'. While Synesius's sophistical talents were in the service of amusement in 'A Eulogy of Baldness', they were put to more serious use in his efforts to calm the often bitter philosophical war between Neoplatonists and Christians. Though a Neoplatonist, he became the bald Bishop of Ptolemais in what is now Libya.

...... ● ......

iii **THE FRENCH PHILOSOPHER** and public intellectual Bernard-Henri Lévy is famous for his luxurious head of hair. He is wealthy, flamboyant, famous as a womanizer. He has many critics, whose remarks he rarely deigns to address; but he does deny having said, 'God is dead, but my hair is beautiful.' Asked by an interviewer why some men make so much of their hair, he replies: 'Because it's really about their virility, maybe? But I don't have a problem with my virility – I really don't.' *See also* BACKBITING vi.

Yet see how *in what good* CONDITION I AM

HAPPINESS *is the* MEANING *and the* PURPOSE *of* LIFE

CHAPTER TWENTY-ONE

HAPPINESS

WISDOM IS NOTHING OTHER THAN THE SCIENCE OF HAPPINESS

- - -

HAPPINESS IS THE SUM TOTAL OF ALL *PARTICULAR PLEASURES*

- · -

Is more often found with those who are

HIGHLY CULTIVATED

in their minds

i **FOR ARISTIPPUS,** happiness and goodness could derive from fine wine, good food or sex with prostitutes – all of these were among Aristippus's passions. Equally, it could come from the exercise of reason. As with many other ancient Greek philosophers, much of what we know about Aristippus is anecdotal evidence from Diogenes Laertius's *Lives and Opinions of Eminent Philosophers*, thought to have been composed during the first half of the third century AD. Diogenes paints Aristippus as, above all, an amiable and – there is no other word for it – *philosophical* man: 'He derived pleasure from what was present, and did not toil to procure the enjoyment of something not present.'

Cyrenaics, as followers of Aristippus were known, perceived human experience as being characterized by the opposites of pleasure and pain. He taught that 'pleasure does not differ from pleasure nor is one pleasure more pleasant than another'; also, 'that there is a difference between "end" and "happiness". Our end is particular pleasure, whereas happiness is the sum total of all particular pleasures, in which are included both past and future pleasures.' Aristippus's teaching on happiness differed from that of the second-century BC Greek Panaetius of Rhodes who identified with the pleasure that follows relief from pain, or the third-century Greek Epicurus who defined it as freedom from discomfort.

Aristippus was a regular at the court of Dionysius I, tyrant of Syracuse, but was equally comfortable in the fleshpots of the city. 'Aristippus was so noted for his mastery over his desires that it is alleged that Plato once stated of Aristippus… "You alone are endowed with the gift to flaunt in robes or go in rags."' One evening Dionysius presented Aristippus with three prostitutes and commanded, 'choose one'. Aristippus replied,

'I choose all three.' The bemused king obliged. Aristippus explained with characteristic wit: 'Paris paid dearly for giving the preference to one out of three.' Aristippus is referring to Dionysius' take on the story from Greek mythology of how Zeus was asked to judge who was fairest among Hera, Athena and Aphrodite. Zeus was reluctant to do so, and asked the Trojan mortal Paris to choose. He judged Helen, thereby sparking the Trojan War. Having chosen all three ladies – and so avoiding the pitfalls inherent in such a choice – Aristippus left with them and, once out of doors, bid them goodnight.

While Aristippus said pleasure was the road to happiness, he also cautioned moderation. The story of the three prostitutes also illustrates his understanding of the concept of freedom. Aristippus's choice was contemptuous of Dionysius the bully, the 'owner' of persons. He respected the choice of a woman to sell herself for money; he did not respect the thinking that gave Dionysius the 'right' to purchase and 'gift' a person to another. Diogenes understood the unusual ethical content of Aristippus's pursuit of pleasure. 'Aristippus found happiness in pleasure, while Socrates found it chiefly in rational enjoyment. Aristippus, however, advocated justice, since injustice does not pay; for it incites retaliation, and awakens in the wrongdoer apprehension of danger; therefore to secure peace of mind, it is advisable to obey the laws.'

...... ● ......

ii **DIOGENES OF SINOPE**, who lived in the fourth century BC, was a founder of Cynicism – the philosophical view that one ought to live one's life in accordance with nature, abjuring possessions, wealth, fame, power. True happiness, according to the Cynics, lay in asceticism. Diogenes lived in a clay jar of the type used to store wine, olive oil or grain. He divested himself of his only two possessions, a bowl and spoon, after observing a poor man using his hands for a bowl. He was banished from his birthplace for defacing currency.

Diogenes outraged contemporaries like Plato in shows of disrespect for their philosophies. He expressed his contempt for social norms by spitting, urinating, defecating and masturbating in public. Dio Chrysostom, the Greek Neoplatonist of the first century AD who is best known for his *Discourses*, titled his eighth discourse 'Diogenes or on Virtue'. He has Diogenes say, 'the noble man holds his hardships to be his greatest antagonists, and with them he is ever wont to battle day and night, not to win a sprig of parsley as so many goats might do, nor for a bit of wild olive, or of pine, but to win happiness and virtue throughout all the days of his life'.

Diogenes compared himself to a dog – in his view, an animal possessed of characteristics more agreeable than those he found in most men. Diogenes says he was called a dog because (against social convention) he ate his lunch in the marketplace. When Plato called him a dog, Diogenes replied, 'Undoubtedly, for I have come back to those who sold me.' At a banquet, a number of diners threw bones at Diogenes. Upon leaving, he cocked his leg against each of them.

Once Alexander the Great came and stood by him, and said, 'I am Alexander, the great king.' 'And I,' said he, 'am Diogenes the dog.' And when he was asked to what actions of his it was owing that he was called a dog, he said, 'Because I fawn upon those who give me anything, and bark at those who give me nothing, and bite the rogues.'

Upon his death, friends of Diogenes set atop his grave a dog carved in marble.

...... ● ......

iii **IN HIS *NICOMACHEAN ETHICS*** (*c.*350 BC) Aristotle said that 'Happiness is the meaning and the purpose of life, the whole aim and end of human existence.' In his *Politics* (*c.*350 BC) he elaborated: 'Happiness, whether consisting in pleasure or virtue, or both, is more often found with those who are highly cultivated in their minds and in their character, and have only a moderate share of external goods, than among those who possess external goods to a useless extent but are deficient in higher qualities.'

...... ● ......

iv **ARISTOTLE'S VIEW** was amplified by Epictetus, a Stoic of the second century AD, who was born a slave: 'It is never possible to make happiness consistent with a longing after what is not present.' His humble beginnings allowed him to form a view of happiness as absence of want, as opposed to an excess of possessions:

For true happiness implies the possession of all which is desired, as in case of satiety with food; there must be no thirst, no hunger. Such is the Cynic honoured with the sceptre and diadem from Zeus; who says, 'That you may see, O mankind, that you do not seek happiness and tranquillity where it is, but where it is not, behold, I am sent an example to you from God; – who have neither estate, nor house, nor

wife, nor children, – nor even a bed, coat, or furniture. And
yet see how in what good condition I am.'

...... ● ......

v **GOTTFRIED WILHELM LEIBNIZ** is a giant among philosophers – a polymath who, in addition to his work in metaphysics and ethics, developed calculus independently of Isaac
Newton, along with numerous other advances in mathematics.
Regarding happiness, Leibniz said: 'Wisdom is nothing other
than the science of happiness, that is to say it teaches us to
attain happiness.' He further defined it as 'the state of a constant joy.' But Leibniz is not blindly optimistic about happiness. He qualifies his definition with the observation:

Whoever is happy, does not indeed feel his joy at all
moments, for he rests sometimes from his reflection, and
also commonly turns his thoughts toward seemly concerns.
It is however enough, that he is in a state to experience joy as
often as he wants to think about it, and that in the meantime,
a joyfulness arises out of it in his being and his actions.
  Joy in the present does not make one happy, if there is no
permanence in it; and one is on the contrary unhappy, who
for the sake of a brief joy falls into a long sadness.

A key component of happiness for Leibniz is that it is not
only an individual feeling, but one that derives from and
includes other people, animals, and inanimate objects: 'Joy is a
pleasure, which the soul feels in itself. The pleasure is the feeling of a perfection or an excellence, be it in us or in something
other; for the perfection of another thing is also pleasant, as

understanding, bravery, and especially, the beauty of other persons; also, as well, of an animal; yes, even of a lifeless creature, a painting, or a work of art.'

...... ● ......

vi BERTRAND RUSSELL was an enormous admirer of Leibniz, upon whom one might say Russell tried to model himself. Russell was one of the twentieth century's most important mathematicians, and wrote broadly across the spectrum of philosophical issues. In *The Conquest of Happiness* (1930) he follows Leibniz in stressing the role that other people play in our own happiness:

... the whole antithesis between self and the rest of the world, which is implied in the doctrine of self-denial, disappears as soon as we have any genuine interest in persons or things outside ourselves. Through such interests a man comes to feel himself part of the stream of life, not a hard separate entity like a billiard-ball, which can have no relation with other such entities except that of collision. All unhappiness depends upon some kind of disintegration or lack of integration; there is disintegration within the self through lack of coordination between the conscious and the unconscious mind; there is lack of integration between the self and society where the two are not knit together by the force of objective interests and affections. The happy man is the man who does not suffer from either of these failures of unity, whose personality is neither divided against itself nor pitted against the world. Such a man feels himself a citizen of the universe, enjoying freely the spectacle that it offers and the joys that it affords, untroubled by the thought of death because he feels himself not really separate from those who will come after him. It is in such profound instinctive union with the stream of life that the greatest joy is to be found.

···GLAD··· **TIDINGS**

HOPE
is what carries us
——— **HIGHER** and ———
FARTHER

A *very* MYSTERIOUS RADIATION

CHAPTER TWENTY-TWO

HOPE

THERE IS NO HOPE
——— *except* ———
IN A NEW BIRTH OF SCIENCE

Only **FAITH** in **HOPE** can save

• *THE WORLD* •

i **THE FRENCH PRODIGY** Jean-Marie Guyau published two distinguished works of philosophy in 1873 at the tender age of seventeen. He died of pulmonary disease at just thirty-three. In his essay 'The Philosophy of Hope', Guyau creates this fable:

> A child saw a butterfly poised on a blade of grass; the butterfly had been made numb by the north wind. The child plucked the blade of grass, and the living flower that was at its tip, still numb, remained attached. He returned home, holding his find in his hand. A ray of sunlight broke through, striking the butterfly's wing, and suddenly, revived and light, the living flower flew away into the glare. All of us, scholars and workers, we are like the butterfly: our strength is made of a ray of light. Not even: of the hope of a ray. One must thus know how to hope; hope is what carries us higher and farther.

...... • ......

ii **AUGUSTINE OF HIPPO** considers hope in the context of his belief in God. With the devil always at his heels, Augustine writes in his *Confessions* (397–400) of his hope that he will be strong enough to resist temptation because, as the Bible teaches, 'the wages of sin is death'. Addressing God, Augustine says: 'there is hope, because thou art faithful and thou wilt not allow us to be tempted beyond our ability to resist, but wilt with the temptation also make a way of escape that we may be able to bear it'. The only way to avoid eternal damnation in hell is to throw himself upon God's mercy. 'My whole hope is in thy exceeding great mercy and that alone.' *See also* TRUTH v.

iii IN HIS *NOVUM ORGANUM SCIENTIARUM* ('new instrument of science', 1620) the Englishman Francis Bacon poured scorn on the Christian hope for heaven, declaring: 'there is no hope except in a new birth of science'. Bacon was an early advocate of scientific method in which scientists pose hypotheses which they test by experiment (*see* TRUTH vi). If their hypothesis is correct, it graduates to the level of knowledge. Hope plays no part.

It did, however, in the work of alchemists, who may be viewed as forerunners of modern scientists. Alchemy was concerned with changing matter – lead, for instance – into gold. Bacon offers a sympathetic view of the alchemist as an essentially hopeful person who is disappointed by failure. The alchemist 'nurses eternal hope and when the thing fails, lays the blame upon some error of his own; fearing either that he has not sufficiently understood the words of his art or of his authors (whereupon he turns to tradition and auricular whispers), or else that in his manipulations he has made some slip of a scruple in weight or a moment in time (whereupon he repeats his trials to infinity)'. Of course, repetition is doomed to failure because it is not based on sound principles; but some good understanding was gleaned along the way.

Bacon compares the alchemist's search to the fable of 'the old man who bequeathed to his sons gold buried in a vineyard, pretending not to know the exact spot; whereupon the sons applied themselves diligently to the digging of the vineyard, and though no gold was found there, yet the vintage by that digging was made more plentiful'.

...... • ......

iv **THE FRENCH EXISTENTIALIST** Gabriel Marcel was forty
when he converted to Catholicism. After Marcel had reviewed
François Mauriac's *Dieu et Mammon* ('God and Mammon',
1958), Mauriac wrote Marcel a letter which asked 'why aren't
you one of us [Catholics]?' Marcel had been meditating for
some time on the possibility of faith without commitment;
Mauriac's letter was the push he needed.

Marcel's work now began to focus on hope as an essential
aspect of the human condition. His existentialism now regarded
every meeting of two persons (subjects) as an opportunity
for what he calls intersubjectivity: the mutual recognition of
each other's subjectivity, or personhood. Each of these human
collisions, Marcel argues, offers an opportunity for hope. In
Tragic Wisdom and Beyond (1973) Marcel attempts to define
hope by contrasting it with desire: 'desire is centred on the
"self", whereas hope is inseparable from love, from what I
have called intersubjectivity'. In Marcel's metaphysics, hope is
the key to 'the universal', to everything:

> the universal is to be found especially in the 'existential
> assurances' encountered in experiences of love, hope, fidel-
> ity, and other related ones, such as belonging. These require
> personal involvement of the most intense kind if they are to
> be experienced in all their significance, but they can by no
> means be lived in isolation. They are experiences of inter-
> subjectivity.

By 'existential assurance' Marcel means something 'primordial', 'which finally is perhaps nothing other than a very mysterious radiation of the *gaudium essendi* [joy in existing]. And
this radiation is hope.' For Marcel, man cannot exist alone,

because his very existence is constituted by others: 'there can be no hope which does not constitute itself through a we and for a *we*'.

...... ● ......

v **THE AMERICAN PRAGMATIST** John Dewey offers a different gloss on hope. Like Marcel he sees the essence of hope as arising from social relations – but not so much between individuals as between individuals and the state. For Dewey hope is related to the acts of thinking and acting; it was essential, he thought, for us to be able to detach ourselves from our personal hopes and experiences to embrace the shared hopes of a community and experiences beyond our individual cognizance. In *Democracy and Education* (1916) he claims that education, properly administered, 'may be made an instrument of realizing the better hopes of men'. A philosophical understanding of the individual's role in relation to the state – through education and informed participation – was the essence of hope for the future of a democratic society.

Like Marcel, Dewey contrasts individual desire with hope. When an individual's hope is driven by desire, it may have an unfavourable outcome for others. He uses an example of a general directing a war as opposed to a neutral observer of it. 'The general who allows his hopes and desires to affect his observations and interpretations of the existing situation will surely make a mistake in calculation.' But even an observer of battle will not think clearly if his observations are filtered through the lens of his preferences: 'While hopes and fears may be the chief motive for a thoughtful following of the war on the part of an onlooker in a neutral country, he too will think ineffectively in the degree in which his preferences modify the stuff of his observations and reasonings.' Dewey is concerned that personal hopes and desires can be the enemy of reflection, of thought. He says there is no 'incompatibility between the fact that the occasion of reflection lies in a personal sharing in what is going on and the fact that the value of the reflection lies upon keeping one's self out of the data'. What is required is detachment.

Hope lies in 'widening of the area of vision through a growth of social sympathies' – detaching oneself from individual desire. Social sympathy is near enough what Marcel means by intersubjectivity (*see* HOPE iv). Dewey talks about 'the almost insurmountable difficulty of achieving this detachment'. By participating in events, our individual thinking can 'develop to include what lies beyond our direct interests'.

Dewey places his hope in science as a tool for the betterment of society:

the coincidence of the ideal of progress with the advance of science is not a mere coincidence. Before this advance men placed the golden age in remote antiquity. Now they face the future with a firm belief that intelligence properly used can do away with evils once thought inevitable. To subjugate devastating disease is no longer a dream; the hope of abolishing poverty is not utopian. Science has familiarized men with the idea of development, taking effect practically in persistent gradual amelioration of the estate of our common humanity.

...... ● ......

vi **A STUDENT** of the German philosopher Martin Heidegger, Hannah Arendt fled Germany after being arrested and briefly detained by Hitler's SS, eventually arriving in the United States (*see also* WAR v). Hope would be a central theme of her work. Her first major publication was *The Origins of Totalitarianism* (1951), followed by *The Human Condition* (1958) in which she outlines the idea of 'natality', the key concept of her philosophy. Natality is the fact of possibility, of hope, that comes into being at the birth of every person in our world.* Natality brings with it the opportunity to act, to change our world. She calls action the 'miracle-working faculty' of man. In *The Human Condition* Arendt says:

> the miracle that saves the world, the realm of human affairs, from its normal, 'natural' ruin is ultimately the fact of natality, in which the faculty of action is ontologically rooted. It is, in other words, the birth of new men and the new beginning, the action they are capable of by virtue of being born

For Arendt, only 'faith in hope' can 'save' the world, and faith in hope is essential to natality. 'Only the full experience of this capacity can bestow upon human affairs faith and hope… It is this faith in and hope for the world that found perhaps its most glorious and most succinct expression in the few words with which the Gospels announced their "glad tidings": "A child has been born unto us."'

---

* Arendt argues against Heidegger, who characterized man's condition as being-towards-death. Hers is more being-towards-life.

MAKING THE **BEST** OF WHAT **YOU'VE GOT**

A DIFFERENT LANDSCAPE FILLED WITH **OBSTACLES**

CHAPTER TWENTY-THREE
ILLNESS

~

Where I am, DEATH *IS*

~

*

Illness changes how one is in the WORLD

SOMETHING *to* LIVE *FOR*

i **THE MOST FAMOUS** living scientist, the British theoretical physicist Stephen Hawking, is equally known for his survival of amyotrophic lateral sclerosis (ALS, also known as Lou Gehrig's disease). ALS is a neurodegenerative disease that has no cure. Its cause is unknown in more than 90 per cent of cases. Life expectancy for someone diagnosed in their twenties (as Hawking was) is two to three years. Against all odds, he has lived more than seventy.

In *My Brief History* (2013) Hawking describes, with typical British sang-froid: 'The realization that I had an incurable disease that was likely to kill me in a few years was a bit of a shock.' Hawking has spent much of his working life on the problem of time; in the two paragraphs of his autobiography he devotes to discussion of his illness, he couches his response to it in relation to past, present and future. The past is invoked when he remembers, 'a boy I vaguely knew' dying 'of leukaemia in the bed opposite me… Whenever I feel inclined to be sorry for myself, I remember that boy.' The present is expressed via a dream of death: 'Before my condition was diagnosed, I had been very bored with life. There had not seemed to be anything worth doing. But shortly after I came out of the hospital, I dreamed that I was going to be executed. I suddenly realized that there were a lot of worthwhile things I could do if I was reprieved.' The future is understood in terms of love: 'What really made the difference was that I got engaged to a girl called Jane Wilde, whom I had met about the time I was diagnosed with ALS. This gave me something to live for.'

…… ● ……

ii **THE NATURE OF 'TIME'** that Hawking evokes in his memoir is 'clock' time, the time of scientific measurement. 'Clock' time is opposed to the nineteenth-century French philosopher Henri Bergson's idea of *la durée*, a continuous subjective or psychological time – time as it is lived and experienced by us, as opposed to the time that is measured by instruments. Bergson's concept of time was not dissimilar to that of his American contemporary William James, who devised the term 'stream of consciousness' to describe how we experience time.

For Hawking, the death sentence turned out only to be a bad dream that inspired him to work hard. No such luck for the British phenomenologist Havi Carel who in 2006 was diagnosed with the incurable lung disease lymphangioleiomyomatosis (LAM) at the age of just thirty-five. Her death sentence is real. She was given ten years to live; there will be no miracle remission.

The effect of the diagnosis – as distinct from the disease itself – has been to collapse the focus of Carel's life to its known end, and to live in that arbitrarily allocated time both in the 'clock' sense of time and in the 'lived' sense of it (*la durée*). 'Serious illness', says Carel, 'is a life-transforming event. This thought did not once occur to me while I was healthy':

> Illness changes everything. It changes not only my internal organs, but my relationship to my body, my relationship to others, their relation to me, to my body... In short, illness changes how one is in the world. Moreover, the world of the ill person changes; it transforms into a different landscape, filled with obstacles. Distances increase. It becomes uncanny. The world of the sick belongs to a different universe from that of the healthy, and the interaction between them is clunky, difficult, abrasive.

As a philosopher, Carel finds solace in the fourth-century BC philosopher Epicurus. Epicureanism advocates the seeking of pleasure while at the same time living a life that does not overreach; it could be summed up as 'making the best of what you've got'. In following Epicurus, Carel believes 'If we can understand ourselves as limited creatures granted a brief existence, if we open ourselves to the possibility of living with an imperfect, even damaged body, we may be able to be ill and at the same time live well. And it is this ability to experience wellbeing despite – or with – illness that I aim to cultivate.'

While Epicurus gives comfort, he does not provide an understanding or explanation of Carel's situation. In order to describe – and therefore better understand – her situation, she turns to the French philosopher Maurice Merleau-Ponty. In *The Phenomenology of Perception* (1945) he described our 'being' as rooted in our experience of ourselves as 'embodied' subjects.* Embracing Merleau-Ponty leads Carel to appreciate how 'Physical change caused by illness is not just that. It does not simply limit mobility, ability to breathe or the function of kidneys or liver. It modifies the ill person's embodied existence and hence her relationship to her world. It is not just the body of the ill person that changes, but her entire way of being and her way of negotiating the world.'

This phenomenological perspective allows the ill person better to understand her personal situation. But it also allows for a wider understanding of what 'illness' is, apart from being the target of technomedicine: it 'should not be divided into its physical aspects (sometimes called disease) and its secondary social, economic and psychological impact. Rather, illness is

---

* Merleau-Ponty believed that our sole experience of the world was given to us through our bodily experience of it.

both the physical changes and their personal, social and temporal effects. The artificial separation serves merely to obscure the essential unity of the human being.' Thus, from the perspective of illness, the philosopher arrives at a notion of health. At the end of the day, however, Carel bows to Heidegger. 'Where I am, death is,' she writes. 'It is a constant presence, a perpetual shadow.'

...... ● ......

iii **THE PERSPECTIVES** on illness given to us by Heidegger and Merleau-Ponty talk about memory as the force that synthesizes our experience of time and the body. Perhaps that is why Alzheimer's disease is so terrifying for its sufferers and so hurtful to their loved ones. There is no memory function to make sense of the linear order of 'clock time' events in one's life or the existential sense of *durée*, of how a personal history has been experience and what its significance is. The sufferer stumbles forward under a great weight of unknowing into a future which more than likely cannot be distinguished from past or present.

...... ● ......

iv **THE LAST NOVEL** written by the Irish-born philosopher and novelist Iris Murdoch, *Jackson's Dilemma* (1995), attracted unusually critical reviews. (One described it as like 'the work of a 13-year-old schoolgirl who doesn't get out enough'.) That same year Murdoch announced she was suffering, for the first time in her long career, from writer's block, which left her in 'a hard, dark place'. The next year she was diagnosed with

Alzheimer's. In his biography of Murdoch, her friend Peter J. Conradi writes of her sense of loss ('I used to write novels,' she told him) and terror ('I don't have a world') in experiencing Alzheimer's. Murdoch's husband, the British literary critic John Bayley, devoted himself to the full-time care of his wife after her diagnosis. He published an account of their last days together, *Iris* (1999), in which he described how they watched the BBC TV children's programme *Teletubbies* together. He recounts how his wife became like 'a very nice 3-year-old', whom he fed, bathed and changed.

 See also WALKING iv *and* vi; WRITING ii.

I've **THROWN** the **POPE** in **PRISON**

I WILL BE *RULING* THE *WORLD* FROM NOW ON

CHAPTER TWENTY-FOUR

INSANITY

I WAS TERROR-STRUCK

MADNESS AND CIVILIZATION

The EXCHANGE BETWEEN **MADNESS** and **REASON**

i **IT COULD BE ARGUED** that Europe produces more meta-physicians while the Anglo-American establishment turns out more logicians. If we asked which country produces more nutty philosophers, it would be a tougher question to answer. A good bet might be France by several lengths with Great Britain beating Germany by three lengths for second place.

The laundry list of mad and depressed philosophers would be tedious were it not so distinguished. The American psychologist and philosopher William James, whose presence is felt everywhere in that country's philosophy, grappled with depression and suffered from suicidal thoughts. The utilitarian John Stuart Mill and the analytic philosophers Bertrand Russell and Ludwig Wittgenstein top the list of stellar British depressives. Russell and Wittgenstein also wrestled with suicidal thoughts.

A rich vein of mental illness runs through French philosophy. Henri de Saint-Simon and his assistant Auguste Comte (*see* ADVICE v) both suffered from depression and attempted suicide. Gilles Deleuze committed suicide by leaping from a fourth-storey window, while his colleague Louis Althusser strangled his wife to death and was held in a psychiatric hospital for three years.

While Germany may not offer superior numbers of mentally ill philosophers, it does have Friedrich Nietzsche, who is perhaps the most spectacular – and tragic – example of an insane philosopher.

...... ● ......

ii **IN 1888 NIETZSCHE** was living in a Turin apartment
owned by Davide Fino, a newsvendor who had a street stall
nearby. Fino was alarmed by his tenant's strange behaviour.
Nietzsche shouted at himself while alone in his room. He tore
up banknotes and threw them in the waste basket. He danced
naked. He demanded that paintings be removed from the walls
of his room so that it would look more like a temple. Students
of Nietzsche might find meaning in this behaviour. Nietzsche
was anti-establishment: destroying banknotes was a protest at
the status quo and at bourgeois worship of money. His room
was a temple, because man was the new God; it was up to us
to find our own morality. Dancing naked (behind closed doors)
is the joyful expression of Zarathustra (*see* WALKING vi).

In 1889 Nietzsche was arrested for making a public distur-
bance. Fino intervened on his behalf and persuaded the police
to let his tenant go. Nietzsche then began writing letters to
friends on the theme of man as God, criticizing national leaders
and anti-Semites. To Jacob Burckhardt: 'I have had Caiaphas*
put in chains. Last year I was crucified in a very drawn-out
fashion by the German doctors. [Kaiser] Wilhelm, Bismarck,
and all anti-Semites are abolished.' To Meta von Salis: 'God
is on the earth. Don't you see how all the heavens are rejoic-
ing? I have just seized possession of my kingdom, I've thrown
the Pope in prison, and I'm having Wilhelm, Bismarck, and
[anti-Semitic politician Adolf] Stocker shot.' And finally, to
his friend the theologian Franz Overbeck: 'The world will be
turned on its head for the next few years'; since 'the old God
has abdicated, I will be ruling the world from now on'. All of
these statements could be lifted from Nietzsche's work, from

---

* Joseph Caiaphas, Jewish high priest rumoured to have organized the plot to kill
Jesus.

any passage in which he proclaims the 'death of God' and the arrival of a new morality for a new man. Stated in letters, they raised suspicion that the author was insane. Upon receipt of his letter, Overbeck arranged for Nietzsche to be taken to a psychiatric asylum in Basel.

For more than a century the received view has been that Nietzsche's dementia was the result of tertiary syphilis. Medical biographers disagree. They can find no evidence of syphilis, and the American psychiatrist Leonard Sax believes that 'Other hypotheses – such as slowly growing right-sided retro-orbital meningioma – provide a more plausible fit to the evidence.' Nevertheless, Nietzsche's mental and physical health declined. Between 1898 and 1900 he suffered three strokes, the last of which killed him.

...... ● ......

iii **IN 1823 THE FRENCH UTOPIAN SOCIALIST** Henri de Saint-Simon, in a fit of depression at not being able to locate a notebook, shot himself six times in the head. Miraculously, he survived with only loss of his sight. He died two years later.

In 1824 the positivist Auguste Comte (*see* ADVICE v) was working as Saint-Simon's secretary. The two had a falling out when Saint-Simon proposed that he publish the first part of *Comte's Course in Positive Philosophy* (six volumes, 1830–42) under his name. Comte fell into a trough of depression and in 1826 was treated in an asylum run by the psychiatrist Jean-Étienne Dominique Esquirol, who diagnosed mania. Comte was subjected to cold-water treatments and blood-letting, but to no avail. In 1827 Comte released himself from Esquirol's care and attempted suicide several times. The most dramatic attempt was a leap from the Pont des Arts in Paris into the River Seine. Comte seems to have been as good a swimmer as Saint-Simon was a bad marksman. He lived for another thirty years.

...... ● ......

iv **IN 1980 LOUIS ALTHUSSER,** a French Marxist philosopher, strangled his wife Hélène Rytmann to death in their apartment in the École Normale Supérieure in Paris. In his autobiography, *The Future Lasts Forever* (1994), he describes the deed:

> I was massaging the front of her neck. I pressed my thumbs into the hollow at the top of her breastbone and then, still pressing, slowly moved them both, one to the left, the other to the right, up towards her ears where the flesh was hard. I continued massaging her in a V-shape. The muscles in my forearms began to feel very tired; I was aware that they always did when I was massaging.
>
> Hélène's face was calm and motionless; her eyes were open and staring at the ceiling. Suddenly, I was terror-struck. Her eyes stared interminably, and I noticed the tip of her tongue was showing between her teeth and lips, strange and still. I had seen dead bodies before, of course, but never in my life looked into the face of someone who had been strangled. Yet I knew she had been strangled. But how? I stood up and screamed: 'I've strangled Hélène!'

Althusser was sedated and taken to the Institut Marcel Rivière, a psychiatric hospital in La Verrière. He was never arrested for his wife's murder. In 1981 a judge ruled he was unfit to plead. The court appointed three psychiatrists to review the case: they concluded he was in a state of dementia when he killed Hélène. The court granted him a *non-lieu* – a determination that there were no grounds for a trial.

...... ● ......

v **MICHEL FOUCAULT'S** *Folie et Déraison: Histoire de la folie à l'âge classique* ('Madness and unreason: a history of insanity in the age of reason') was published in France in 1961, and in English in an abridged edition in 1964, under the title *Madness and Civilization. Histoire de la folie* was Foucault's doctoral thesis, and it broke with the orthodoxies of phenomenology and existentialism to offer an original analysis of how society viewed (or created) 'madness' at different moments in history. Insanity is studied as an evolving concept which arises as a result of social and legal structures he would later refer to as the 'discourse of power'. Foucault was not unfamiliar with mental illness, having been severely depressed as a child. He made his first suicide attempt when he was twenty-two, and tried again on several occasions.

Foucault defended his thesis in the Salle Louis Liard at the Sorbonne. University rules required a public defence of the work, and the room was packed for the event. Foucault chose the philosopher and physician Georges Canguilhem as his *rapporteur* (sponsor). *Histoire de la folie* is, by any standard, an unusual doctoral thesis. Foucault was criticized for making broad generalizations unsupported by specific argument, yet the distinguished jury was dazzled by Foucault's work, as was the audience (*see also* NICKNAMES xi). Foucault's fame was established then and there. Pierre Macherey, a student of

Althusser's, had never heard of Foucault before that day, but for the rest of his life he purchased every one of Foucault's books on its day of publication.

There has been much speculation about Foucault's suicidal tendencies in the context of his behaviour as a gay man. Fond of the San Francisco bathhouse and leather bar scene, he contracted AIDS, from which he died. His biographer James Miller quotes Foucault's remark about how he'd spend his fortune if he won the lottery:

> I'd set up an institute where people who wanted to die could come and spend a weekend, a week or a month, enjoying themselves as far as possible, perhaps with the help of drugs, and then disappear... In his 1979 essay ['The Simplest of Pleasures'], he imagines 'suicide-festivals' and 'suicide-orgies' and also a kind of special retreat where those planning to commit suicide could look 'for partners without names, for occasions to die liberated from every identity'.

Modern thinking about insanity has had three key moments. Hippocrates was the first to ascribe natural causes to mental illness (as opposed to the supernatural, 'divine madness' attribution of the ancient world). The second moment occurred towards the end of the eighteenth century when medicine began to define various forms of insanity and to assign specific causes to them. Foucault's achievement in *Histoire de la folie* was to suggest that psychiatry is not a pure and uninterested branch of science that determines who is mad and who is sane; the diagnosis of insanity is, rather, a social and political act.

The
CONCEPTION
of a
CLEAR
AND
ATTENTIVE
MIND

HIS PRE-EMINENCE
IS DUE TO HIS
MUSCLES
OF INTUITION
BEING THE
STRONGEST

CHAPTER TWENTY-FIVE

INTUITION

I sometimes FEEL
that I AM
RIGHT

It is
INTUITION
that
IMPROVES
the
WORLD

INTUITION IS THE OUTCOME
OF AN EARLIER
— INTELLECTUAL —
EXPERIENCE

i   **THE TWENTIETH-CENTURY** Russian Marxist philosopher
A. G. Spirkin defined intuition as 'the capacity for grasping the
truth through direct apprehension of it without any grounds in
reasoning'. While philosophy is ultimately concerned with reasoning, virtually every school of thought, from the pre-Socrat-
ics to the present, counts intuition as an important moment on
the road to knowledge. The exception is analytic philosophy,
which considers the concept of intuition as having no meaning.
For Spirkin, however, 'Intuition and logic-governed reason are
inseparable in any form of human creativity; their union is a
necessary element in the birth of the truth.' *See also* TRUTH i;
BELIEF i.

...... ● ......

ii   **RENÉ DESCARTES** considered intuition the purest mental
act. In his abandoned work *Rules for the Direction of the
Mind* (published posthumously in 1684) he wrote: 'By "intuition" I do not mean the fluctuating testimony of the senses or
the deceptive judgement of the imagination as it botches things
together, but the conception of a clear and attentive mind,
which is so easy and distinct that there can be no room for
doubt about what we are understanding.' For Descartes, intuition is a starting place for thought, unencumbered by sense
impressions or assumptions. To intuit is to be in the realm of
pure intellect, the place from which truth may be discovered.

...... ● ......

iii THE ECONOMIST JOHN MAYNARD KEYNES, a keen student of Isaac Newton, noted that while the great physicist was a dedicated experimentalist, it was his intuition that led to great discoveries. All great scientists did experiments, says Keynes; but Newton's 'peculiar gift was the power of holding continuously in his mind a purely mental problem until he had seen straight through it. I fancy his pre-eminence is due to his muscles of intuition being the strongest and most enduring with which a man has ever been gifted.' Keynes said that the ability to hold a scientific or philosophical problem in one's mind with total focus and concentration was only given to some thinkers. Even then, to focus hard for more than a few hours was beyond the reach of most. Newton was different because he 'could hold a problem in his mind for hours and days and weeks until it surrendered to him its secret. Then being a supreme mathematical technician he could dress it up, how you will, for purposes of exposition, but it was his intuition which was pre-eminently extraordinary.' Newton's friend the English mathematician Augustus De Morgan remarked that Newton was 'so happy in his conjectures as to seem to know more than he could possibly have any means of proving'. Newton's proofs were 'dressed up afterwards', says Keynes; 'they were not the instrument of discovery'. Intuition was.

...... ● ......

iv ALBERT EINSTEIN, whose theories of relativity give us the best explanation we presently have of our physical world, put intuition above all mental faculties. He wrote to a colleague in 1949, 'A new idea comes suddenly and in a rather intuitive way. But intuition is nothing but the outcome of earlier intellectual experience.' In 1918 Einstein addressed the Physical Society of Berlin on the occasion of the German theoretical physicist Max Planck's sixtieth birthday. He said: 'The supreme task of the physicist is to arrive at those universal elementary laws from which the cosmos can be built up by pure deduction.' But, he cautioned, 'there is no logical path to these laws; only intuition, resting on sympathetic understanding of experience, can reach them'.

So, how can an intuitive approach yield certainty, Einstein asks. 'In this methodological uncertainty, one might suppose that there were any number of possible systems of theoretical physics all equally well justified; and this opinion is no doubt correct, theoretically. But the development of physics has shown that at any given moment, out of all conceivable constructions, a single one has always proved itself decidedly superior to all the rest.'

Even if we are prone to value intuition as a real and good thing, the question still lingers: how did Einstein know how to choose the right system of theoretical physics? In a 1929 interview, he attempts to elaborate further on the question of believing (intuition) versus knowing (proof). 'I believe in intuitions and inspirations,' he said. 'I sometimes feel that I am right. I do not know that I am.' Einstein was content to let others do the proving. 'When two expeditions of scientists, financed by the Royal Academy, went forth to test my theory of relativity, I was convinced that their conclusions would tally with my hypothesis. I was not surprised when the eclipse of May 29, 1919, confirmed my intuitions.' He remarked, 'I would have been surprised if I had been wrong.' Einstein explains that his flashes of intuitive brilliance rest on a bedrock of hard work and experience. 'Every man knows that in his work he does best and accomplishes most when he has attained a proficiency that enables him to work intuitively. That is, there are things which we come to know so well that we do not know how we know them... Perhaps we live best and do things best when we are not too conscious of how and why we do them.' Perhaps the peculiar nature of Einstein's genius was his ability to look at what he called 'unrelated facts' and to wonder how they could be shown to be related. Einstein believed logic alone could never find answers that could only be grasped intuitively: 'it is intuition that improves the world, not just following a trodden path of thought. Intuition makes us look at unrelated facts and then think about them until they can all be brought under one law.' Following the well-trodden path can often mean 'holding on to what one has instead of searching for new facts. Intuition is the father of new knowledge, while empiricism is nothing but an accumulation of old knowledge. Intuition, not intellect, is the "open sesame" of yourself.'

...... ● ......

v **HENRI BERGSON** (*see also* ILLNESS ii *and* LAUGHING vi) was the greatest exponent of intuition as a tool for discovering what something is, to arrive at the essence of an object of study. In his *Introduction to Metaphysics* (1903) he defines intuition as

the kind of intellectual sympathy by which one places oneself within an object in order to coincide with what is unique in it and consequently inexpressible. Analysis, on the contrary, is the operation which reduces the object to elements already known, that is, to elements common both to it and

other objects. To analyse, therefore, is to express a thing as a function of something other than itself.

While Bergson's approach has declined in popularity with the rise of analytic philosophy and attacks upon it by that school's co-founder Bertrand Russell, he was arguably the first international philosopher-superstar.

When Henri Bergson came to New York to lecture in 1913, his presence was celebrated like that of a famous actor or general. Fashionable matrons vied for space with students at his lectures. Gentlemen fought over seats. So great was the interest that, as one observer put it, parts of the city were choked by 'the first traffic jam of the brand-new automotive age'.

THE
ORIGIN
OF
JUSTICE
is the making
OF
COVENANTS

Justice implies
SUPERIOR CHARACTER
and intelligence

THE GREATEST *of*
VIRTUES

CHAPTER TWENTY-SIX

JUSTICE

A
GOVERNMENT
without
– **LAWS** –
is a
MYSTERY
in
POLITICS

i **WHEN WE ARE FRUSTRATED** by an injustice we call it stupid, even evil. When we splutter with anger and frustration we are in good company. In Plato's *Republic* (380 BC) Socrates says that 'justice implies superior character and intelligence while injustice means deficiency in both respects. Therefore, just men are superior in character and intelligence and are more effective in action. As injustice implies ignorance, stupidity and badness, it cannot be superior in character and intelligence.'

Aristotle takes a different view of justice, arguing that it is not an individual virtue in itself, but arises only through its extension to others. In Book V of his *Nicomachean Ethics* (*c.*350 BC) he says, 'Justice, then, is complete virtue, but not absolutely, but in relation to our neighbour.' It is this social or communal quality of justice that makes it, for Aristotle, 'the greatest of virtues'. Why? Because 'it is complete virtue in its fullest sense, because it is the actual exercise of complete virtue. It is complete because he who possesses it can exercise his virtue not only in himself but towards his neighbour also.' Aristotle observes that 'many men can exercise virtue in their own affairs, but not in their relations to their neighbour. This is why the saying of Bias of Priene* is thought to be true, that "rule will show the man".' Aristotle follows Bias in arguing that 'justice, alone of the virtues, is thought to be "another's good", because it is related to our neighbour; for it does what is advantageous to another'. In this sense, justice is selfless. It is the extension of justice to a neighbour that defines its uniqueness as a virtue. 'What the difference is between virtue and justice in this sense is plain from what we have said; they are the same but their essence is not the same; what, as a relation

---

* Bias of Priene was a sixth-century BC advocate famed for defending what is right. He is counted among the 'Seven Sages' of Greece.

to one's neighbour, is justice is, as a certain kind of state without qualification, virtue.'

...... ● ......

ii **THOMAS HOBBES** (*see* GOVERNING ii) viewed man as a selfish individual with a warlike nature. Hobbesean man uses force to get what he desires, and only superior force will deter him. Justice is not a naturally occurring virtue for Hobbes: it arises solely out of agreements ('covenants') made between men. In *Leviathan* (1651) he wrote:

> Although the origin of justice is the making of covenants, there can't be any actual injustice until the reason for such fear be taken away, which can't be done while men are in the natural condition of war. So the labels 'just' and 'unjust' can have application only when there is some coercive power to compel all men equally to perform their covenants, through the terror of some punishment greater than the benefit they expect from breaking their covenant, and thereby to ensure that men get the benefits they contract for, this being their compensation for giving up some of their rights. There is no such power before the commonwealth is created.

Justice is a matter of enforcing prevailing agreements. The overarching covenant that protects all other agreements is that by which government (the commonwealth) is agreed among men.

For Hobbes, justice is primarily about the protection of property:

> Where there is no 'own', that is, no property, there is no

injustice; and where there is no coercive power erected, that is, where there is no commonwealth, there is no property, all men having right to all things; therefore where there is no commonwealth, there nothing is unjust. So that the nature of justice consists in the keeping of valid covenants; but the validity of covenants begins not but with the constitution of a civil power sufficient to compel men to keep them; and then it is also that property begins.

...... ● ......

iii **JOHN LOCKE'S** liberal view of justice extended beyond individual property rights. In *Two Treatises of Government* (1689) he asked, 'Consider what civil society is for'? 'It is', he wrote, 'set up to avoid and remedy the drawbacks of the state of nature that inevitably follow from every man's being judge in his own case.' It protects against self-interest and protects the interests of the less powerful in society 'by setting up a known authority to which every member of that society can appeal when he has been harmed or is involved in a dispute – an authority that everyone in the society ought to obey'. Where 'people who don't have such an authority to appeal to for the settlement of their disputes they are still in the state of nature' that Hobbes describes prior to the establishment of the commonwealth.

For Locke, justice is partly about the defence of property. He acknowledges that, at base, 'justice gives every man a title to the product of his honest industry, and the fair acquisitions of his ancestors descended to him'. In this statement Locke recognizes two kinds of property – wages accrued through labour and hereditary estates. His concept of justice embraces

everyone from day labourers to the landed gentry. But justice
also entails charity for Locke. His concept of charity is a kind
of redistribution of wealth: 'charity gives every man a title to
so much out of another's plenty as will keep him from extreme
want, where he has no means to subsist otherwise'. Justice also
involves protection of the poor: 'a man can no more justly
make use of another's necessity to force him to become his
vassal, by withholding that relief God requires him to afford
to the wants of his brother, than he that has more strength can
seize upon a weaker, master him to his obedience, and with a
dagger at his throat offer him death or slavery'.

For Locke, laws and the mechanisms of their just application are the state. 'Where there is no longer the administration
of justice for the securing of men's rights,' he says, 'nor any
remaining power within the community to direct the force, or
provide for the necessities of the public, there certainly is no
government left.' He concludes: 'a government without laws is,
I suppose, a mystery in politics inconceivable to human capacity, and inconsistent with human society'.

...... ● ......

iv **THE EIGHTEENTH-CENTURY** Scottish philosopher
David Hume argued for the utility of justice. In *An Enquiry
Concerning the Principles of Morals* (1751), he claims 'public
utility is the SOLE origin of justice' and that 'the beneficial
consequences of this virtue are the SOLE foundation of its
merit'. All justice must be applicable to all men, even those 'in
political society' (politicians must not be above the law). Those
who commit crimes are to have their rights 'suspended for a
moment'.

> **When any man, even in political society, renders himself by his crimes, obnoxious to the public, he is punished by the laws in his goods and person; that is, the ordinary rules of justice are, with regard to him, suspended for a moment, and it becomes equitable to inflict on him, for the BENEFIT of society, what otherwise he could not suffer without wrong or injury.**

For Hume, 'the rules of equity or justice depend entirely on the particular state and condition in which men are placed, and owe their origin and existence to that utility'. He warns that conditions of 'extreme abundance or extreme necessity' can result in 'rendering justice totally USELESS'. Protecting justice means finding 'a medium amidst all these extremes'.

Like his above-cited predecessors, Hume focuses on the protection of property as the first job of justice because it is the most useful. He says that 'few enjoyments are given us from the open and liberal hand of nature; but by art, labour, and industry, we can extract them in great abundance. Hence the ideas of property become necessary in all civil society.'

...... ● ......

v **IMMANUEL KANT'S DEFINITION OF JUSTICE** in his *Groundwork of the Metaphysics of Morals* (1785) begins with his concept of respect, which is a feeling 'self-wrought by a rational concept, and, therefore, is specifically distinct from... inclination or fear. What I recognise immediately as a law for me, I recognise with respect.' This variety of respect 'signifies the consciousness that my will is subordinate to a law, without the intervention of other influences on my sense. The immediate determination of the will by the law, and the consciousness of this, is called respect, so that this is regarded as an effect of the law on the subject, and not as the cause of it.'

Respect, says, Kant, 'is properly the conception of a worth which thwarts my self-love'. This lays the groundwork for a justice that is impartial, and in no way based on the interests of one individual or group. The law is not to be handed down by God or by kings, but, rather, is something that 'we impose on ourselves and yet recognise as necessary in itself'. Further, 'moral interest consists simply in respect for the law'.

For Kant, it is reason alone which creates the laws that underpin justice. 'The common reason of men in its practical judgements perfectly coincides with this and always has in view the principle here suggested.'

...... ● ......

vi **G. W. F. HEGEL IS CRITICAL OF JUSTICE** as a concept. 'At one time,' he writes (in *Elements of the Philosophy of Right*, 1820) the 'administration of justice, which is concerned with the private interests of all members of the state, was... turned into an instrument of profit and tyranny'. This was made possible partly because the persons who benefited from crooked justice were powerful, and partly because 'the law was buried in pedantry and a foreign tongue, and knowledge of legal processes was similarly buried in involved formalities'. The law was above and beyond ordinary persons, who often felt it offered no remedies or protections for them.

For Hegel, the key to administering true justice is to make it public: 'an integral part of justice is the confidence which citizens have in it, and it is this which requires that proceedings shall be public.' Hegel talks about 'the right of publicity', which 'depends on the fact that (i) the aim of the court is justice, which as universal falls under the cognisance of everyone, and (ii) it is through publicity that the citizens become convinced that the judgment was actually just'.

...... ● ......

vii **JOHN STUART MILL** tackled the idea of justice in *Utilitarianism* (1863). Of all philosophers, Mill offers one of the clearest and most succinct explanations of it:

> **the idea of justice supposes two things; a rule of conduct, and a sentiment which sanctions the rule. The first must be supposed common to all mankind, and intended for their good. The other (the sentiment) is a desire that punishment may be suffered by those who infringe the rule. There is involved, in addition, the conception of some definite person who suffers by the infringement; whose rights (to use the expression appropriated to the case) are violated by it.**

Mill counts among the basic animal desires in man the one which is naturally predisposed to retaliate against injury so that 'the sentiment of justice appears to me to be, the animal desire to repel or retaliate a hurt or damage to oneself, or to those with whom one sympathizes'. The mechanism by which this sentiment is 'widened so as to include all persons' he calls 'the human capacity of enlarged sympathy', to which he adds 'the human conception of intelligent self-interest'.

Justice for Mill arises from the possession of rights: to have a right is 'to have something which society ought to defend me in the possession of'. The main reason Mill cites is that of utility. If 'the objector' does not find sufficient reason in utility, Mill next directs him to that 'animal element, the thirst for retaliation', which he argues leads back to 'the extraordinarily important and impressive kind of utility which is concerned'. He continues: 'The interest involved is that of security, to every one's feelings the most vital of all interests.' Security is essential, says Mill, because it involves what he calls 'immunity from evil':

Nearly all other earthly benefits are needed by one person, not needed by another; and many of them can, if necessary, be cheerfully foregone, or replaced by something else; but security no human being can possibly do without; on it we depend for all our immunity from evil, and for the whole value of all and every good.

viii IN *A THEORY OF JUSTICE* (1971), the American philosopher John Rawls, the most influential theorist of justice in the modern period, takes issue with utilitarianism (the argument that what is right is what gives the greatest benefit to the greatest number of people). He argues that it 'aggregates' human happiness and therefore does not comprise a universal theory of justice. In its place, Rawls erects a theory which he calls 'justice as fairness'.

'In justice as fairness society is interpreted as a cooperative venture for mutual advantage,' says Rawls. 'The circumstances of justice', he continues, 'may be described as the normal conditions under which human cooperation is both possible and necessary.'

Justice is the first virtue of social institutions, as truth is of systems of thought. A theory however elegant and economical must be rejected or revised if it is untrue; likewise laws and institutions no matter how efficient and well-arranged must be reformed or abolished if they are unjust. Each person possesses an inviolability founded on justice that even the welfare of society as a whole cannot override... in a just society the liberties of equal citizenship are taken as settled; the rights secured by justice are not subject to political bargaining or to the calculus of social interests.

Equality under the law, and justice itself, are compromised by the accrual of great wealth in the hands of a few, so that the 'difference between rich and poor makes the latter even worse off, and this violates the principal of mutual advantage'.

Against thinkers like Hobbes, whose theory of justice includes 'self-evident' concepts like natural law, Rawls argues that 'a conception of justice cannot be deduced from self-evident premises or conditions on principles; instead, its justification is a matter of the mutual support of many considerations, of everything fitted together into one coherent view'. That is, justice is a man-made thing created in a particular set of circumstances. The concept of justice is 'defined, then, by the role of its principles in assigning rights and duties and in defining the appropriate division of social advantages. A conception of justice is an interpretation of this role.'

Justice, for Rawls, is founded on the principle of equal rights: 'each person is to have an equal right to the most extensive basic liberty compatible with a similar liberty for others'. This includes a robust social and economic structure in which 'social and economic inequalities are to be arranged so that they are both (a) reasonably expected to be to everyone's advantage, and (b) attached to positions and offices open to all'. Inclusiveness is key to Rawls's concept of justice.

Against the argument that some are born more talented or wealthier than others, Rawls says that justice 'requires that the higher expectations of the more advantaged contribute to the prospects of the least advantaged'. Therefore, 'no one deserves his greater natural capacity nor merits a more favorable starting place in society'. He concludes, 'to each according to his threat advantage does not count as a principle of justice'.

Looking for a single word to sum up Rawls's thought, one probably couldn't improve upon 'decency'.

A **FIT** of **LAUGHTER** indulged to **EXCESS** almost always produces a **VIOLENT** reaction

--- A ---
COMEDY
IS FAR MORE LIKE
REAL LIFE
THAN A DRAMA IS
— • —

CHAPTER TWENTY-SEVEN

LAUGHING

It is **SCHADENFREUDE**
which remains the worst trait in
HUMAN NATURE

LAUGHTER AT THE DEFECTS OF OTHERS IS A SIGNE OF PUSILLANIMITY

AMUSEMENT
is
RELAXATION

i **DEMOCRITUS** had the nickname 'the laughing philosopher' (*see* NICKNAMES i). He left us no essay on laughter, but the jolly thinker immortalized in busts and many paintings is generally believed by historians to have been amused by the antics of his fellow men. I nearly wrote 'simply' amused by the antics of his fellow men – but there is nothing simple about laughter. It is a complex phenomenon that has exercised Western philosophy since its beginnings in ancient Greece. Laughter can be at the expense of others; it can be at our own expense; it can occur as an inappropriate response (to tragic news, for instance); it can result from what philosophers call 'incongruity' (Q: What's purple and goes 150 miles per hour? A: An Italian sports plum.) These examples only begin to suggest the complexities of laughter as studied by philosophers.

...... ● ......

ii **PLATO WAS SUSPICIOUS** of laughter, which he thought was often a derisory judgement of the less fortunate passed by a person mistakenly convinced of his own superiority. Such persons, Plato says in *The Republic* (380 BC), are 'ignorant of their own stature'. In his rules of poetry Plato states 'persons of worth, even if only mortal men, must not be represented as overcome by laughter, and still less must such a representation of the gods be allowed'. State officials must not laugh: 'Neither ought our guardians to be given to laughter. For a fit of laughter which has been indulged to excess almost always produces a violent reaction.' Laughter is excess, the absence of moderation, loss of self-control.

Aristotle largely agreed with Plato on the subject of laughter. In his *Nicomachean Ethics* (*c*.350 BC) he remarked:

Those who carry humour to excess are thought to be vulgar buffoons, striving after humour at all costs, and aiming rather at raising a laugh than at saying what is becoming and at avoiding pain to the object of their fun.

Like Plato, Aristotle says that laughter is derisory and demeans its objects. Laughing 'too much' is a sign that one has been 'defeated by violent and excessive pleasures'. Laughter for Aristotle is both a self-control issue and a political one, since too much laughter interferes with 'work' and, by implication, the orderly running of the state: 'amusement is a relaxation, since it is a rest from work; and the lover of amusement is one of the people who go to excess in this'.

...... ● ......

iii **THOMAS HOBBES** (see GOVERNING ii) thought laughter to be of sufficient importance to include a section on it in the 'Human Nature' chapter of *The Elements of Law, Natural and Politic* (1640). He defines laughter as a 'passion': 'the passion of laughter is nothing else but a sudden glory arising from sudden conception of some eminency in ourselves, by comparison with the infirmities of others, or with our own formerly'. In this respect, Hobbes follows Plato and Aristotle in noticing that laughter is often laughing at the expense of someone less fortunate than ourselves, and a false declaration of 'eminence'. We 'take it heinously to be laughed at or derided' because it is the equivalent of being 'triumphed over'.

In *Leviathan* (1651) Hobbes judges that malicious laughter is a sign of deficient character, an act committed by 'those who are forced to keep themselves in their own favour, by

observing the imperfections of other men. And therefore much
Laughter at the defects of others is a signe of Pusillanimity.'
Hobbes's analysis of laughter leads him to a moral imperative:
'For of great minds, one of the proper workes is, to help and
free others from scorn; and compare themselves onely with
the most able.'

...... ● ......

iv **IN *THE CRITIQUE OF PURE REASON*** (1781; 1787)
Immanuel Kant (*see* DUTY iii) attempted to describe the psychological and physical actions of laughter:

> **Laughter is an affection arising from a strained expectation
> being suddenly reduced to nothing. This very reduction, at
> which certainly understanding cannot rejoice, is still indirect-
> ly a source of very lively enjoyment for a moment. Its cause
> must consequently lie in the influence of the representation
> upon the body and the reciprocal effect of this upon the
> mind. This, moreover, cannot depend upon the representa-
> tion being objectively an object of gratification (for how can
> we derive gratification from a disappointment?) but must
> rest solely upon the fact that the reduction is a mere play of
> representations, and, as such, produces an equilibrium of the
> vital forces of the body.**

Kant gives an example of a laughter-inducing situation.
There is an Indian sitting with an Englishman who observes a
bottle of beer being opened. Froth flows from the bottle. This
amuses the Indian. The Englishman asks what is so wonderful
about froth flowing from a bottle of beer. The Indian replies,

'Oh, I'm not surprised myself at its getting out, but at how you ever managed to get it all in.' Here is Kant's analysis of why the scene induces laughter: 'it gives us hearty pleasure. This is not because we think ourselves, maybe, more quick-witted than this ignorant Indian,* or because our understanding here brings to our notice any other ground of delight. It is rather that the bubble of our expectation was extended to the full and suddenly went off into nothing.' If Kant is right about the joke being about 'nothing', how is it that 'nothing' creates laughter? It is because, he argues,

> the joke must have something in it capable of momentarily deceiving us. Hence, when the semblance vanishes into nothing, the mind looks back in order to try it over again, and thus by a rapidly succeeding tension and relaxation it is jerked to and fro and put in oscillation. As the snapping of what was, as it were, tightening up the string takes place suddenly (not by a gradual loosening), the oscillation must bring about a mental movement and a sympathetic internal movement of the body. This continues involuntarily and produces fatigue, but in so doing it also affords recreation (the effects of a motion conducive to health).

...... ● ......

v **ARTHUR SCHOPENHAUER** disagrees with Kant about the point of a joke being 'nothing', or an absence. He argues that what Kant calls 'nothing' is the 'something' that induces laughter. He agrees with Plato and Aristotle that laughter is

---

* Kant's derogatory remarks about persons of colour are well documented, and are discussed in this book under RACISM i and ii.

often at the expense of others, and, in *Parerga und Paralipomena* (1851), he denounces it forcefully:

> it is Schadenfreude, a mischievous delight in the misfortunes of others, which remains the worst trait in human nature. It is a feeling which is closely akin to cruelty, and differs from it, to say the truth, only as theory from practice.

Despite his label as a pessimist, there is a certain wry humour in Schopenhauer's critical view of the human species. Most philosophers consider laughter a social phenomenon (partly because derisory laughter is predicated on an us-versus-them group perspective); but Schopenhauer was an advocate of solitary laughter. He thought the inability to laugh alone indicated 'dullness of mind':

> I am not surprised that people are bored when they are alone; they cannot laugh when they are alone, for such a thing seems foolish to them. Is laughter, then, to be regarded as merely a signal for others, a mere sign, like a word? It is a want of imagination and dullness of mind generally (ἀναισθησία καὶ βραδυτὴς ψυχῆς), as Theophrastus* puts it, that prevents people from laughing when they are alone. The lower animals neither laugh when they are alone nor in company.

...... ● ......

---

* A philosopher of the peripatetic school (*see* WALKING i) who lived in the fourth century BC.

vi HENRI BERGSON IDENTIFIED LAUGHING as a human phenomenon (*Laughter*, 1900). Animals don't make fun of men, but men make fun of the 'human qualities' to be found in our anthropomorphized views of animals. To laugh at someone means to be emotionally detached from the object of laughter. Laughter is a social activity: people laugh together, and a social bond between them is established. If we discover that we cannot laugh along with others, there is a good chance that we are the butt of the laughter. 'A man, running along the street, stumbles and falls; the passers-by burst out laughing. They would not laugh at him, I imagine, could they suppose that the whim had suddenly seized him to sit down on the ground. They laugh because his sitting down is involuntary.' Bergson, following Plato, notices that behind laughter is 'an unavowed intention to humiliate':

> laughter, even on the stage, is not an unadulterated enjoyment; it is not a pleasure that is exclusively aesthetic or altogether disinterested. It always implies a secret or unconscious intent, if not of each one of us, at all events of society as a whole. In laughter we always find an unavowed intention to humiliate, and consequently to correct our neighbour, if not in his will, at least in his deed. This is the reason a comedy is far more like real life than a drama is.

I have
HEARD
that one should
DIE
in
SILENCE

YOU ARE
STRANGE
FELLOWS; WHAT IS
WRONG
WITH YOU?

CHAPTER TWENTY-EIGHT

MARTYRDOM

CRITO, WE OWE
A COCK TO
ASCLEPIUS

THINKING BECOMES A
COURAGEOUS ACT

i   **YOU ARE STRANGE fellows; what is wrong with you? I sent
     the women away for this very purpose, to stop their creating
     such a scene. I have heard that one should die in silence. So
     please be quiet and keep control of yourselves.**

This is Socrates chiding his friends Crito of Alopece and
Apollodorus of Phaleron who were weeping as they waited to
watch the execution of their friend by drinking hemlock.* He
was speaking in Plato's dialogue *Phaedo* named after Phaedo
of Elis, who was also present.

Socrates' is the most famous death in Western philosophy.
He was condemned in 399 BC for refusing to recognize state-
authorized gods and 'corrupting' the youth of Athens. At the
appointed hour he accepted the poison cup from an apothecary
of whom he inquired what the experience would be like. The
apothecary told him his limbs would grow heavy, he would lie
down and death would follow. Socrates spoke for as long as he
could about the soul and the afterlife. His last words: 'Crito,
we owe a cock to Asclepius. Do pay it. Don't forget.' *See also*
ADVICE iii *and* GRIEF i.

...... ● ......

ii   **SOCRATES' DEATH** teaches us that philosophy can be a
     dangerous business. Real thinking necessarily involves disa-
     greement with others; and when those others hold power and
     are not willing to be challenged, the wages of thought can be
     death. Philosophers are martyrs, too.

---

* The Greek death penalty is both a suicide and a state-directed homicide, as
the condemned man must self-administer the poison. The effect of hemlock is
paralysis. The respiratory system fails and death is caused by asphyxia.

The Egyptian philosopher and mathematician Hypatia was born in the middle of the fourth century AD, 750 years after Socrates' execution. Much had happened during that time. The Romans eclipsed the Greeks, creating the largest empire the world had seen; Christianity replaced Greek polytheism and became the state religion of the Roman Empire in the East and West. At the same time, the ideas of Plato continued to hold sway.

Hypatia was a Neoplatonist who developed the ideas of Plotinus, who taught a monist philosophy centred on the principal of the 'one' – the concept of a central idea that transcends all things. Plotinus' metaphysical system was based around the triad of the 'one', the intellect and the soul. Hypatia's most famous student is Synesius (*see also* HAIRCUTS ii), who reconciled Plotinus' thought with Christian belief, particularly with reference to the triune God (father, son and Holy Spirit).

In 415 Orestes, the prefect of Alexandria, and Cyril, Bishop of Alexandria, were locked in a feud that arose over Jewish dancing exhibitions in the city, which drew large crowds and were a frequent cause of civil disorder. When Orestes published an edict regulating public assembly, Jews and Christians alike were angered. After a Christian follower of Bishop Cyril was tortured on the orders of Orestes on a charge of sedition, Cyril threatened retaliatory sanctions against the Jews. This triggered clashes between the two communities and a rash of tit-for-tat bloodletting, which escalated after a Jewish mob spread false reports of a fire at a Christian church. Under cover of darkness Jews killed Christians who responded to the alarm. Cyril rounded up the Jews of Alexandria, took their property and banished them. Orestes objected to the expulsion of the Jews because he thought it weakened his city. Then, 500 monks from the monastery at Nitria marched on Alexandria, attacking Orestes. A citizen named Ammonius who came to Orestes' aid was tortured and killed by the monks, who had falsely branded Orestes a 'pagan' (he was a baptized Christian). Orestes declared Ammonius a martyr. This further infuriated the Christians.

Hypatia became embroiled in Orestes' quarrel with Cyril because Orestes had frequently consulted Hypatia on questions both philosophical and civil. The public mistrusted her wide learning. Being an astronomer as well as a mathematician and philosopher, Hypatia was known to use the astrolabe, a tool for locating and predicting movements of planets and stars. The rabble said she had been using a 'magical' device, and she was denounced as a pagan. Rumours were also put about that Hypatia advised Orestes to take a position against Cyril.

A Christian mob kidnapped Hypatia and brought her to the Caesareum, a Christian church that was originally a temple to Julius Caesar commissioned by his lover Cleopatra VII. They stripped her naked and murdered her by flaying her alive with the sharp edges of roof tiles. The mob then dismembered Hypatia's body and took her limbs to Cinaron, where they were burned. In the words of a modern biographer of Hypatia: 'With Hypatia's death, Alexandria lost its secular tradition almost entirely. What little mathematical activity remained in the empire tended to be conducted elsewhere.'

...... ● ......

iii THE GERMAN PHILOSOPHER Moritz Schlick was the founder of logical positivism, a method of doing philosophy that required empirical verification of truths. He also headed the Vienna Circle (*see* BACKBITING v), a discussion group composed of philosophers, mathematicians and scientists that focused on Wittgenstein's *Tractatus Logico-Philosophicus* (1921). On 22 June 1936 Johann Nelböck, a former student of Schlick's, put four bullets in his teacher's chest on one of the central staircases of the University of Vienna, killing him instantly. The facts are simple, the interpretation of them complex.

Schlick's murder occurred in the context of Austrofascism. Shortly after Hitler's rise to power in 1933, Austria declared fascist rule with a new constitution on 1 May 1934 (the new government was right wing and authoritarian, but not yet Nazi). Most members of the Vienna Circle had already fled Austria for the safety of universities in the United States and Great Britain. Among them were Rudolf Carnap (UCLA), Philipp Frank (Harvard), Richard von Mises (Harvard), Otto Neurath and Olga Hahn-Neurath (Oxford), Friedrich Waismann (Oxford) and Rose Rand (Cambridge). Only Hans Hahn, Victor Kraft, Theodor Radakovic and Schlick himself stayed in Vienna.

From 1925 to 1931 Nelböck was Schlick's postgraduate student (his thesis was on *The Importance of Logic in Empiricism and Positivism*). In 1931 Nelböck and his girlfriend Sylvia Borowicka threatened to kill Schlick. Schlick went to the police and Nelböck was confined to the Steinhof psychiatric hospital for three months' evaluation. He was diagnosed a paranoid schizophrenic. Early in 1932 Nelböck again threatened Schlick's life, and was sent to the psychiatric hospital. Four years later Nelböck carried out his threat.

Nelböck gave prosecutors three accounts of his motive for the crime. The first was his insistence that Schlick was having an affair with Borowicka. The second was his claim that Schlick threatened to tell his employer he had been sent to a psychiatric hospital. (Nelböck was teaching in an adult education college; he told police that a colleague who was a Catholic conservative and supporter of the Austrofascist government said Schlick was planning to denounce Nelböck, with the likely consequence that he would lose his job.) Nelböck's third argument in his defence was that Schlick's anti-metaphysical philosophy had called his Christian beliefs into question, and had 'interfered with his moral restraint' – i.e. that Schlick had only himself to blame for his murder. In 1937 Nelböck was sentenced to ten years in prison. After Austria's annexation by Germany in 1938 he was released after serving less than two years.

Schlick was a Protestant, but many of his philosophical colleagues were Jews. Sharing the views of Jewish thinkers in 1938 Vienna was enough for public opinion and the court to judge Schlick and others like him 'worse' than Jews, because they wilfully entertained 'Jewish ideas'. The Catholic weekly *Schönere Zukunft* commented that 'Schlick embodied the Jewish characteristics associated with the anti-metaphysical philosophical movement to the highest degree, and expressed hope that his murder would result in a peaceful solution of the "Jewish Question"'.

Nelböck's counsel argued successfully on appeal:

that by his act and the resulting elimination of a Jewish teacher who propagated doctrines alien and detrimental to the nation he rendered National Socialism a service and also

suffered for National Socialism as a consequence of his act. Since the world-view, the rightness of which he recognized even then and out of which he committed his act, is now the ruling national ideology, he considers it a hardship if he still has to remain in a disadvantaged position because of an act which sprang from his world-view.

What the deaths of Socrates, Hypatia and Schlick demonstrate is that when a philosophical idea becomes concretized as ideology, or a religious belief turns to dogma, thinking becomes a courageous and or potentially dangerous act.

 See also RACISM i; VANITY i.

WE HOPE FOR NOTHING
WE FEAR EVERYTHING

It is a PLACE where I can't BE and where I can't NOT BE

CHAPTER TWENTY-NINE
MELANCHOLY

BLACK BILE

The NATURE of THE BRAIN BECOMES DRY and COLD

MELANCHOLICS are in perpetual NEED OF MEDICINE

i **ARISTOTLE TALKED ABOUT 'MELANCHOLICS'** rather than melancholy. 'Why is it', he asks, 'that all those who have become eminent in philosophy or politics or poetry or the arts are clearly melancholics?'

What do we mean by melancholy? The modern definition is 'a feeling of pensive sadness, typically with no obvious cause'.* Historically, melancholy derives from the Greek μέλαινα χολή (melaina kholé), which means 'black bile'. Hippocrates thought that health was governed by four 'humours' – blood, yellow bile, black bile and phlegm. In this system black bile was associated with autumn, earth, the spleen and the qualities of cold and dry. The melancholic was despondent, quiet, analytical, serious. Aristotle talks about creative persons as being 'affected by diseases caused by black bile'; he says, 'If they are not careful, they can become extremely melancholic.' What is it, in Aristotle's view, to be melancholic? Melancholy has two aspects, mania and depression. He cites the examples of Heracles,† who murdered his family; and Ajax,‡ who committed suicide. When the condition of melancholy is tempered, it opens the door to creativity. The ancient melancholic personality is easily identified as the 'clinically' depressed patient of today, who is subject to manic depression.

Nowadays doctors control depression with drugs (selective serotonin reuptake inhibitors (SSRIs) which control the amount of serotonin§ in the brain; serotonin and norepi-

---

* *Oxford English Dictionary.*

† In Greek mythology, the son of Zeus, renowned for his strength.

‡ Son of Telamon, who was the son of Aeacus and grandson of Zeus; cousin of Achilles.

§ A monoamine neurotransmitter thought to affect feelings of wellbeing and happiness.

nephrine reuptake inhibitors (SNRIs) increase the availability of serotonin and norepinephrine). But the ancient Greeks also relied on drug treatment. Aristotle wrote that 'Melancholics are in perpetual need of medicine. Depending on coincidence, they can become the victim of either an extreme exuberance or deep sorrow. And through medical therapy these extremes become less pronounced.' Ancient pharmaceutical treatments included extracts from the poppy and mandrake* plants, in addition to hypericum oil.† A diet of milk and barley gruel was prescribed, as were baths and massages. Music was also recommended. The goal of modern medicine is to quash melancholy/depression; the point of classical treatment was not to eradicate it, but to temper it.

...... • ......

ii 'MELANCHOLY IS DUE to the first attack by the devil on the nature of man since man disobeyed God's command by eating the apple.' That was the view of Hildegard of Bingen, the medieval German Benedictine abbess long referred to as 'Saint Hildegard', but whose canonization was only formally declared by Pope Benedict XVI in 2012. Hildegard was a true polymath – visionary, author, composer and philosopher. In addition she is considered the originator of natural science in Germany, and possessed a wide knowledge of plants and animals. Her medical views were influenced more by Christian mythology than they were by the naturalistic theories of the ancient Greeks. In her *Book of Holistic Healing* (written 1151–58) she borrows

---

* A member of the nightshade family whose forked root resembles the human form. Ancients said it shrieked when pulled from the ground.

† A natural antidepressant also known as St John's wort.

some of the language of humoural pathology, but marries it with an interpretation of the Christian creation myth. She describes melancholics as

people who are dour, nervous and changeable in their mood so that in their case there is no single constant disposition. They are like a strong wind that does harm to all plants and fruits. That is, a phlegm grows in them that is neither moist nor thick, but lukewarm. It is like a slime that is sticky and can be stretched to various lengths. It causes bile that came into being at the very beginning out of Adam's semen through the breath of the serpent since Adam followed his advice about eating the apple.

Like Hippocrates, Hildegard views black bile as the physical cause of melancholy. She starts with the medical judgement that 'Bile is black, bitter, and releases every evil, sometimes even a brain sickness. It causes the veins in the heart to overflow.' But she quickly trades medical for theological language, arguing that black bile

causes depression and doubt in every consolation so that the person can find no joy in heavenly life and no consolation in his earthly existence. This melancholy is due to the first attack by the devil on the nature of man since man disobeyed God's command by eating the apple. From this meal, this melancholy developed in Adam and in all his posterity and it is the cause of all serious disease in humans.

For Hildegard melancholy manifests itself differently in men and women. In a section titled 'The Melancholic Man' she writes:

There are men whose brain is fat. Their scalp and blood vessels are entangled. They have a pale facial colour. Even their eyes have something fiery and snake-like about them... their behaviour with women is as improper and undisciplined as animals and snakes... they really love no one; rather they are embittered, suspicious, resentful, dissolute in their passion, and as unregulated in their interaction with women as a donkey. If they ever refrain from their desire, they easily become sick in the head so that they become crazy... The influence of the devil rages so powerfully in the passion of these men that they would kill the woman with whom they are having sexual relations if they could.

Of 'The Melancholic Woman' Hildegard takes a less disapproving view:

These women are heedless and dissolute in their thoughts and of evil disposition if they are grieved by any irritation. Since they are unstable and irresponsible, on occasion they also suffer from melancholy. During the monthly menses they lose much blood, and they are infertile because they have a weak, fragile womb. For that reason, they can neither receive, retain, nor warm the male seed. For that reason they are more healthy, more powerful, and happier without a mate than with one because they become sick from relations with a husband... If their monthly menses ever stops earlier than corresponds to the womanly nature, they get arthritis, swollen legs, or headaches that cause melancholy... If they receive no help and are not freed from their sufferings by God's help or through a medicine, they will soon die.

iii 'WE HOPE FOR NOTHING, we fear everything.' Thus did the Italian Renaissance priest and Neoplatonist Marsilio Ficino describe the plight of the melancholic.

Ficino's accomplishments were many, and his greatest was very great indeed: he produced the first Latin translation of Plato's entire corpus. His life's work was an attempt to synthesize Christianity and Platonism, an enormous intellectual effort. One of the things he discovered about persistent intellectual effort is that it could bring on bouts of melancholia. In *Three Books of Life* (1482) – a curious mix of medical, astrological and philosophical advice on health – he identified three causes for such episodes of melancholia: celestial, natural and human. By celestial, Ficino really means astrological. Following the humoural pathology which links Saturn with black bile, Ficino writes: 'Mercury, who invites us to investigate doctrines, and Saturn, who makes us persevere in investigating doctrines and retain them when discovered, are said by astronomers to be somewhat cold and dry... just like the melancholic nature, according to physicians.' The natural (or scientific) cause

> seems to be that for the pursuit of the sciences, especially the difficult ones, the soul must draw in upon itself from external things to internal as from the circumference to the centre... Now to collect oneself from the circumference to the centre and to be fixed in the centre, is above all the property of the Earth itself,* to which black bile is analogous. Therefore black bile continually incites the soul both to collect itself together into one and to dwell on itself and to contemplate itself.

---

* The Copernican revolution was still some decades away, so Ficino believes the Earth is at the centre of our solar system.

In discussing the third cause, the human, Ficino essentially argues that brain work promotes melancholy: 'Because frequent agitation of the mind greatly dries up the brain, therefore, when the moisture has been mostly consumed – moisture being the support of the natural heat – the heat also is usually extinguished; and from this chain of events, the nature of the brain becomes dry and cold, which is known as the earthy and melancholic quality.' He then analyses the blood, which 'is necessarily rendered dense, dry and black' by thinking. This leads to poor digestion and lack of exercise (as a result of which 'superfluities are not carried off'). Ficino concludes:

All these things characteristically make the spirit melancholy and the soul sad and fearful – since, indeed, interior darkness much more than exterior overcomes the soul with sadness and terrifies it. But of all learned people, those especially are oppressed by back bile, who, being sedulously devoted to the study of philosophy, recall their mind from the body and corporeal things and apply it to incorporeal things. The cause is, first, that the more difficult the work, the greater concentration of mind it requires; and second, that the more they apply their mind to incorporeal truth, the more they are compelled to disjoin it from the body. Hence their body is often rendered as it if were half-alive and often melancholic.

...... • ......

iv **IN DEDICATING HIS ESSAY** 'OF THE AFFECTION OF FATHERS TO THEIR CHILDREN' to a friend, Michel de Montaigne explains how melancholy was the impetus for his famous collection *Essays* (1580):

> 'Tis a melancholic humour, and consequently a humour very much an enemy to my natural complexion, engendered by the pensiveness of the solitude into which for some years past I have retired myself, that first put into my head this idle fancy of writing.

Montaigne said that he was not a natural melancholic; how, then, might he have slipped into a mood of black biliousness? One suggestion is that, like Ficino, Montaigne believed that too much brainwork promotes melancholy. In his essay 'OF THE EDUCATION OF CHILDREN', he cites Epicurus' advice to Menoeceus:

> 'That neither the youngest should refuse to philosophise, nor the oldest grow weary of it.' Who does otherwise, seems tacitly to imply, that either the time of living happily is not yet come, or that it is already past. And yet, for all that, I would not have this pupil of ours imprisoned and made a slave to his book; nor would I have him given up to the morosity and melancholic humour of a sour ill-natured pedant.

If a parent encourages a 'solitary and melancholic complexion' in a child, he is in danger of becoming 'overmuch addicted to his book'. Montaigne cautions that 'to nourish that humour in him... renders him unfit for civil conversation, and diverts him from better employments'. And, he adds, 'how many have

I seen in my time totally brutified by an immoderate thirst after knowledge?'

While Montaigne protested that he is not melancholic by nature, in his essay 'APOLOGY FOR RAIMOND SEBOND' he admits to the occasional flirtation with it:

> I am one while for doing every thing, and another for doing nothing at all; and what pleases me now would be a trouble to me at another time. I have a thousand senseless and casual actions within myself; either I am possessed by melancholy or swayed by choler; now by its own private authority sadness predominates in me, and by and by, I am as merry as a cricket.

Montaigne says: 'I am of the opinion that there is design, consent, and complacency in giving a man's self up to melancholy... there is some shadow of delight and delicacy which smiles upon and flatters us even in the very lap of melancholy. Are there not some constitutions that feed upon it?' But, in the end, Montaigne comes back to his original position that 'I am in my own nature not melancholic'. Instead, he pleads, he is 'meditative'; 'there is nothing I have more continually entertained myself withal than imaginations of death, even in the most wanton time of my age'.

...... ● ......

v 'FROM MELANCHOLY dispositions,' said the seventeenth-century scholar and cleric Robert Burton, 'no man living is free, no stoic, none so wise, none so happy, none so patient, so generous, so godly, so divine, that can vindicate himself; so well composed, but more or less, some time or other he feels the smart of it. Melancholy in this sense is the character of mortality.'

Burton's *The Anatomy of Melancholy* (1621) surveys the history of the condition, discussing its many sources and offering a variety of cures. Burton explains the humoural roots of melancholy, but he also examines causes of which Hildegard of Bingen would approve, including 'A Digression of the nature of Spirits, bad Angels, or Devils, and how they cause Melancholy'. Like Ficino and Montaigne, Burton – himself one of the most distinguished scholars of the age – focuses on 'Love of Learning, or overmuch study. With a Digression of the misery of Scholars, and why the Muses are Melancholy.'*

Burton's suggestions for the 'rectification' of melancholy include recommendations about diet and the use of various herbs and medicines. But the most interesting of Burton's remedies have to do with altering personal circumstances, choices and behaviours. He recommends living in a situation that is 'hot and moist, light, wholesome, pleasant &c'. The environment must be rectified 'Artificially, by often change of air, avoiding winds, fogs, tempests, opening windows, perfumes, &c.' He advises moderate physical exercise ('hawking, hunting, riding, shooting, bowling, fishing, fowling, walking in fair fields'; see also WALKING ii) and moderate mental exercise ('chess, cards, tables &c, to see plays, masks, &c, serious studies, business, all honest recreations').

More important, perhaps, is Burton's counsel regarding what we would nowadays call 'self-help'. The melancholic, Burton

---

* It would be difficult to cite a contemporary of Burton's who had more learning (or books; Burton's personal library contained more than two thousand volumes). Ficino's translations into Latin of the entire corpus of Plato easily qualifies as 'love of learning' or even as 'overmuch study'.

says, must use 'all good means of help', primarily 'confessing to a friend'. He should avoid 'all occasions of his infirmity'* and – perhaps the most difficult advice to follow – 'Not giving way to passions, but resisting to his utmost.' From his friends the melancholic should seek 'By fair and foul means, counsel, comfort, good persuasion, witty devices, fictions, and, if it be possible, to satisfy his mind,' Burton recommends 'Music of all sorts' along with 'Mirth and merry company'. That is the positive aspect of Burton's self-help regime.

There is also what we might term a 'negative' aspect of Burton's self-help regime: a list of things to avoid. First among these is 'vain fears', followed by 'sorrows for death of friends, or otherwise'. Here Burton gives some insight into the ancient Greeks' advice against immoderate mourning: it is a gateway to melancholy (*see also* GRIEF ii). He proscribes the vices of envy, hatred, malice, emulation, ambition and self-love. He advocates against 'repulses, abuses, injuries, contempts, disgraces, contumelies,† slanders, and scoffs, &c'.

Burton counted romantic love as a chief cause of melancholy. His long consideration of it in *The Anatomy of Melancholy* is mainly composed of classical quotes ('every story is full of men and women's insatiable lust'). First-hand accounts of love are absent from the book perhaps because, as a fellow of Oxford University at the time, Burton was not allowed to marry.

Of love, Burton remarks that, like drunkenness, it 'cannot be concealed'. He recounts the story of Demophon (King of Athens) and his wife Phyllis (daughter of a Thracian king, perhaps Sithon): 'when he is gone, he thinks every minute an hour,

---

* What today's counsellors might call 'triggers' that bring on a bout of melancholy/depression.

† Insulting language or behaviour.

every hour as long as a day, ten days a whole year, till he see her again. She looks out at window [sic] still to see whether he come, and by report Phillis went nine times to the seaside that day, to see if her Demophoon were approaching.' Burton describes the melancholy Phyllis experiences in her husband's absence:

> She is ill at ease, and sick till she see him again, peevish in the meantime; discontent, heavy, sad, and why comes he not? where is he? why breaks he promise? why tarries he so long? sure he is not well; sure he hath some mischance; sure he forgets himself and me; with infinite such. And then, confident again, up she gets, out she looks, listens, and inquires, hearkens, kens; every man afar off is sure he, every stirring in the street, now he is there, that's he... the longest day that ever was, so she raves, restless and impatient.

'The symptoms of the mind in lovers are almost infinite, and so diverse, that no art can comprehend them,' says Burton. 'Though they be merry sometimes, and rapt beyond themselves for joy: yet most part, love is a plague, a torture, a hell, a bitter sweet passion at last... fair, foul, and full of variation, though most part irksome and bad.' He quotes Augustine of Hippo as saying that romantic love causes 'biting cares, perturbations, passions, sorrows, fears, suspicions, discontents, contentions, discords, wars, treacheries, enmities, flattery, cozening, riot, impudence, cruelty, knavery' (*see also* SEX v). Despite all, however, Burton maintains, in his bachelor way: 'Yet for all this, amongst so many irksome, absurd, troublesome symptoms, inconveniences, fantastical fits and passions which are usually incident to such persons, there be some good and graceful qualities in lovers, which this affection causeth.'

At the end of the day, Burton's 'Cure of Love-Melancholy' is 'Labour, Diet, Physic, Fasting'. Melancholic lovers to this day follow his prescription. As for Burton himself, he is rumoured to have hanged himself in his rooms in Christ Church.*

...... ● ......

vi **SIGMUND FREUD** published a short paper on 'Mourning and Melancholia' in 1917 in which he wrote:

> **The distinguishing mental features of melancholia are a profoundly painful dejection, cessation of interest in the outside world, loss of the capacity to love, inhibition of all activity, and a lowering of the self-regarding feelings to a degree that finds utterance in self-reproaches and self-reviling, and culminates in a delusional expectation of punishment.**

In 2014 the English writer Jenny Diski gave an account of her lifetime of depression in an essay entitled 'Blackness Ever Blackening':

> **It is reaching some place deep inside, a physically experienced cavernous place enclosed by the barrier, as it seems, of my skeleton and skin, and something in addition that forces out the air of the room a little way beyond my physical**

---

* In his *Brief Lives*, written in the late seventeenth century, John Aubrey wrote: 'Mr. Robert Hooke of Gresham College told me that he lay in the chamber in Christ Church that was Mr. Burton's, of whom 'tis whispered that, non obstante all his astrologie and his booke of Melancholie, he ended his dayes in that chamber by hanging him selfe.'

self. It is a place where I can't be, and where I can't not be. It is negative upon negative. Blackness ever blackening. Obscurity and obstacle always increasing, arriving at a point where nothing can be retrieved, mended – and then more and further, beyond my capacity to imagine more. A struggle that only and always resolves itself into a further impossibility, to infinity, eternity; a terrifying forever, in the most inexplicably inhuman sense of the word.

Le Colonisateur de
BONNE VOLONTÉ

The WEEPING **PHILOSOPHER**

CHAPTER THIRTY
NICKNAMES

—THE—
WRANGLER

•
DOCTOR
MIRABILIS
•

— THE RIDDLER —

i **ARISTOTLE, MARTIN LUTHER,** Jeremy Bentham and Auguste Comte were all given the remarkably unoriginal nickname 'the Philosopher' by their friends and colleagues. In general, the ancient Greeks did rather better than that. The pre-Socratic philosopher Heraclitus of Ephesus rejoiced in no fewer than three nicknames: 'the Obscure', 'the Riddler' and 'the Weeping Philosopher'. Only fragments remain of his work *On Nature*, which was composed in a poetic, aphoristic style. He is best remembered for his statement 'no man ever steps in the same river twice, for it's not the same river and he's not the same man'. This gnomic proclamation refers to our experience of time, and provided much of the impetus for Martin Heidegger's *Being and Time* (1927). The fourth-century Greek Timon of Phlius gave Heraclitus the nickname 'the Riddler', adding that *On Nature* was written 'rather unclearly'. As may be inferred from the riparian statement quoted above, the thrust of Heraclitus's thought is that all is in flux; there is nothing but change. Which brings us to his third nickname, 'the Weeping Philosopher'. Heraclitus despaired of the ordinary person's lack of interest in thinking, or inability to follow philosophy. This pessimistic (and elitist) view led him to quit Ephesus and wander outside the city gates, where he is reported to have been found eating grass and weeping in despair.

The Thracian thinker Democritus of Abdera, who lived a century after Heraclitus, was called 'the Laughing Philosopher' for two reasons. One is that he was an advocate of cheerfulness; the other is that the follies of his fellow men often drove him to laughter.

...... ● ......

ii **THE EXTENT OF PLATO'S LEGACY** to Western civilization was famously summed up by A. N. Whitehead – mathematician, philosopher and a notable influence on the young Bertrand Russell – in his *Process and Reality: An Essay in Cosmology* (1929): 'The safest general characterization of the European philosophical tradition is that it consists of a series of footnotes to Plato.' 'Plato' is actually a nickname (his given name was Aristocles). The Greek word 'platon' means 'broad'. Diogenes Laertius reasons that Ariston of Argos, Plato's wrestling coach, gave him the nickname 'Plato' either because of his stocky figure, his broad knowledge, or his broad forehead.

...... ● ......

iii **IN ANCIENT TIMES** the Phoenician city of Tyre, on the coast of what is now the southern part of Lebanon, was famed for its production of a rare and expensive purple dye. Tyrian purple, as the dye was known, was produced from the secretions of the sea snail and was reserved, in many cultures, for the use of royalty or nobility. It was in Tyre, around AD 234, that a boy was born who would become a celebrated Neoplatonist, logician and the author of such works as *Philosophy from Oracles and Against the Christians* (which would provoke the ire of the Christian Roman emperor Constantine). His parents gave their son the name Malchus (meaning 'king'). In due course Malchus made his way to Athens, to be at the centre of learning, and became a student of Cassius Longinus, a fellow Syrian and leading rhetorician. Longinus gave Malchus a nickname that stuck so hard that history knows him only by it. That nickname was 'Porphyrius' (Porphyry in modern parlance), which means 'purple' in Greek, and may well be a reference to the colour with which the philosopher's home town is asso-ciated. In the early 260s Porphyry travelled to Rome, drawn there by the presence of the eminent Neoplatonist Plotinus, whose works he would edit and publish. Little is known of Porphyry's later life or the circumstances of his death. The creator of his clever nickname, however, is known to have met a violent end. In AD 273 Longinus was executed on the orders of the Roman emperor Aurelian for advising Zenobia, queen of Palmyra (whose empire included present-day Syria and Egypt), to seek independence from Rome. According to the later Byzantine historian Zosimus, Longinus met his end with exemplary courage and dignity.

...... ● ......

iv **THE NICKNAMES OF MEDIEVAL THINKERS** tend to be more serious than the light-hearted ones of the Greeks. Perhaps this was because medieval philosophy was largely indistinguishable from theology, and humour did not play a large role in its discourse. The Persian-born Islamic thinker Al-Ghazali was so revered by his eleventh-century contempo-raries that he was referred to as *Hujjat al-Islam*, or 'the Proof of Islam'. Al-Ghazali 'corrected' a growing Neoplatonist influ-ence on Islam; but he was also a conciliator who bridged the gap between orthodox Islam and Sufism. An abridged version of his key work *Revival of the Religious Sciences* was pub-lished as *The Alchemy of Happiness*. There he argued that the exercise of thought, the use of reason, leads man to a greater spiritual understanding of God.

The Islamic thinker we refer to as Averroes was born in 1126 in Córdoba in Al-Andalus* and spent his life attempting to reintroduce Greek thought – specifically, the philosophy of Aristotle – to the Muslim world. Averroes' given name is Ibn Rushd, which was translated in Hebrew as Aben Rois or Rosh, hence Averroes. His commentaries on Aristotle are so authoritative that they earned him the nickname 'the Commentator'. Because his philosophical ideas directly contradicted those of Al-Ghazali and his followers, Averroes was banished from Marrakesh, capital of the Almohad caliphate which ruled over North Africa and Islamic Spain for much of the twelfth and thirteenth centuries, and many of his works were burned. Latin translations of Averroes' works helped promote the influence of Aristotle on Western thought.

...... • ......

v **EARLY TWELFTH-CENTURY** Córdoba was also the birthplace of the Jewish philosopher, astronomer and physician Maimonides. When the fundamentalist Berber Almohads conquered Córdoba in 1148, life for Christians and Jews became markedly less comfortable than it had been in the earlier centuries of Muslim rule in Al-Andalus. Maimonides was compelled to adopt an itinerant existence, travelling around southern Spain before settling in Fez, in Morocco. He eventually made his home in Egypt, where he found fame as a physician (his writings show him to be conversant with the symptoms of asthma, diabetes, hepatitis and haemorrhoids) and became leader (*nagid*) of the Egyptian Jewish community.

---

* The name for those parts of the Iberian peninsula that were governed by Muslims during the period from 711 until 1492, when Ferdinand and Isabella completed the Christian *Reconquista*.

Just as Al-Ghazali was the greatest codifier of Islamic law, so Maimonides established the reference for Talmudic law in his *Mishneh Torah* (1170–80). His philosophical views, as opposed to his interpretations of Jewish law, are expressed in his *Guide for the Perplexed* (1190).

Maimonides has two nicknames: the implausibly macho-sounding 'RamBam', an acronym of 'Rabbi Moshe ben Maimon' ('Our teacher Moses son of Maimon'); and 'the Great Eagle' (a reflection of his soaring mastery of the Oral Torah). In the commonly used Latinized form of his name, the Hebrew word 'ben' – meaning 'son of' – is replaced by the Greek-style suffix '-ides' to give 'Moses Maimonides'.

...... ● ......

vi **DURING THE CHRISTIAN** High Middle Ages, it was customary to endow celebrated doctors of theology and law with epithets that designate their particular qualities of excellence. The French scholastic Francis of Mayrone, distinguished debater at the Sorbonne, was *Doctor Acutus* (acute) or *Magister abstractionum* ('Master of abstractions'); William of Ockham, the English Franciscan who devised the problem-solving principle known as 'Ockham's razor',* was Doctor *Invincibilis* ('invincible'); another Franciscan, the Shropshire-born Alexander of Hales, was *Doctor Irrefragibilis* ('not to be refuted'); Roger Bacon, yet another Englishman and an early proponent of empiricism, was *Doctor Mirabilis* ('astounding'); the shadowy Frenchman John of Bassolis was *Doctor Ordinatissimus* ('most methodical'); the Italian Bonaventure

---

* 'Ockham's razor' generally recommends that in explaining something, no more assumptions should be made than are absolutely necessary.

(canonized by the Counter-Reformation pope Sixtus V) was *Doctor Seraphicus* (the seraphim being first among the nine orders of angels); the Majorcan-born logician Ramon Llull was *Doctor Illuminatus* ('illuminated'); Henry of Ghent was *Doctor Solemnis* ('solemn'); John of Duns (aka Duns* Scotus), born in the Scottish Borders town of that name, whose idea of the 'univocity of being' was to be enormously influential, was *Doctor Subtilis* ('subtle'); the German Dominican Albertus Magnus was *Doctor Universalis* ('universal'); Jean Ruysbroeck, a Flemish mystic, was *Doctor Divinus Ecstaticus* ('ecstatic'); and last but not least another English Franciscan, Haymo of Faversham, rejoiced in the epithet *Inter Aristotelicos Aristotelicissimus* ('most Aristotelian among the Aristotelians').

With the coming of the Renaissance a scintilla of humour creeps back into philosophical nicknaming. The original 'Renaissance man' is the Italian Galileo Galilei (*see* TRUTH vi). He was nicknamed 'the Wrangler' while still a student for his willingness to question the church dogma of the scholastics and for his courage in argument. In 1615 he famously defended the Copernican view of a heliocentric universe, drawing the wrath of the Inquisition.

...... ● ......

vii **THE FRENCH ENLIGHTENMENT** philosopher, novelist and essayist Voltaire created more than one name for himself. He was born – in 1694 – François-Marie Arouet, to François and Marie-Marguerite Arouet (he was given the name Arouet

---

* The word 'dunce' originally meant a follower of Duns Scotus. Its modern sense of a 'stupid person' arose in the sixteenth century, when the 'Scotists' were ridiculed by humanists and reformers as enemies of the new learning.

even though he was the bastard son of the chevalier Guérin de Rochebrune). The Arouets nicknamed him 'Zozo'. When he was twenty-four, after spending eleven months imprisoned in the Bastille for suggesting that the Duke of Orleans (who was then Regent of France, during the minority of Louis XV) practised incest with his daughter, he gave himself the name Voltaire. The name is an anagram of 'AROVET LI', the Latin spelling of his surname 'Arouet' and the initial letters of *'le jeune'* ('the young'). Some historians claim the adoption of the name Voltaire signalled a break with his family and his past, but it is also a near anagram of 'Airvault', the name of his family's chateau in Poitou. Not content with having a given name and two nicknames, Voltaire also wrote under 178 *noms de plume*, including Firmin Abauzit, Dominico Zapata and Dr Good Natur'd Wellwisher. *See also* WRITING iii.

...... • ......

viii AS A CHILD, the Dane Søren Kierkegaard – Christian existentialist and author of critical texts on morality, ethics, psychology and the philosophy of religion – was mischievous in the extreme. For one of his cousins, he was 'a frightfully spoiled and naughty boy who always hung on his mother's apron strings'. Another cousin noted his tendency to sulk. Kierkegaard was nicknamed 'the fork' because, when asked what he would most like to be, he had identified that item of cutlery as his preference. On being pressed as to the reasons for his unusual ontological choice, the freckled Søren responded, 'Well, then I could "spear" anything I wanted on the dinner table!' To the rejoinder 'But what if we come after you?' the future author of *Fear* and *Trembling* and *The Sickness Unto*

Death shot back: 'Then I'll spear you.' The nickname stuck, thanks to Kierkegaard's precocious tendency to make barbed and satirical remarks.

...... ● ......

ix **IN HIS PUBLISHED WORKS,** Kierkegaard would explore a range of complex philosophical problems from different viewpoints, and he used pseudonyms to present these various viewpoints and to interact with each other in dialogue. These pseudonyms included:

> *Johannes de silentio* (Latin, 'John of the silence'), author of *Fear and Trembling* (the title refers to Philippians 2:12 – 'Wherefore, my beloved, as ye have always obeyed, not as in my presence only, but now much more in my absence, work out your own salvation with fear and trembling').

> *Vigilius Haufniensis* (Latin, 'the watchman of Copenhagen'), author of *The Concept of Anxiety: A Simple Psychologically Orienting Deliberation on the Dogmatic Issue of Hereditary Sin*.

> *Nicolaus Notabene* (Latin, 'note well'), author of *Prefaces*.

> *Hilarius Bookbinder*, editor of *Stages on Life's Way*.

> *Johannes Climacus*, author of *Philosophical Fragments and Concluding Unscientific Postscript to the Philosophical Fragments*. (Johannes Climacus may be a reference to a seventh-century Christian monk, who believed that an individual is

converted to Christianity by way of a ladder, one rung (or virtue) at a time. Kierkegaard, unlike Climacus, believed the individual makes a 'leap to faith'.

...... ● ......

x *DER ALLZERMALMENDE* ('the all-destroying') was the nickname given by Moses Mendelssohn to his philosophical giant of a friend, the Enlightenment thinker Immanuel Kant, who, in constructing his system, challenged the greatest thinkers on the most universal problems in philosophy. Among other systematizing Germans, G. W. F. Hegel had such a sombre demeanour that his fellow students called him *der Alte* ('the old man'), while the precocious Friedrich Nietzsche was called 'the little pastor' as a child – ironically in view of his later association with the statement 'God is dead' (*see* GOD vii) – on account of his piety.

In terms of his influence, Martin Heidegger was to the twentieth-century German philosophical tradition what Hegel had been to the nineteenth (*see also* BACKBITING iv). The students taught by Heidegger at the University of Freiburg im Breisgau include such philosophical luminaries as Hannah Arendt, Günther Anders, Hans Jonas, Karl Löwith, Charles Malik, Herbert Marcuse and Ernst Nolte. According to Löwith, he and his fellow students dubbed Heidegger 'the little magician from Messkirch' (Heidegger's birthplace in Baden-Württemberg) on account of their teacher's mesmerizing presence in the lecture hall:

He was a small dark man who knew how to cast a spell insofar as he could make disappear what he had a moment

before presented. His lecture technique consisted in building up an edifice of ideas which he then proceeded to tear down, presenting the spellbound listeners with a riddle and then leaving them empty-handed. This ability to cast a spell at times had very considerable consequences: it attracted more or less psychopathic personality types, and, after three years of guessing at riddles, one woman student took her own life.

Heidegger, as a card-carrying member of the Nazi party, remained in Germany throughout the Second World War.

Staying at home was not, however, a safe option for the many Jewish or fervently anti-Nazi German artists and intellectuals of the time. Two exiled philosophers of the 'Frankfurt School', Theodor Adorno and Max Horkheimer, settled in the early 1940s in Pacific Palisades, on the Westside of the city of Los Angeles. So popular was the district with exiled German and Austrian writers and artists (the philosophers' neighbours included the dramatist Bertolt Brecht and the Viennese twelve-tone composer Arnold Schoenberg, whose work had been demonized as 'degenerate' by the Nazis) that the novelist Thomas Mann labelled it 'German California'. Adorno and Horkheimer collaborated to produce *Dialectic of Enlightenment* (1944), a critique of what the Frankfurt School social theorists saw as the failure of the Enlightenment, since hailed as a core text of modern critical theory. Two of the twentieth century's foremost thinkers on aesthetics and philosophy, Adorno and Horkheimer employed pet names for each other that some might find surprising: Adorno called Horkheimer *Mammut* ('Mammoth'), while Horkheimer's nickname for Adorno was *Nilpferd* ('Hippopotamus').

xi **JEAN-PAUL SARTRE,** the bespectacled, wall-eyed French existentialist, was known as *Kobra* (after the venomous snake whose hood, when flared, resembles a pair of eyeglasses); Sartre called his lifelong partner Simone de Beauvoir *Castor* ('beaver'). Their contemporary, the Algerian-born French novelist Albert Camus, had possibly the longest nickname of any philosopher: *Le Colonisateur de Bonne Volonté* ('the well-meaning colonist'). He earned the nickname for his controversial effort to broker a truce between Algerian Muslims and the Front Français that would spare civilians from fighting in the Algerian War of Independence (1954–62).

The French post-structuralist Michel Foucault (*see* INSANITY v) was given the nickname *Fuchs* (German for 'fox') by his friend the semiologist Jean Molino. Foucault earned the nickname because he 'was slyer than the others, and because foxes dig more deeply than others'.

Of all philosophers' nicknames, perhaps the English ethicist G. E. (Gerald Edward) Moore's (*see also* BACKBITING i) is the most puzzling: his wife called him Bill.

The
WHIRLIGIG
of
REPRESENTATION
GOES MAD

GIVING UP ON
ONE'S OWN
WILL
IS ONLY IN
ONE ASPECT
NEGATIVE

CHAPTER THIRTY-ONE

OBFUSCATION

The
AUTHENTIC
TRUTH

We have deduced
SENSATION
as an
ACT OF EGO

THE DESIRE FOR
— **RECOGNITION** —
DOMINATES THE DESIRE THAT IS
TO BE RECOGNIZED

i **SOCRATES PRIDED HIMSELF** on making his arguments clear. He used ordinary language that ordinary people could understand. For more than two thousand years, philosophers generally followed this trend.

And then German idealism happened (*see* CONSCIOUSNESS iv). For some reason the Germans started inventing new words and took to writing tortuous sentences that were longer than an Englishman's paragraph and tended to obscure rather than explain the subject at hand.

...... ● ......

ii **IT ALL STARTED** with Johann Gottlieb Fichte, a founder of German idealism. This piece, on the ego, is moderately obscure; idealism-lite, if you will:

> We have deduced sensation as an act of the Ego, whereby it relates a foreign something in itself to itself, and posits it as its own. The act, sensation, we now know, and also its object, that which enters sensation. But we do not yet know the *sensating*, that is, the Ego, active in that relation; nor do we know yet the opposite activity of the Non-Ego which was excluded in the sensation. Let us now seek to know of them.

...... ● ......

iii **AFTER FICHTE,** the key Germans all followed the obscurantist style, notable among them being Friedrich Wilhelm Joseph Schelling. But the king of obscurantism – possibly the author of the most obscure philosophical texts ever written – was G. W. F. Hegel. One can choose at random. Browsing his 1807 classic *The Phenomenology of Mind*, one finds Hegel discussing the problem of giving up one's will:

> ...giving up one's own will is only in one aspect negative; in principle, or in itself, it is at the same time positive, positing and affirming the will as an other, and, specifically, affirming the will as not a particular but universal. This consciousness takes this positive significance of the negatively affirmed particular will to be the will of the other extreme, the will, which, because it is simply an 'other' for consciousness, assumes the new form of advice, or counsel, not through itself, but through the third term, the mediator. Hence its will certainly becomes, for consciousness, universal will, inherent and essential will, but is not itself in its own view this inherent reality.

...... ● ......

iv **THE OBSCURANTIST** mantle passes to Martin Heidegger, a founder of existentialism (*see also* BACKBITING iv). In this passage from his 1927 magnum opus *Being and Time* he reflects on the will-related problem of 'resoluteness':

> *Does resoluteness, in its own inmost existentiell tendency of being [Seinstendenz], itself point ahead to anticipatory resoluteness as its own most authentic possibility?* What if resoluteness, following its own meaning, were brought into its authenticity only when it no longer projects itself upon arbitrary possibilities merely lying near by, but rather upon the most extreme possibility that lies ahead of every factical potentiality of being of Dasein, and, as such, more or

less enters without distortion every potentiality-of-being of Dasein factically seized upon? What if resoluteness, as the *authentic* truth of Dasein, reached the *certainty authentically belonging to it* only in the anticipation of death? What if all the factical '*anticipatoriness*' of resolve were authentically understood, that is, existentially *caught up with* only in the anticipation of death?

...... ● ......

v JEAN-PAUL SARTRE, founder of the French branch of existentialism, was much influenced by Heidegger. In this passage from *Critique of Dialectical Reason* (1960) he attempts to define 'scandal':

Scandal is the Other as the formula of a series. But as soon as the first manifestations of scandal have occurred (that is to say, the first acts of someone acting for the Others in so far as he is Other than himself), they create the living unity of the audience against the author, simply because the first protester, through his unity as an individual, realises this unity for everyone in transcendence (*la transcendance*). Moreover, it will remain a profound contradiction in everyone, because this unity is that of all the Others (including himself) as Others and by an Other: the protester was not revealing or expressing popular opinion; rather, he was expressing, in the objective unity of a direct action (shouts, insults, etc.), what still existed for everyone only as the opinion of the Others, that is to say, as their shifting, serial unity. But once the scandal has been reported and discussed, it becomes, in the eyes of those who did not witness it, a synthetic event which gave the audience which saw the play that night a temporary unity as an organism. Everything becomes clear if we situate the non-grouped who discover themselves to be a collective through their impotence in relation to the group which they reveal.

...... ● ......

vi **THE FRENCH PSYCHOANALYST** and philosopher Jacques Lacan reinterpreted Sigmund Freud for the twentieth century, using his insights not only for clinical treatment, but also as a method to be applied more widely as a critical tool inside structuralism, to study how language operates in literature, culture and politics (*see also* DREAMS iv). Here he discusses desire in the context of transference, in which a client of a psychoanalyst redirects emotions to a substitute, the psychoanalyst:

The necessary and sufficient reason for the repetitive insistence of these desires in the transferrance and their permanent remembrance in a signifier that repression has appropriated – that is, in which the repressed returns – is found if one accepts the idea that in the determinations the desire for recognition dominates the desire that is to be recognized, preserving it as such until it is recognized.

...... ● ......

vii THE FRENCH POST-STRUCTURALIST Jacques Derrida (*see also* CONSCIOUSNESS vi) set out in his book *Of Grammatology* to explore the 'condition of all linguistic systems'. Below is an example of what that exploration yielded:

> It is because arche-writing, movement of differance, irreducible arche-synthesis, opening in one and the same possibility, temporalization as well as relationship with the other and language, cannot, as the condition of all linguistic systems, form a part of the linguistic system itself and be situated as an object in its field. (Which does not mean it has a real field *elsewhere*, *another* assignable *site*.) Its concept could in no way enrich the scientific, positive and 'immanent' (in the Hjelmslevian* sense) description of the system itself.

...... ● ......

viii THE FRENCH POST-STRUCTURALIST Jean Baudrillard was a Marxist who rejected the profit motive of capitalism. In *Symbolic Exchange and Death* (1976) he develops the idea of hyperreality – a modern condition of our consciousness in which fact and fiction are so blended together we can hardly tell one from the other. This idea would seem an ideal candidate for clear exposition using ordinary language. But what Baudrillard writes is:

> Hyperrealism is only beyond representation because it functions entirely within the realm of simulation. There, the whirligig of representation goes mad, but with an implosive

---

* Louis Trolle Hjelmslev was a Danish scholar and a member of the Copenhagen School, a centre of linguistic structuralism in the mid-twentieth century.

insanity which, far from being ex-centric, casts longing eyes at the centre, toward its own repetition en abîme. Like the distancing effect within a dream, which tells one that one is dreaming, but only in [sic] behalf of the censor, in order that we continue dreaming, hyperrealism is an integral part of a coded reality, which it perpetuates with modifying.

...... ● ......

ix **THE AMERICAN CRITICAL THEORIST** Frederic Jameson sets out to analyse Honoré de Balzac's use of the omniscient narrator device:

The constitutive feature of the Balzacian narrative apparatus, however, is something more fundamental than either authorial omniscience or authorial intervention, something that may be designated as libidinal investment or authorial wish-fulfillment, a form of symbolic satisfaction in which the working distinction between biographical subject, Implied Author, reader, and characters is virtually effaced. Description is one privileged moment in which small investments may be detected and studied, particularly when the object of the description, as in the following evocation of a provincial townhouse, is contested, and focuses antagonistic ambitions within the narrative itself.

...... ● ......

x IT HAS THUS become apparent that physical 'reality', no less than social 'reality', is at bottom a social and linguistic construct; that scientific 'knowledge', far from being objective, reflects and encodes the dominant ideologies and power relations of the culture that produced it; that the truth claims of science are inherently theory-laden and self-referential; and consequently, that the discourse of the scientific community, for all its undeniable value, cannot assert a privileged epistemological status with respect to counter-hegemonic narratives emanating from dissident or marginalized communities.

We have by now come to accept that this is the sort of verbiage we can expect from some of the most celebrated philosophers from Kant to Derrida. And some of us might wonder, 'what does it really mean?' Absolutely nothing, says the American physics professor Alan Sokal, who wrote the above in an article titled 'Transgressing the Boundaries: Towards a Transformative Hermeneutics of Quantum Gravity', published in the peer-reviewed academic journal *Social Text* in 1996.* The article has since come to be known as 'Sokal's Hoax'. His intention was to prove that what passes for academic writing is often egregious nonsense. He succeeded.

---

* No. 46/47, pp. 217–52 (Spring/Summer 1996). A peer-reviewed journal is one in which a committee of one's academic peers reviews an article for accuracy and absence of plagiarism.

NATURE FORMED YOU WITH THE SAME **SPIRIT**, THE SAME **REASON**, THE SAME **VIRTUES**

Seeing her made me WONDER *and ask questions about her* COLOUR

CHAPTER THIRTY-TWO
RACISM

FAIR KINGS *do not want any* SLAVES

THEY CALLED THOSE PEOPLE **BRUTES** *CURSED BY HEAVEN*

i   **WHAT IS OUR JUDGEMENT** of the intellectual attainment
and general character of someone who writes:

> I am apt to suspect the negroes and in general all other spe-
> cies of men (for there are four or five different kinds) to be
> naturally inferior to the whites. There never was a civilized
> nation of any other complexion than white, nor even any
> individual eminent either in action or speculation. No ingen-
> ious manufactures amongst them, no arts, no sciences.

Or:

> The Negroes of Africa have by nature no feeling that rises
> above the trifling. Mr. Hume challenges anyone to cite a sin-
> gle example in which a Negro has shown talents, and asserts
> that among the hundreds of thousands of blacks who are
> transported elsewhere from their countries, although many
> of them have even been set free, still not a single one was
> ever found who presented anything great in art or science
> or any other praiseworthy quality, even though among the
> whites some continually rise aloft from the lowest rabble,
> and through superior gifts earn respect in the world. So fun-
> damental is the difference between these two races of man,
> and it appears to be as great in regard to mental capacities
> as in colour... The blacks are very vain but in the Negro's way,
> and so talkative that they must be driven apart from each
> other with thrashings.

These might be considered the words of a racist thug, a white
supremacist. The first quotation is from David Hume, in a foot-
note to the 1753 edition of his essay 'Of National Characters'

(1748); the second is from Immanuel Kant's *Observations on the Feeling of the Beautiful and Sublime* (1764).

Were Hume and Kant 'racists'? Would it be an error to call them 'white supremacists'? The evidence is incontrovertible. Given their indisputable contributions to Western thought, what can be said in their defence? Perhaps that they represented the prevailing opinion of the time? That everyone 'thought' 'that way'? Would that get them off the hook?

Not really. France boasts two exceptions to the 'prevailing thought' defence: Olympe de Gouges, playwright and feminist; and the Marquis de Condorcet, political philosopher and mathematician.

In 1781 Condorcet published the pamphlet 'Reflections on Negro Slavery', in which he addresses the entire black race:

My Friends,

Although I am not the same colour as you, I have always regarded you as my brothers. Nature formed you with the same spirit, the same reason, the same virtues as whites.

Seven years later, de Gouges offered further evidence of a contemporary exception to the racism of Hume and Kant. In December 1789 de Gouges' anti-slavery play *L'Esclavage de Nègres, ou l'Heureux naufrage* ('Black Slavery, or the Fortunate Shipwreck'), was performed at the Comédie-Française.* It ran for only three performances. In February 1788 de Gouges had published an essay 'Réflexions sur les hommes nègres' ('Reflections on the negroes') in which she said:

---

* The play was written in 1784. Its original title was *Zamore et Mirza*.

I have always been interested in the deplorable fate of the Negro race. I was just beginning to develop an understanding of the world, at that age when children hardly think about anything, when I saw a Negress for the first time. Seeing her made me wonder and ask questions about her colour. People I asked did not satisfy my curiosity and my reason. They called those people brutes, cursed by Heaven. As I grew up, I clearly realized that it was force and prejudice that had condemned them to that horrible slavery, in which Nature plays no role, and for which the unjust and powerful interests of Whites are alone responsible.

In contrast to Hume and Kant, de Gouges was of the opinion that 'People are equal everywhere. Fair kings do not want any slaves.'

In August 1789 the National Constituent Assembly passed the defining document of the French Revolution, *The Declaration of the Rights of Man and of the Citizen*. Noting the lack of women's rights in the declaration, de Gouges published in 1791 her *Declaration of the Rights of Woman and the Female Citizen*. As the revolution gained steam de Gouges became increasingly critical of it. She was arrested and held for three months before being sentenced to death on 2 November 1793. She was executed by guillotine the next day.

A warrant for Condorcet's arrest was issued in October 1793. He went into hiding. On 25 March 1794 he attempted to leave Paris, but was arrested two days later. On his second day in prison, he was found dead in his cell. Opinion differs as to whether he took his own life with poison given him by a friend, or was murdered.

ii **WHILE THE PRE-SOCRATIC GREEKS** were busy inventing Western philosophy in the sixth century BC, the multi-authored Upanishads were being composed on the Indian subcontinent. The Upanishads explore ideas central to the development of Hinduism, Buddhism and Jainism, and lay the groundwork for the Vedanta and Samkhya philosophies. These texts, composed by men and women of colour, have largely been ignored by Western thinkers. An exception was the German Arthur Schopenhauer, who studied the Upanishads daily. Rejecting the racism of Hume and Kant, Schopenhauer wrote in 1851: 'The highest civilization and culture, apart from the ancient Hindus and Egyptians, are found exclusively among the white races.' Schopenhauer found the idea of white supremacy absurd. He said that Adam, the first man, was black. Therefore:

> Since Jehovah created him in his own image, then he too should be depicted as black in works of art, although one can leave him the traditional white beard since the thin beard depends not on the black colour but merely on the Ethiopian race. Indeed, the oldest images of the Madonna and Christ child, those found in the Levant and even in a few ancient Italian churches, have a dark complexion. In fact the whole chosen people of God was black or certainly brown and is still now darker than we who stem from pagan tribes that immigrated earlier... That the white complexion is a degeneration and unnatural is evidenced by the disgust and repugnance it evinced in some peoples of the African interior when they first saw it.

...... ● ......

iii **IN 1929,** at the age of fifty-seven, Bertrand Russell wrote in *Marriage and Morals*:

> In extreme cases, there can be little doubt of the superiority of one race to another. North America, Australia and New Zealand certainly contribute more to the civilisation of the world than they would do if they were still peopled by aborigines. It seems on the whole fair to regard Negroes as on the average inferior to white men, although for work in the tropics they are indispensable, so that their extermination (apart from the question of humanity) would be highly undesirable.

Twenty-two years later, the seventy-nine-year-old sage reflected in *New Hopes for a Changing World*: 'It is sometimes maintained that racial mixture is biologically undesirable. There is no evidence whatever for this view. Nor is there, apparently, any reason to think that Negroes are congenitally less intelligent than white people, but as to that it will be difficult to judge until they have equal scope and equally good social conditions.'

...... ● ......

iv **UNIVERSITIES BECOME** more diverse every year. Yet a recent survey shows that blacks account for 1.32 per cent of the total number of people professionally affiliated as graduate students or faculty in United States philosophy departments. Blacks make up 0.88 per cent of PhD students and 4.3 per cent of tenured philosophy professors are black.

The figures for the United Kingdom are even lower. The

government Higher Education Statistics Agency figures for 2011 show that of 14,385 British professors (across all disciplines), only fifty are black – that is, 0.4 per cent.

The frenzy **GRIPPED** *me and I* **SURRENDERED** *myself entirely to lust*

— THERE — GOES A *GREAT* MIND **RUINED** BY *SEX*

CHAPTER THIRTY-THREE

— NOTHING —
SHAMES
A MAN **MORE** THAN TO BE SEEN BY HIS **BELOVED** COMMITTING AN **INGLORIOUS** ACT

The THOUGHT *of it is so* REVOLTING

POLYMORPHOUSLY *PERVERSE*

i   **THE AUSTRIAN** physician and father of psychoanalysis Sigmund Freud (*see also* DREAMS iv) disturbed late nineteenth-century Western civilization with his suggestion that everything depends upon sex. Our childhood formation, our motives as adults, our behaviour in every sphere, said Freud, boils down to this one urge.

More alarmingly Freud proposed that we are all born 'polymorphously perverse'. At birth, he argues, our sexuality recognizes no socially or religiously imposed rules. We are bisexual, homosexual, heterosexual, incestuous by nature. He proposed three stages of human sexual development – anal, oral and phallic – that occur between birth and the age of five, after which our sexuality falls in line with social expectations. Or not.

...... ● ......

ii   **A GREEK** from the fifth century BC would agree with Freud and blink in astonishment at the medieval and modern obsession with demonizing sex that is not heterosexual and confined to Christian marriage. The ancient Greeks did not have words to denote 'heterosexual', 'homosexual' or 'bisexual'. In ancient Greece, one loved beauty, in things and people. The gender of a person was not relevant to a discussion about sex unless the purpose of the union was procreation. Male same-sex love was part of the fabric of most ancient Greek society. Typically, same-sex relations fell under the heading of what is now criminalized as pederasty. It was common for a young freeman to choose a boy between twelve and seventeen (or when facial hair appeared) and engage him in a courtship ritual. The dominant, older man (the *erastes*, or lover) would share knowledge and contacts with his *eromenos* (beloved). In sex, the *erastes*

would take the dominant role, the *eromenos* the passive role.
Freemen were generally not to assume the passive role in sexual
intercourse after reaching manhood.

...... • ......

iii **THE STEREOTYPICAL IMAGE** of homosexual men
as effeminate is contradicted in the fourth century BC by the
Sacred Band of Thebes, an army troop comprised of 150 pairs
of male lovers. It was an elite unit that excelled in the Battle
of Leuctra (371 BC), which shattered the power of Sparta; but
the historian Plutarch reports that all 300 of the Sacred Band
were slaughtered by Philip II of Macedon, father of Alexander
the Great, in the Battle of Chaeronea (338 BC). In Plato's
Symposium (*c*.385–370 BC) Phaedrus argued on behalf of the
Sacred Band that Eros, oldest of the gods, inspired each of
the paired male lovers to excel on the battlefield by demon-
strating his bravery in an attempt to win further admiration
from the beloved. 'Nothing shames a man more than to be seen
by his beloved committing an inglorious act,' says Phaedrus.
'A handful of such men, fighting side by side, would defeat
practically the whole world.'

...... • ......

iv **EPICURUS**, whose philosophy counselled happiness, even
pleasure (to be attained by the absence of fear and pain), was
asked by a correspondent for advice about how to deal with
a persistent desire for sexual intercourse. Epicurus replied:

I learn from your letter that carnal disturbances make you

excessively inclined to sexual intercourse. Well, so long as
you do not break any laws or disturb well-established conventions or annoy any of your neighbours or wear down your
body or use up your funds, you may carry out your own plans
as you like. However, it is impossible not to be affected by at
least one of these things. Sex never benefited any man, and
it's a marvel if it hasn't injured him!

...... ● ......

v 'THE FRENZY GRIPPED ME and I surrendered myself
   entirely to lust... I was tossed and spilled, floundering in the
   broiling sea of... fornication.' Not a lurid sex novel, but Saint
   Augustine in his *Confessions*. In contrast to the sexual freedom
   of ancient Greece the medieval Church prohibited sex except
   in certain circumstances: it must be heterosexual, within marriage and practised only for the purpose of procreation. The
   fornicator of Hippo embraced chastity with the zeal of a convert, even abjuring sex within marriage (of which he did not
   approve): 'I have decided that there is nothing I should avoid
   so much as marriage. I know nothing which brings the manly
   mind down from the heights more than a woman's caresses
   and that joining of bodies without which one cannot have a
   wife.' *See also* MELANCHOLY v.

...... ● ......

vi IMMANUEL KANT, in his *Lectures on Ethics*: 'The desire
   which a man has for a woman is not directed towards her
   because she is a human being, but because she is a woman; that
   she is a human being is of no concern to the man; only her sex

is the object of his desires. Human nature is thus subordinated.'

Kant shares the view of the Church that sex between a man and a woman without the aim of procreation is evil. Kant's reasoning is that

> each of them dishonours the human nature of the other. They make of humanity an instrument for the satisfaction of their lusts and inclinations, and dishonour it by placing it on a level with animal nature. Sexuality, therefore, exposes mankind to the danger of equality with the beasts.

...... ● ......

vii **A GEOMETRY CLASS** conducted by the founder of modern political philosophy would appear, on the face of it, to be an unusual context in which to engage in a session of forthright self-abuse. In an unpublished work, John Aubrey, better known for his sequence of affectionate and influential Restoration pen-portraits entitled *Brief Lives* (1680–93, first published 1813) relates an unsavoury episode from the 1640s recounted to him by the distinguished thinker Thomas Hobbes:

> Mr Hobbes told me that G., Duke of Buckingham at Paris... desired him to read geometry. Mr. Hobbes read geometry, and his Grace did not apprehend, which Mr. Hobbes wondered at. At length Mr. Hobbes observed that his Grace was at masturbation – his hand in his codpiece. This is a very improper age at that reason for learning.

The misbehaving student was the teenaged George Villiers, 2nd Duke of Buckingham, later to find fame as a Restoration

rake and as a member of the 'cabal' of high councillors of King
Charles II in the late 1660s.

Some two and half centuries later, the eleven-year-old
Bertrand Russell was introduced to the works of the Greek
mathematician Euclid (*see also* TRUTH iii), so-called 'father of
geometry', by his brother Frank. Russell, who would endure
a lonely adolescence, found the pull of masturbation as hard
to resist as George Villiers, though there is no evidence that
his – apparently compulsive – onanism formed an accompani-
ment to his reflections on conical sections and the congruence
of triangles. The sheer rigour of Euclidean geometry did, however, leave an enduring mark on Russell, who went on to read
for the Mathematical Tripos at Trinity College, Cambridge,
gaining first-class honours as a 'wrangler' in 1893 and becoming a fellow just two years later. His first mathematical book,
An Essay on the Foundations of Geometry, was published in
1897, and showed the influence of Immanuel Kant. Kant had
claimed, in *The Critique of Pure Reason* (1781; 1787), that
elementary mathematics, like arithmetic, is synthetic a priori,
but in his *Metaphysics of Morals* (1797) the Prussian philosopher turned his fire on the evils of masturbation: 'That such
an unnatural use (and so misuse) of one's sexual attributes is a
violation of one's duty to himself and is certainly in the highest
degree opposed to morality strikes everyone upon his thinking
of it. Furthermore, the thought of it is so revolting that even
calling such a vice by its proper name is considered a kind of
immorality...'

Kant would, one imagines, have been disgusted by the conduct of the young Austrian who turned up unannounced at
Russell's rooms at Trinity in October 1911, and who would
become Russell's philosophical protégé. Ludwig Wittgenstein,

author of the *Tractatus Logico-Philosophicus* and icon of twentieth-century analytic philosophy, reports in his diary that he was a chronic masturbator, indulging in the practice as many as eight times a day. *See also* BACKBITING iii.

...... ● ......

viii BERTRAND RUSSELL soon outgrew his onanistic tendencies and turned his attention to women. He had four wives and was widely known as a philanderer. His mistresses included Lady Ottoline Morrell, who stopped sleeping with him because of his foul breath.

Perhaps the greatest philanderer in British philosophy was the logical positivist A. J. Ayer, Grote Professor of the Philosophy of Mind and Logic at University College London and then Wykeham Professor of Logic at Oxford. A colleague there is alleged to have remarked, 'There goes a great mind ruined by sex.'

The sexual antics of Russell and Ayer were a matter of public gossip because of their status: Russell was the first British philosophy superstar of the twentieth century; Ayer was the second, eclipsing Russell.

...... ● ......

ix RUSSELL AND AYER were notoriously contemptuous of the French existentialists Jean-Paul Sartre and Simone de Beauvoir, who enjoyed even greater superstar status. The couple were known for a lifelong love affair that allowed 'contingent loves' (i.e. sex with other people). Beauvoir's great 'other' love was the American crime novelist Nelson Algren; Sartre's lovers, too numerous to mention, included schoolgirls and a Soviet 'translator' (spy).

What marked their promiscuity was their taste for under-age female pupils. Sartre and Beauvoir regularly had sex with selected lycée students (usually de Beauvoir first, then Sartre and others of their group). De Beauvoir was banned from teaching in 1941 after a student's mother complained to the authorities. Both of them were among the sixty-nine signatories of a letter to *Le Monde* dated 26 January 1977 supporting abolition of the age of consent (other prominent French intellectuals who signed the letter included Roland Barthes, Gilles Deleuze, Félix Guattari, Jean-François Lyotard and the future minister of education Jack Lang).

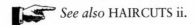 *See also* HAIRCUTS ii.

PHILOSOPHY — IS A — **COMBATIVE** SPORT

INTERNATIONAL sporting contests lead to ——— **ORGIES of** ——— **HATRED**

SPORT may show the MAN who HAS and who HAS NOT *COURAGE*

CHAPTER THIRTY-FOUR

SPORT

HE KNEW THAT THOSE WHO KNEW *nothing of* *FOOTBALL* KNEW NOTHING OF *LIFE*

The **COMMONALITIES** between

· *BOXING* ·

and **PHILOSOPHY** are **MANY**

i   **IN NOVEMBER 1945,** during the first months of the Cold
War, the Soviet football team Moscow Dynamo visited the UK
for a series of friendly matches against British clubs. In the
aftermath of their tour, the essayist and novelist George Orwell
wrote: 'I am always amazed when I hear people saying that
sport creates goodwill between the nations, and that if only
the common peoples of the world could meet one another at
football or cricket, they would have no inclination to meet on
the battlefield.' Orwell was amazed by this sentiment because,
in his view, 'international sporting contests lead to orgies of
hatred'. 'At the international level,' Orwell wrote, 'sport is
frankly mimic warfare.' Orwell disliked the competitive nature
of international sport because it required one side to be victori-
ous, the other to lose face and the flames of rivalry constantly
to be stoked.

It was for precisely these reasons that Plato saw sport as an
essential part of the curriculum and as a national duty. In his
last dialogue *Laws* (348 BC), he advocated that soldiers

> shall have contests one with another in every part of the
> country, seizing upon posts and lying in ambush, and imitat-
> ing in every respect the reality of war; fighting with boxing-
> gloves and hurling javelins, and using weapons somewhat
> dangerous, and as nearly as possible like the true ones, in
> order that the sport may not be altogether without fear, but
> may have terrors and to a certain degree show the man who
> has and who has not courage.

In these 'contests' Plato did not mind if death occurred from
time to time. 'If anyone dies in these mimic contests, the homicide is involuntary, and we will make the slayer, when he has

been purified according to law, to be pure of blood, considering that if a few men should die, others as good as they will be born; but that if fear is dead, then the citizens will never find a test of superior and inferior natures, which is a far greater evil to the state than the loss of a few.' So, for Plato, sport was a deadly serious business of the type that Orwell feared.

...... ● ......

ii **IN *LAWS*,** Plato has an Athenian remark that watching sport keeps the spark of youth alive in older persons:

> Our young men break forth into dancing and singing, and we who are their elders deem that we are fulfilling our part in life when we look on at them. Having lost our agility, we delight in their sports and merry-making, because we love to think of our former selves; and gladly institute contests for those who are able to awaken in us the memory of our youth.

...... ● ......

iii **IN THE SECOND CENTURY AD** Lucian of Samosata (*see* EXTRATERRESTRIALS vii) produced a dialogue called *Anacharsis*, an imaginary conversation between Solon, a reforming Greek statesman of the sixth century BC, and the Scythian* 'barbarian' Anacharsis. The dialogue shows Solon explaining and defending athletic contests as a useful and important institution. Anacharsis remarks:

---

* Scythia was an area of central Eurasia east of the Black Sea.

Why do your young men behave like this, Solon? Some of
them grappling and tripping each other, some throttling,
struggling, intertwining in the clay like so many pigs wallowing. And yet their first proceeding after they have stripped
– I noticed that – is to oil and scrape each other quite ami-
cably; but then I do not know what comes over them – they
put down their heads and begin to push, and crash their fore-
heads together like a pair of rival rams. There, look! that one
has lifted the other right off his legs, and dropped him on
the ground; now he has fallen on top, and will not let him
get his head up, but presses it down into the clay; and to
finish him off he twines his legs tight round his belly, thrusts
his elbow hard against his throat, and throttles the wretched
victim, who meanwhile is patting his shoulder; that will be a
form of supplication; he is asking not to be quite choked to
death... Now I want to know what is the good of it all. To me
it looks more like madness than anything else. It will not be
very easy to convince me that people who behave like this
are not wrong in their heads.

Solon replies: 'Be reassured, my dear sir; these proceedings are
not madness; it is no spirit of violence that sets them hitting
each other, wallowing in clay, and sprinkling dust. The thing
has its use, and its delight too, resulting in admirable physical
condition.'

Late in the dialogue, Solon goes on to speak of the wider
socio-political benefits of sporting contests:

It seems, Anacharsis, that you have never yet done any
thinking about the proper way to direct a state; otherwise
you would not disparage the best of institutions. If ever you

make it your object to find out how a state is to be organized
in the best way possible, and how its citizens are to reach the
highest degree of excellence, you will then praise these exer-
cises and the rivalry which we display in regard to them, and
champions would have taken advantage of the offer. You will
know that they have much that is useful intermingled with
the hardships, even if you think our energy is spent on them
for nothing.

...... ● ......

iv ONE OF THE LEADING contemporary philosophers of
sport is Gordon Marino, a Kierkegaard scholar who is also
a boxer. For Marino, boxing teaches composure in the face
of fear, providing an important life lesson. He also argues
that 'The commonalities between boxing and philosophy are
many.' For instance, he argues, 'philosophy is a combative
sport. Arguments or reading of texts that you might have spent
years working on are probed and tested by colleagues who are
not always friendly. I have often joked that I would prefer a
punch in the snoot to some of the shots that you can take when
you deliver a paper at a conference.' For Marino, boxing is
a type of Socratic 'non-narcissistic self-examination'. It 'is a
great vehicle of self-knowledge. In the ring, you soon come
to know your anger and your fear, as well as how far you are
willing to go in your effort to succeed.' Marino cites a moral
purpose in boxing that goes beyond the individual's mastery
of himself. He uses boxing as a metaphor to criticize what he
sees in American culture as the widespread failure to teach the
young how to 'modulate' their emotions. 'Americans', he says,
'for the most part live in a culture of release in which passion

and spontaneity are worshipped. Beyond being told that troublesome feelings are medical problems, our young people receive scant instruction in modulating their emotions. As a result, there are very few opportunities to spar with heavyweight emotions such as anger and fear.'

From Marino's perspective, the sport of boxing can instil positive values in the individual which, collectively, improve the nation. Marino's fellow American philosopher of sport William Morgan sees present-day sport as evidence of moral decline. Following the Scottish-born ethicist Alasdair MacIntyre whose *After Virtue* (1984) influences much thinking in the philosophy of sport, Morgan says that MacIntyre 'famously claimed that every moral theory and scheme of moral beliefs presupposes a sociology'. In Morgan's view, 'the present sociology that informs morality in contemporary America imperils the moral life, indeed, makes it difficult for people even to think in moral terms. And I argue that this story of the decline of moral life is writ large in contemporary American sports.' For Morgan, sports 'are no mere reflection of larger society's growing indifference to moral considerations but, in part because of their prominent standing in contemporary society, both a conspicuous exemplification of such moral callousness and important sign of things to come'. Against Plato's praise of sport and its role in helping form the moral backbone of a nation, Morgan sees contemporary sports with their cheating, doping and abuse scandals as 'an attack on the moral life'. He thinks criticism of sport is an urgent task for philosophy because in American sports there is 'a war on the moral life waged within their precincts', and 'the stories that we Americans tell about ourselves would lose much of their resonance, their capacity to unite and move us, if moral considerations no longer figured in them'.

v **ALBERT CAMUS** was an enthusiastic footballer in his youth. As a teenager he was goalkeeper for the Racing Universitaire Algerios (RUA) junior team. Reflecting on that experience in a piece he wrote for his old university magazine in 1948 (by which time he was an established novelist and star in the French literary firmament), he wrote: 'After many years during which I saw many things, what I know most surely about morality and the duty of man I owe to sport and learned it in the RUA.'

Camus' words have generally been interpreted as a form of homage to football, a celebration, perhaps, of the collaborative, selfless virtues of interpassing; of the value of resilience and fortitude, of trying one's hardest until the final whistle blows. But if one probes a little deeper into Camus' article one finds the following: 'I learned that a ball never arrives from a direction you expected it. That helped me in later life, especially in mainland France, where nobody plays straight.' So there is wariness in Camus' words – an alertness to the game's potential for deceit as well as heroism. Camus was a good player, and might have turned professional if he had not contracted tuberculosis when he was seventeen. Football's loss was literature's gain.

...... ● ......

vi **JACQUES DERRIDA** (*see* OBFUSCATION vii), another star of French philosophy born in Algeria, also loved football. Derrida played for the same team as Camus, Racing Universitaire Algerios. He loved football more than his studies:

My passion for sport in general and football in particular dates back to the time when going to school meant heading

off with a pair of football boots in your satchel. I had a real fetish [*culte*] for those boots. I waxed them and took better care of them than of my exercise books. Football, running, baseball (taught us by the Americans), matches against the Italian POWs, this is what kept us busy; our education was much less important.

The Canadian law professor Allan C. Hutchinson views Derrida as 'a frustrated man of action' for whom 'the philosophical life was only a consolation for a more fulfilled life as sporting hero':

It is as a footballer of attacking flair, not as an intellectual of defensive legend, that I will remember Derrida best. While it is hard to imagine the suave Derrida in the garishly-coloured synthetic shirt of his favourite team with a number '7' and 'Derrida' emblazoned on the back, there is a genuine excitement at the prospect of him tantalising and tormenting the opposition in his own version of 'the beautiful game'. He knew that those who knew nothing of football knew nothing of life.

...... ● ......

vii **C. L. R. JAMES,** a Trinidad-born Marxist, social theorist and historian, wrote what many consider to be the best book on cricket, the semi-autobiographical *Beyond a Boundary* (1963), which poses the question: 'What do they know of cricket who only cricket know?' Like Plato and Solon, James recognized that the significance of sport goes beyond mere entertainment. He observes: 'the Greeks were the most politically minded and intellectually and artistically the most creative of all peoples. It is surprising to find that they hero-worshipped the athletes to a degree which would shock our modern seekers after autographs. To our hypocritical "only a game" they would have replied with scorn and quick anger.'

Cricket, he argues, raises fascinating philosophical issues regarding the individual and the group:

> two individuals are pitted against each other in a conflict that is strictly personal but no less strictly representative of a social group. One individual batsmen faces an individual bowler. But each represents his side. The personal achievement may be of the utmost competence or brilliance. Its ultimate value is whether it assists the side to victory or staves off defeat. This has nothing to do with morals. It is the organisational structure on which the entire spectacle is built... the batsman facing the ball does not merely represent his side. For that moment, to all intents and purposes, he is his side. The fundamental relations of the One and the Many, Individual and Social, Individual and Universal, leader and followers, representatives and ranks, the part and the whole, is structurally imposed on the players of cricket.

...... ● ......

viii FOOTBALL IS NOT JUST ABOUT fit young men with fancy haircuts. In 2013, the Italian midfielder Andrea Pirlo, who was instrumental in his country's victory in the 2006 FIFA World Cup final, published an autobiography with the Cartesian-sounding title, *Penso Quindi Gioco* ('I Think, Therefore I Play'). However, the 'philosopher' with whom Pirlo seems most impressed is not Descartes but Pep Guardiola, who managed Barcelona between 2008 and 2012, and who in 2010 made an unsuccessful attempt to sign Pirlo from AC Milan. It was the combustible Barcelona striker Zlatan Ibrahimović, a Swede of Bosnian extraction, who had originally dubbed Guardiola 'the philosopher', in a crude attempt to insult the refined, thoughtful – and widely admired – Catalan coach. But Pirlo interpreted the word in rather more complimentary terms than Ibrahimović:

> Being a philosopher is to think, seek wisdom and have principles that guide and influence what you do. It's to give meaning to things, find your way in the world, believe that in the end, in every instance, good will overcome evil even if there's a bit of suffering along the way. Guardiola has taken all that and applied it to football, an imperfect science. He racked his brains and dispersed the fog, more through hard work than mere thought. What he's achieved hasn't been about miracles, rather a gentle programming of his players. His style is crèma catalana – easily digestible. It's virtual reality mixed with real life; a swim between the shores of fantasy and reality...

In selecting a title for his own autobiography (also published in 2013), Ibrahimović spurned the aphoristic probing of Pirlo for a less reflective statement on the self: *I am Zlatan* was his choice. None of the great philosophers has – overtly at least – espoused solipsism (this being the view or theory that the self is all that can be known to exist). It might be argued, however, that Descartes' account of the nature of mind is conducive to the development of solipsistic patterns of thought, the ego revealed by Descartes' cogito being a solitary consciousness, which is not necessarily located in any body, and can be assured of its own existence exclusively as a conscious mind.

In 2013, the then Queens Park Rangers midfielder Joey Barton, whose career has been marked by a number of controversial incidents and disciplinary problems (including a six-month prison sentence for common assault), began a part-time philosophy degree at Roehampton University in south-west London. He commented in December 2014: 'I carry a bag of books around with me at all times. I'm reading Machiavelli's *The Prince*. All the stuff in class at the moment is about dualism, materialism and Epicurus' Letter to Menoeceus.'

REASON IS THE DISCOVERY OF **TRUTH** or **FALSEHOOD**

WE ARE TOO WEAK TO DISCOVER **THE TRUTH** BY **REASON** ALONE

CHAPTER THIRTY-FIVE

TRUTH

To say that that which is, is and that which is NOT *is* NOT, *is* TRUE

TRUTHS are so close to the MIND, as soon as you OPEN your eyes you will SEE them

I AM *what* I AM

i 'GOD CREATED THE WORLD in six days around six thousand years ago' and 'Iraq possesses/possessed weapons of mass destruction' are examples of statements held to be true by many people. Both are patently false. How do we know? In the first example, unquestionable and verifiable scientific data tell us our solar system is around 14.6 billion years old. In the second example, the US authorities who promulgated the untruth have been revealed as liars. The invasion of Iraq in 2003 – predicated on that lie – proved that the country had no weapons of mass destruction. The cost of believing the myth of creationism is to accommodate a society of wilfully stupid persons who cannot differentiate between fact and fiction, making them woefully ill qualified for the burden of responsibility that citizenship places upon them. The cost of the invasion of Iraq in 2003 is more than half a million dead Iraqis and a terrorist recruitment gift that exceeded their wildest dreams.

'Truth' has a claim to being the prime object of philosophy, yet philosophers have never reached an absolute agreement about what truth is, or even how to go about looking for it. If they did agree, philosophy probably would have gone out of business a long time ago.

The above statements about the age of our planet (the 'world') and the existence of weapons of mass destruction are made with language. Language is a tricky thing: it is our main means of communicating with one other, but the meaning of what is said with it is often open to interpretation. Mathematics, on the other hand, lays claim to being a universal 'language'. It is composed of non-emotive figures, symbols and characters used to denote a state of affairs that is evident to anyone, anywhere, irrespective of what language they speak, who knows how to interpret them. Both means are employed in the search for truth. *See also* BELIEF i; GOD i; INTUITION i.

...... • ......

ii **FOR PLATO,** truth is what corresponds with the reality around us. Hence, the judgement 'the sky is blue on a sunny day' is incontrovertibly true for Plato (and for the majority of us). The statement corresponds with an actual state of affairs, hence the 'correspondence theory' of truth. Aristotle put it like this in his *Metaphysics*: 'To say that [either] that which is, is not or that which is not is, is a falsehood; and to say that that which is, is and that which is not is not, is true.' Or, as the cartoon character Popeye says, 'I am what I am'.*

...... • ......

iii **THE GREEK MATHEMATICIAN EUCLID** found a way to establish certain irrefutable truths using geometric proofs instead of language. The beauty of his proofs is that, once posed, they are self-evident and do not rely on the translation problems associated with language for their communication. Euclid's five postulates are:

1. A straight line segment can be drawn joining any two points.
2. Any straight line segment can be extended indefinitely in a straight line.

---

* When Moses asked God who he was, God replied: 'I am that I am'. Exodus 3:4, King James Version.

3. Given any straight lines segment, a circle can be drawn having the segment as radius and one endpoint as centre.

4. All right angles are congruent.*

5. If two lines are drawn which intersect a third in such a way that the sum of the inner angles on one side is less than two Right Angles, then the two lines inevitably must intersect each other on that side if extended far enough. This postulate is equivalent to what is known as the Parallel Postulate.

Each of these postulates can be illustrated with a pencil, ruler and compass. Euclid's uncovering of self-evident truth and the means of its expression helped set the stage for mathematically-inclined truth seekers like the twentieth-century British philosopher Bertrand Russell.

Euclid established the concept of 'public truth' (as opposed to the idea of 'private truth' which might arise from arguments about the same subject conducted by multiple participants. 'Euclid's assumptions', however, 'are not intended to be granted by you or me or any other particular person; they are intended to be universally acceptable. Likewise, the steps of Euclid's proofs are not intended to convince any particular person; they are intended to be beyond anyone's reproach.' *See also* SEX vii.

...... ● ......

iv **THAT SELF-EVIDENT** truth is the best kind – assuming for the moment that more than one type of truth exists – was an assumption held by the founding fathers of the United States when they wrote in that country's constitution: 'We hold these

---

* That is, they coincide exactly when superimposed.

truths to be self-evident, that all men are created equal, that they are endowed by their Creator with certain unalienable Rights, that among these are Life, Liberty and the pursuit of Happiness.' But the founding fathers move way beyond the genuine irrefutability of Euclidian postulates with a series of propositions over which they wave the self-evident wand. The chief problem that arises from this is the problem of God ('the Creator', who is assumed to exist). Introducing God moves the conversation to the realm of the supernatural.

...... ● ......

v **PHILOSOPHY**, as it developed from the metaphysics and mathematics of ancient Greece, became a naturalistic pursuit. Christian thought, exemplified by scholastic philosophers like Thomas Aquinas, brought with it a series of developments in logic and dialectical reasoning that have endured despite their reliance on a belief in the supernatural. When Aquinas argues that the number of angels that can fit on the point of a needle is infinite, he uses a logical argument that is valid. It does, however, rely on the premise that God and angels exist (*see* GOD iv).

In his *Confessions* (397–400) Augustine of Hippo wrote 'we are too weak to discover the truth by reason alone'. The great twelfth-century scholastic logician Peter Abelard* declared in *Sic et Non* (*Yes and No*, 1121), 'through doubting we are led to inquire, and by inquiry we perceive the truth'. But for Abelard, doubt had boundaries one was not permitted to cross: for the scholastics, all truth was dependent upon belief in God.

---

* The twelfth-century logician is famous for his secret marriage to Héloïse of Argenteuil who bore his child. As punishment Héloïse was sent to a convent by her uncle, and Abelard was castrated by the uncle's henchmen.

vi **SCIENTISTS** like Nicolaus Copernicus, Galileo Galilei and
Isaac Newton were pioneers of a new age of truth ushered in
by the scientific revolution during the sixteenth and seventeenth centuries. The Renaissance (fourteenth to seventeenth
centuries) finds philosophy moving from the medieval to the
modern period with developments in thought which tested the
Church's grip on truth.

  From the twelfth through the nineteenth centuries the Church
instituted a series of tribunals, or inquisitions, whose aim was
to protect the faith against heresy and ideas that challenged
Church teaching. Penalties could be a severe as death (burning
at the stake) or as mild as forbidding Catholics to read the
works of certain thinkers. In 1904 the Inquisition was renamed
the Supreme Sacred Congregation of the Holy Office; in 1965
it was renamed again as the Congregation for the Doctrine of
the Faith.

  In 1543 Copernicus published *On the Revolutions of the
Celestial Spheres* (1543), which argued that the sun is at the
centre of our solar system and that the Earth moves around
it. In 1616 the Roman Inquisition (the Supreme Sacred
Congregation of the Roman and Universal Inquisition) concluded that Copernicus' truth was 'foolish and absurd in
philosophy'. His proposition that the sun was at the centre of
our solar system was judged 'formally heretical'. The fact that
Earth moved around the sun was held to be 'at least erroneous
in faith'. The Roman Inquisition also tried Galileo in 1633. It
stopped just short of calling him a heretic, declaring instead
that he was 'vehemently suspected of heresy'. It banned his
work, *Dialogue Concerning the Two Chief World Systems*,
and sentenced him to house arrest, under which he died. The
Italian philosopher Giordano Bruno was found guilty of heresy

by the Inquisition in 1600 after a trial lasting seven years. He was burned at the stake in Rome's Campo de' Fiori. His crime was to have extrapolated the Copernican model to suggest that the stars were, in fact, suns surrounded by planets, and that those planets might support life. He also proposed that the universe is infinite.

About half of the post-Renaissance philosophers mentioned in this book had their works placed on the Catholic *Index Librorum Prohibitorum*, the papacy's list of forbidden and heretical books. These included Erasmus, Michel Eyquem de Montaigne, Thomas Hobbes, René Descartes, Blaise Pascal, Baruch Spinoza, John Locke, Bishop Berkeley, Voltaire, David Hume, Jean-Jacques Rousseau, Denis Diderot, Immanuel Kant, John Stuart Mill and Jean-Paul Sartre. If the Church had succeeded in its desire to squash the truths published in these works, might we still be living in a world of feudal lords presiding over ignorant peasants, all labouring under a Europe-wide regime based on superstition and lies?

The fact is that truth, once discovered, is impossible to put down.

...... • ......

vii **THE NEW SCIENTIFIC DESCRIPTIONS** of the reality of our situation in the cosmos were given by thinkers who could be described as 'materialists', who believed that matter is the basic substance of the universe. During the eighteenth century the nature of what matter is became the subject of intense philosophical study which led to the position of 'idealism'. Idealists generally hold that what is real is only made so through human perception. The Anglo-Irish George Berkeley, who served as Bishop of Cloyne, developed the philosophy of subjective idealism which challenged the materialist view. In 1710 Berkeley wrote in *The Principles of Human Knowledge*:

> Some truths are so close to the mind, and so obvious, that as soon as you open your eyes you will see them. Here is an important truth of that kind:
>
>> All the choir of heaven and furniture of the earth, in a word all those bodies that compose the mighty structure of the world, have no existence outside a mind; for them to exist is for them to be perceived or known; consequently so long as they aren't actually perceived by (i.e. don't exist in the mind of) myself or any other created spirit, they must either have no existence at all or else exist in the mind of some eternal spirit; because it makes no sense – and involves all the absurdity of abstraction – to attribute to any such thing an existence independent of a spirit.
>
> To be convinced of this, you need only to reflect and try to separate in your own thoughts the existence of a perceptible thing from its being perceived – you'll find that you can't.

In Germany, Immanuel Kant would develop the philosophical position known as transcendental idealism, and after him G. W. F. Hegel and others continued this line of thinking about how we, each through our individual subjectivity, constitute what is true, meaningful and real (as opposed to an independently existing set of objects in the world). *See also* CONSCIOUSNESS iii *and* iv.

viii **BY CONTRAST**, the Scottish philosopher David Hume argued that all our ideas – and therefore our knowledge of truth – come from our sensory experiences of things outside of us. In his *An Enquiry Concerning Human Understanding* (1748) he writes that 'curiosity, or the love of truth', is 'the first source of all our inquiries'. He elaborates: 'Reason is the discovery of truth or falsehood. Truth or falsehood consists in an agreement or disagreement either to the real relations of ideas, or to real existence and matter of fact.' So, as with Plato, the statement 'the sky is blue' describes a true state of affairs. However, Hume also allows that our 'passions, volitions and actions' are 'original facts and realities, complete in themselves'.

With the anti-truth efforts of the Inquisition in mind, along with the problem of deference to received opinion on matters of 'morality', Hume offers this criticism as a guide for those who would pursue truth:

> There is no method of reasoning more common, and yet none more blameable, than, in philosophical disputes, to endeavour the refutation of any hypothesis, by a pretence of its dangerous consequences to religion and morality. When any opinion leads to absurdities, it is certainly false; but it is not certain that an opinion is false, because it is of dangerous consequence. Such topics, therefore, ought entirely to be forborne; as serving nothing to the discovery of truth, but only to make the person of an antagonist odious.

...... ● ......

ix **PART OF THE APPEAL** of mathematical approaches to truth is that the vagaries of religion and metaphysics, with their reliance upon language, do not apply. Mathematicians argue that the logical structure of their approach offers a universal 'language' that is clear and incontrovertible. They are joined by logical positivists whose goal in pursuing truth is to separate the wheat from the chaff, as it were; to distinguish, as A. J. Ayer put it, between sense and non-sense.

In *Language, Truth and Logic* (1936) Ayer dismisses as nonsense all metaphysical arguments because they cannot be verified; they are no more than the results of 'mystical feeling' or grammatical errors:

> although the greater part of metaphysics is merely the embodiment of humdrum errors, there remain a number of metaphysical passages which are the work of genuine mystical feeling; and they may more plausibly he held to have moral or aesthetic value. But, as far as we are concerned, the distinction between the kind of metaphysics that is produced by a philosopher who has been duped by grammar, and the kind that is produced by a mystic who is trying to express the inexpressible, is of no great importance: what is important to us is to realize that even the utterances of the metaphysician who is attempting to expound a vision are literally senseless; so that henceforth we may pursue our philosophical researches with as little regard for them as for the more inglorious kind of metaphysics which comes from a failure to understand the workings of our language.

The approach of Ayer and his fellow logical positivists is to take some of the fun out of philosophy: no more arguments about what is *to be*, for instance. No more discussions about God. The appeal to Ayer's followers is that much of the two-thousand-year-old philosophical agenda could be erased, dissolved – because there was nothing to say about it. Truth was now circumscribed within very narrow, manageable boundaries. *See also* BACKBITING v.

...... ● ......

x **THE AMERICAN PHILOSOPHER** Richard Rorty did much, through candour and common sense, to bridge the gulf between the metaphysicians of continental philosophy and the logicians and positivists of analytic thought. In *Contingency, Irony, and Solidarity* (1989) he wrote: 'Truth cannot be out there – cannot exist independently of the human mind – because sentences cannot so exist, or be out there. The world is out there, but descriptions of the world are not. Only descriptions of the world can be true or false. The world on its own unaided by the describing activities of humans cannot.'

MANY men have got a **GREAT** *name from the* **FALSE** *opinions of the* **CROWD**

VANITY IS SO ANCHORED IN THE HEART OF MAN

CHAPTER THIRTY-SIX

VANITY

THERE IS NO MORE MANIFEST VANITY THAT TO WRITE OF IT SO **VAINLY**

POPULAR FAVOUR is **NEVER CONSTANT**

i   IN AD 523 the politician and philosopher Boethius was sentenced to death for treason by the Ostrogothic king Theodoric
the Great.* While awaiting execution Boethius composed *The
Consolation of Philosophy*, a treatise on fortune, death and
other matters, which became one of the most popular works
of the Middle Ages. The eighteenth-century English writer
Edward Gibbon described it as 'a golden volume not unworthy
of the leisure of Plato or Tully [Cicero]'.

Vanity is, in Boethius's view, a trait both deceitful and base.
'Many men have got a great name from the false opinions of
the crowd,' he writes; 'And what could be baser than such a
thing?' A man of true worth, he argues, would blush to hear
false praise. Of the man who deserved praise because of his
just merit, he asks, 'what can they add to the pleasure of a
wise man's conscience? For he measures his happiness not by
popular talk, but by the truth of his conscience.' Writing in the
pre-internet age, Boethius dismisses fame by saying that it is
essentially *local* in nature: 'there must be yet more lands into
which the renown of a single man can never come; wherefore
it follows that the man, whom you think famous, will seem to
have no such fame in the next quarter of the earth'. 'Popular
favour', Boethius says, 'comes not by any judgement, and is
never constant.'

Awaiting execution on the orders of a king, Boethius reflects
on the vanity of noble birth. 'Who can but see how empty a
name, and how futile, is noble birth? For if its glory is due
to renown, it belongs not to the man. For the glory of noble
birth seems to be praise for the merits of a man's forefathers.
But if praise creates the renown, it is the renowned who are

---

* Theodoric was ruler of Italy (AD 493–526), having overthrown and killed
Odoacer, who had himself deposed the last Western Roman emperor in 476.

praised. Wherefore, if you have no renown of your own, that of others cannot glorify you.' The only value of a hereditary monarchy, says Boethius, is that it might set a standard for successive rulers to live up to. 'If there is any good in noble birth, I conceive it to be this, and this alone, that the highborn seem to be bound in honour not to show any degeneracy from their fathers' virtue.'

Sources vary on whether the club or the sword was employed to execute Boethius. He is buried – fittingly for a man whose masterpiece is seen by many as the last great literary creation of Late Antiquity – in the same church* as St Augustine of Hippo.

...... ● ......

ii **MICHEL DE MONTAIGNE** opens his essay 'OF VANITY' (1580) with this admission: 'There is, peradventure, no more manifest vanity than to write of it so vainly.' He treats the subject with irony and humour, proclaiming, 'I make it my business to bring vanity itself in repute, and folly too, if it produce me any pleasure; and let myself follow my own natural inclinations, without carrying too strict a hand upon them.' His fellow countryman Blaise Pascal, as a scientist and a Christian, argued that man needed more than a purely mechanistic model of the universe in order to make sense of the world. In his thought number sixty-seven, 'The vanity of the sciences', he wrote that 'Physical science will not console me for the ignorance of morality in the time of affliction. But the science of ethics will always console me for the ignorance of the physical

---

* San Pietro in Ciel d'Oro, in Pavia.

sciences.' Pascal was occupied by what he called the 'search for the true good', of which he remarked: 'Ordinary men place the good in fortune and external goods, or at least in amusement. Philosophers have shown the vanity of all this and have placed it where they could.' While Pascal hopes that philosophers, of all people, might be above vanity, he knows better.

> **Vanity is so anchored in the heart of man that a soldier, a soldier's servant, a cook, a porter brags and wishes to have his admirers. Even philosophers wish for them. Those who write against it want to have the glory of having written well; and those who read it desire the glory of having read it. I who write this have perhaps this desire, and perhaps those who will read it.**

...... ● ......

iii **FRIEDRICH NIETZSCHE** deals with vanity in a series of aphoristic jabs designed to shock the reader out of any sense of moral complacency. In *The Dawn* (1881) he defines vanity as 'the dread of appearing to be original. Hence it is a lack of pride, but not necessarily a lack of originality.' In his view, 'Passionate people think little of what others may think; their state of mind raises them above vanity.'

The question of vanity is at the heart of Nietzschean ethics. The truly moral man *becomes* moral; he does not submit to moral teaching: 'One becomes moral, but not because one is moral! Submission to morals may be due to slavishness or vanity, egoism or resignation, dismal fanaticism or thoughtlessness.' The acts of the unthinking moral person – the creation of laws, the waging of war – are often the result of vanity, which is a striving for the illusion of power. 'Whatever may be the influence in high politics of utilitarianism and the vanity of individuals and nations, the sharpest spur which urges them onwards is their need for the feeling of power.'

For Nietzsche, the pursuit of knowledge is predicated upon an absence of vanity. Of preachers and professors, the so-called teachers of morals, he wrote:

The relatively small success which teachers of morals have met with may be explained by the fact that they wanted too much at once, i.e. they were too ambitious and too fond of laying down precepts for everybody. In other words, they were beating the air and making speeches to animals in order to turn them into men; what wonder, then, that the animals thought this tedious!

In place of vanity, Nietzsche would have magnanimity: 'the noblest virtue of a great thinker is his magnanimity, which urges him on in his search for knowledge to sacrifice himself and his life unshrinkingly, often shamefacedly, and often with sublime scorn, and smiling'.

IF ONE JUST
KEEPS ON
WALKING,
EVERYTHING
WILL BE
ALLRIGHT

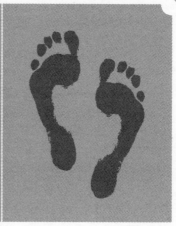

CHAPTER THIRTY-SEVEN

WALKING

MY MIND ONLY
MOVES WHEN
— MY —
FEET DO

I CAN
MEDITATE
ONLY WHEN
WALKING

DELECTABLE RECREATION

i **THE ADJECTIVE 'PERIPATETIC'**, which describes someone who walks from place to place, derives from Aristotle's style of teaching. He would wander about the Lyceum, students in tow, sharing his observations on the natural world and discussing with them questions of politics, ethics and aesthetics. The peripatetic school derives its name from two pleasingly related words: the *peripatoi*, or colonnades, of the Lyceum; and *peripatetikos* which, in Greek, means walking.

Aristotle not only taught while he walked, he also observed and researched. A man of the world who knew that colleagues and competitors could often be 'snakes', Aristotle observed that 'just as tall men walk with their spines bellied (undulated) forward, and when their right shoulder is leading in a forward direction their left hip rather inclined backwards, so that their middle becomes hollow and bellied (undulated), so we ought to conceive snakes as moving in concave curves (undulations)'.

...... ● ......

ii **THE SEVENTEENTH-CENTURY** anatomist of melancholy Robert Burton was cheerful on the subject of walking, which he praised as a 'delectable recreation':

> ...the most pleasant of outward pastimes is that is Areteaus,* *deambulatio per amoena loca,*† to make a petty progress, a merry journey now and then with some good companions, to visit friends, see cities, castles, towns... to walk amongst orchards, gardens, bowers, mounts, and arbours, artificial

---

* Aretaeus of Cappadocia was a Greek physician of the first century AD.
† 'Strolling through pleasant scenery'.

wildernesses, green thickets, arches, groves, lawns, rivulets, fountains, and such-like pleasant places, like the Antiochian Daphne, brooks, pools, fishponds, between wood and water, in a fair meadow, by a river-side, *ubi variae avium cantationes, florum colores, pratorum frutices,** etc., to disport in some pleasant plain, park, run up a steep hill sometimes, or sit in a shady seat, must needs be a delectable recreation.

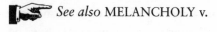 *See also* MELANCHOLY v.

...... ● ......

iii **JEAN-JACQUES ROUSSEAU'S** novel *Emile, or On Education* (1761) includes a chapter titled 'Profession of Faith of the Savoyard Vicar'. The Roman Catholic Archbishop of Paris, Christophe de Beaumont, condemned the novel as heretical. (He thought Rousseau advocated the heresy of indifferentism, the belief that no one religion is better than another.) Protestant authorities also found *Emile* objectionable. There were warrants for Rousseau's arrest. He fled to Môtiers, in Switzerland. Villagers stoned the house in which he was a guest. He escaped to England in 1766, where he stayed in Staffordshire with a friend of the Scottish philosopher David Hume.

When the furore died down, Rousseau returned to France in 1767. He took to walking. Between 1776 and 1778 he composed *Reveries of a Solitary Walker*, published in 1782. The book is organized in ten walks. The first begins, 'So here I am, all alone on this earth, with no brother, neighbour, or friend, and no company but my own.' His project was to make 'a

---

* 'To enjoy the songs of the birds, the colour of the flowers, the verdure of the meadows'.

faithful record of my solitary walks and the reveries that fill them when I let my mind wander quite freely and my ideas follow their own course unhindered and untroubled'.

Rousseau said walking was necessary to his very ability to think. 'I can meditate only when walking,' he writes; 'as soon as I stop, I can no longer think, for my mind moves only when my feet do.' Rousseau equated walking with personal freedom. For Rousseau walking was also an act of self-creation. He speaks of the more pedestrian benefits of the walk, noting 'The pleasant sights of the countryside, the unfolding scene, the good air, a good appetite, the sense of wellbeing that returns as I walk', then arrives at the higher purpose of walking: 'all of this releases my soul, encourages more daring flights of thought, impels me, as it were, into the immensity of being, which I can choose from, appropriate, and combine exactly as I wish'.

...... ● ......

iv **ANGST-DRIVEN** Søren Kierkegaard dressed like a dandy and walked with a corkscrew gait. He declared that his mind only worked in conjunction with his legs. His voluminous output is a testament to the miles he walked.

The dour Dane – author of *Fear and Trembling* (1843), *The Sickness Unto Death* (1849) and *The Concept of Anxiety* (1844) – thought of life as not so much a journey, but, rather, as the road on which that journey occurs. In 'The Road is How', he says that comparing life to a road has some value, but that it might be better to think about how life is not like a road. On the one hand, the road has a physical reality whether or not it contains pedestrians. 'The road is the road,' he observes laconically. It is what it is, and nothing more. That is, until it is transformed by the walker. 'In the spiritual sense,' he writes, 'the road comes into existence only when we walk on it. That is, the road is how it is walked.'

Another reason Kierkegaard cited for walking was health. It was typical of his philosophical outlook to cite the nature of the health-giving walk in both positive and negative terms; that is as a cure for illness and as a prophylaxis against it. In an 1847 letter to his friend Henrietta Lund he offers this advice: 'Above all, do not lose your desire to walk. Everyday, I walk myself into a state of wellbeing and walk away from every illness. I have walked myself into my best thoughts, and I know of no thought so burdensome that one cannot walk away from it.' He tells her that health and salvation are exclusively available as a result of walking. The opposite of walking, sitting still, is the cause of illness. 'The more one sits still,' he writes, 'the closer one comes to feeling ill.'

Kierkegaard was a fop and a snob who was dismissive of people who didn't interest him, and he was intensely critical of walkers who didn't measure up to his standard. In *The Concept of Irony* he describes the walking of 'provincials' as 'wretched, ridiculous and tasteless' and declares that most stage actors don't know how to do it properly. Someone who doesn't walk is 'suspect' ('It will not tolerate a man to stand still and become immersed in himself, to walk slowly is already suspect'). But the Italians, he laconically judged, know how to walk.

Kierkegaard's motto: 'If one just keeps on walking, everything will be all right.'

...... ● ......

ᵛ **THE MOST FAMOUS** and influential American walker is
the transcendentalist philosopher Henry David Thoreau. His
essay 'Walking', which was published a month after his death
in 1862, is one of the founding documents of what might
loosely be described as the environmental movement.

Thoreau pursued walking with physical intensity and spiritual zealotry, at least four hours per day. He had contempt
for those with idle legs. He pointed to the mechanic and shop-
keeper, and those who spent their day with legs crossed, as
examples of person who deserve credit for not having committed suicide. For Thoreau, the sedentary life was death. To
the credit of the rest of the human race, Thoreau claimed to
have known 'but one or two' persons in his entire life who
understood what he called 'the art of Walking'.

The highest form of walking in Thoreau's opinion was sauntering. Most readers of this book would define sauntering as
the act of walking at a slow or leisurely pace, perhaps with no
particular destination in mind. The Romanian-born Canadian
etymologist Ernest Klein proposed that 'saunter' derives from
the mid-fourteenth-century Anglo-French *sauntrer*, which derives in turn from the French *s'aventurer*, 'to take risks', but the
Oxford English Dictionary cautions that this interpretation is
'unlikely'.

The editors of the *OED* overlooked Thoreau's two charming
and highly plausible explanations of the word's origins. First
he suggests it 'is beautifully derived "from idle people who
roved about the country, in the middle ages, and asked charity,
under pretence of going *à la sainte terre*" – to the holy land, till
the children exclaimed, "There goes a *sainte-terrer*", a saun-
terer – a holy-lander'. His second explanation is that it comes
from *sans terre*, which means a landless person. Such a person

would be truly blessed for Thoreau, being *in* nature rather than owning it. With no particular home, everywhere would be his home. Thoreau preferred the first theory, not only because he judged it the most probable, but because he believed 'every walk is a sort of crusade, preached by some Peter the Hermit in us, to go forth and reconquer this holy land from the hands of the Infidels'.

The 'holy land' to which Thoreau refers is the world in which we find ourselves, our natural inheritance. The infidels are those who would destroy it: industrialists, clear-cutters, burners, strip miners and poisoners. He imagines himself and his fellow saunterers as members of a new order of walkers, 'not the Knight but Walker Errant'. With astonishing prescience he foresaw the Green Movement as 'a sort of fourth estate – outside of Church and State and People'.

We should go forth on the shortest walk, perchance, in the spirit of undying adventure, never to return; prepared to send back our embalmed hearts only, as relics to our desolate kingdoms. If you are ready to leave father and mother, and brother and sister, and wife and child and friends, and never see them again; if you have paid your debts, and made your will, and settled all your affairs, and are a free man; then you are ready for a walk.

...... ● ......

vi FRIEDRICH NIETZSCHE was one of philosophy's great walkers. In *Twilight of the Idols* (1889) he wrote: 'all truly great thoughts are conceived by walking'. It is perhaps no coincidence that Nietzsche was drawn to the works of Thoreau, making Thoreau the first American exporter of philosophical ideas back to the old world.

After resigning his professorship at the University of Basel owing to chronic ill health (including violent migraines and severe indigestion) Nietzsche travelled frequently, in search of good health, and spent several summers near St Moritz in south-eastern Switzerland. His routine was to rise at dawn, wash with cold water, drank warm milk, then write until 11 a.m. Then, with notebook in pocket, he set out for a brisk two-hour walk, pausing occasionally to write. He took a late lunch at the Hôtel Alpenrose to avoid other diners, then continued walking until 4 or 5 p.m. During one of his walks along Lake Silvaplana he encountered a giant, pyramid-shaped rock. The moment was to become the inspiration for *Thus Spake Zarathustra* (1883–91), in which Nietzsche turns traditional morality upside down:

I now wish to relate the history of *Zarathustra*. The fundamental idea of the work, the *Eternal Return*, the highest form of a Yea-saying to life that can ever be attained, was first conceived in the month of August 1881. I made a note of the idea on a sheet of paper, with the postscript 'six thousand feet beyond man and time'. That day I happened to be wandering through the woods alongside the Lake of Silvaplana, and I halted not far from Surlei, beside a huge rock that towered aloft like a pyramid. It was then that the thought struck me.

Nietzsche's hero is a constant walker, quite literally followed by his adherents. When Zarathustra declares he must walk alone, they make him the gift of a walking stick, the handle of which is a golden globe with a snake coiled around it.

Zarathustra was Nietzsche himself, the walking philosopher, who declared: 'I have learned to walk: ever since, I let myself run. I have learned to fly: ever since, I do not want to be pushed before moving along. Now I am light, now I fly, now I see myself beneath myself, now a god dances through me.'

Before GOD
HE HOPES ONLY
for MERCY

– – THE – –
WISE
MAN WILL WAGE
JUST WARS
– • –

Primordial
VIOLENCE

CHAPTER THIRTY-EIGHT

WAR

PEACE
must be the
GOAL

THERE MUST BE
SERIOUS
PROSPECTS OF
SUCCESS

i **PHILOSOPHERS** have been soldiers from the very beginning. Socrates was an infantryman, serving in battles at Potidaea (432–429 BC), Delium (424 BC) and Amphipolis (422 BC). Xenophon was a soldier and a mercenary. In the twentieth century, Ludwig Wittgenstein, Paul Feyerabend and Stuart Hampshire were all soldiers. By contrast, Bertrand Russell was a pacifist. He said that, 'Of all evils of war the greatest is the purely spiritual evil: the hatred, the injustice, the repudiation of truth, the artificial conflict.'

...... ● ......

ii **AUGUSTINE OF HIPPO** was among the first Western thinkers to use the phrase 'just war' in making the Christian argument for war in his *De Civitate Dei* (*City of God*, early fifth century AD): 'But, say they, the wise man will wage just wars. As if he would not all the rather lament the necessity of just wars, if he remembers that he is a man; for if they were not just he would not wage them, and would therefore be delivered from all wars.' Defending killing in a 'just war', Augustine says

> They who have waged war in obedience to the divine command, or in conformity with His laws, have represented in their persons the public justice or the wisdom of government, and in this capacity have put to death wicked men; such persons have by no means violated the commandment, 'Thou shalt not kill.'

Thomas Aquinas built on Augustine's just war theory by claiming that for a war to be just it must meet three criteria:

- It must be waged by a 'proper authority', such as the state.
- The action must have as its motivation the setting right of an injustice (i.e. the recovery of territory that has been taken, or to halt an evil perpetrated by another government or group within a state).
- Its goal must be peace.

In 1992 the *Catechism of the Catholic Church* updated Aquinas's teaching. Now, war is justified if *four* conditions are met:

- The damage inflicted by the aggressor on the nation or community of nations must be lasting, grave, and certain.
- All other means of putting an end to it must have been shown to be impractical or ineffective.
- There must be serious prospects of success.
- The use of arms must not produce evils and disorders graver than the evil to be eliminated (the power of modern means of destruction weighs very heavily in evaluating this condition).

The Catholic Church continues to update its teaching on war. Its latest effort is the *Compendium of the Social Doctrine of the Church* (2004).

...... • ......

iii **THE PRUSSIAN GENERAL** and military theorist Carl Philipp Gottfried von Clausewitz brought to bear the weight of Enlightenment philosophy on the study of war. While not a follower of Hegel, Clausewitz used the kind of dialectical reasoning made famous by Hegel. Hegelian dialectic posits a *thesis*; reaction against the thesis, a contradiction (or *antithesis*); resolved by a *synthesis* created from the tension between thesis and antithesis. In his book, Clausewitz proposes that war is:

- Thesis: 'an act of force to compel our enemy to do our will'.
- Antithesis: the famous aphorism 'war is merely the continuation of policy by other means'.
- Synthesis: war is 'a fascinating trinity – composed of primordial violence, hatred, and enmity, which are to be regarded as a blind natural force; the play of chance and probability, within which the creative spirit is free to roam; and its element of subordination, as an instrument of policy, which makes it subject to pure reason'.

...... ● ......

iv **THE AUSTRIAN PHILOSOPHER** Ludwig Wittgenstein was in England when the First World War broke out. He returned to Vienna to do his duty, enlisting in the Austro-Hungarian army. After serving in an artillery workshop, Wittgenstein was posted to the Russian front where he served with valour for two years. He earned many decorations, including one for bravery while attacking a British position. He continued at the front in Italy, then Austria.

On the first day of his service, Wittgenstein began writing thoughts in pencil in a notebook that would eventually be published as *Tractatus Logico-Philosophicus* (1921), one of the founding documents of analytic philosophy. The war had a profound effect on Wittgenstein, who did not return to

England (and philosophy) until 1929. He worked at various occupations, including teaching in a rural school in Austria. He was forced to resign after regularly inflicting severe corporal punishments on his students.

...... • ......

v **THE RISE OF NAZISM** in Germany and subsequent aggressive war waged by Hitler led to a worldwide conflict and the murder of millions of innocents targeted 'unfit' or 'impure' by Hitler's regime: Jews, communists, gypsies, homosexuals and those who did not agree with the Führer's plan for world domination. This was a conflict that tested philosophers (*see also* MARTYRDOM iii). How did they respond?

A quarter of Germany's philosophers belonged to the Nazi Party, including Martin Heidegger, who unsuccessfully sought control of the teaching of philosophy in German universities by attempting to curry favour with the regime. The fundamental challenge for philosophers in Germany after Hitler's rise to power in 1933 was what position to take as government policies promoted persecution of Jews and others and, ultimately, genocide.

Heidegger joined the Nazi Party in 1933 and was elected rector of Freiburg University after the forced resignation of his teacher Edmund Husserl, a Jew who had converted to Lutheranism. After finishing his address Heidegger gave a double Nazi salute. He began and ended his lectures at Freiburg with a Nazi salute which was returned by his students. Of course Jews were no longer allowed at the university. Several of Heidegger's most prominent students were Jews.

One of Heidegger's students was Hannah Arendt, a Jew who

had been his lover. Embracing Nazism, Heidegger refused to recognize her. She fled Germany soon after her arrest by the Gestapo. In France she was put in the concentration camp in Gurs. She escaped to Portugal, and eventually arrived in New York in 1941. Ten years later she published *The Origins of Totalitarianism* (1951), which explained how terror is organized, and how communities respond to it.

Heidegger had been a student of the German phenomenologist Edmund Husserl. He worked closely with Husserl, editing his papers for publication and working as his teaching assistant. He was succeeded by Edith Stein. Her thesis was *On the Problem of Empathy* (1917), a subject which put her directly at odds with a systemic suppression of empathy. A Jew, Stein converted to Roman Catholicism. She became a nun. The Nazis chased her from Germany, and finally caught up with her at a convent in The Netherlands in 1942. She was taken to Auschwitz where she was gassed with her sister.

...... ● ......

vi **THE GERMAN THEOLOGIAN** Dietrich Bonhoeffer believed that Christians had a duty to act against evil. His response to Hitler was to join the Abwehr (German intelligence) and became involved in a cell that nurtured resistance to Hitler. He used ecumenical connections in the United Kingdom to inform authorities there about resistance activities in Germany. Bonhoeffer was privy to numerous Abwehr plots to assassinate Hitler. In his posthumously published *Ethics* (1949), Bonhoeffer hints at his justification as a Christian endorsing a plot to assassinate a murderous tyrant:

> When a man takes guilt upon himself in responsibility, and no
> responsible man can avoid this, he imputes this guilt to him-
> self and to no one else; he answers for it; he accepts respon-
> sibility for it. He does not do this in the insolent presumptu-
> ousness of his own power, but he does it in the knowledge
> that this liberty is forced upon him and that in this liberty
> he is dependent on grace. Before other men the man of free
> responsibility is justified by necessity; before himself he is
> acquitted by his conscience; but before God he hopes only
> for mercy.

Bonhoeffer was hanged with various Abwehr conspirators,
including the Abwehr chief Admiral Wilhelm Canaris, at
Flossenbürg concentration camp.

...... • ......

vii CARL SCHMITT, one of the twentieth century's most influential legal theorists of war, joined the Nazi Party on 1 May
1933. On 10 May he encouraged the burning of books by
Jewish authors. Unlike some who maintained after the war that
they merely 'went along' with Nazism, Schmitt was a fanatical
anti-Semite and fervent Nazi who developed some of the legal
foundations of the Third Reich. He drew upon the Roman
notion of *auctoritas*, literally translated in English as 'authority', to justify the power of the Führer. Beyond the concept of
mere authority, the principle of *auctoritas* also implied an element of charisma, and the justification to act in an emergency.

It is from *auctoritas* that Schmitt derives Hitler's justification for taking exceptional measures to deal with exceptional
crises by the use of emergency powers. In June 1934 Schmitt

was made editor-in-chief of the Nazi legal journal *Deutsche Juristen-Zeitung*. In July, a few days after the *Röhm-Putsch* (or Night of the Long Knives) in which Hitler had between 100 and 150 of his opponents in the Sturmabteilung (the paramilitary wing of the Nazi Party) murdered and a thousand more arrested, Schmitt published an article '*Der Führer schützt das Recht*' ('The Leader Protects the Law') in which he justifies Hitler's action as 'the highest form of administrative justice'.

At the end of the war Schmitt was interned by American forces in Germany. Despite a year of attempts at 'de-nazification', Schmitt would not budge. He lived on, barred from academic employment, and died in 1985 at the age of ninety-six. Schmitt is important today because his ideas gained in popularity with the rise of neoconservatism in the United States where his views on war and the justification of exceptional actions found a new audience. Like a legal Doctor Strangelove, Schmitt 'went through a curious revival by theorists on the left, and, after 9/11, interest in him ratcheted up again, largely because of his writings that support untrammeled executive power in the face of emergency'. Many writers noticed the 'Schmittian' character of the Bush administration's constitutional arguments on issues such as torture.

...... ● ......

viii **THE AUSTRIAN PHILOSOPHER** of science Paul Feyerabend served in the German army as an officer (lieutenant) in France and on the Eastern Front in the Second World War. He was wounded during the retreat from the USSR and awarded the Iron Cross. He emigrated to the United States where he had a thirty-year career at the University of California at Berkeley.

In his book *Against Method* (1975) Feyerabend takes an 'anarchist' view of science which rejects the idea of universal methodological rules. He loathed dogma and promoted the idea of plurality. In his autobiography *Killing Time* (1995) Feyerabend talks about how his notion of plurality allowed him to flirt with the idea of joining the SS*, the reasons behind that thinking: 'an SS man looked better and spoke better and walked better than ordinary mortals; aesthetics, not ideology, was my reason. (I remember feeling a strong erotic undercurrent while discussing the matter with a fellow soldier.)' Feyerabend uses the example of Hitler's charisma to explain his enduring conviction for an anarchical attraction to what he calls 'strange views':

> I concluded an essay on Goethe (a school assignment) by linking him to Hitler. There was no insight behind this manoeuvre, no deeply felt conviction; the desire for a good grade certainly played no role; nor had I fallen for Hitler's 'charisma,' as had artists, philosophers, scientists, and millions of ordinary men and women. So what made me do it? I assume it was the tendency (still with me) to pick up strange views and push them to the extreme.

Clausewitz speaks of the 'fog of war' – the uncertainty of one's position in relation to the enemy, the confusion that can result from fast and deadly action all around one. Feyerabend's *Killing Time* describes the fog of his war memory. Extraordinarily, he remembers only three instances of killing

---

* Or *Schutzstaffel*, Hitler's feared paramilitary arm that was most responsible for the Holocaust in which six million Jews and other enemies of the state were murdered.

while serving on the Eastern Front, where thirty million were killed. The first was noticing that a fellow soldier had been run over by a tank ('he lay there flat, like a piece of cardboard'); the others are described in this passage:

> We heard artillery and saw fires, but we never saw a single Russian soldier. There were no civilians, either – with two exceptions. On one occasion a huge infantryman I had noticed before herded civilians, men and women, into a cellar about two hundred meters from when I was standing, and threw a hand grenade after them. 'What did he do that for?' my neighbour asked. On another occasion a small, mean-looking individual shot a civilian right in the head. These events did not shock me – they were too strange for that; yet they have stayed with me, and they make me shiver when I think of them today.

In between battles Feyerabend entertained his fellow soldiers with a series of lectures on Nazi ideology. The ideas of Friedrich Nietzsche had been corrupted by the Nazi philosopher Alfred Bäumler who attempted to link Nietzsche to National Socialism: Feyerabend's lectures followed false readings of Bäumler. Feyerabend had not been a member of the Nazi Party and so was allowed to pursue his academic career without being subjected to the de-nazification process.

...... ● ......

ix **THE ENGLISH ETHICIST** Stuart Hampshire was a contemporary of Feyerabend, though his experience of war was very different. In 1940 he enlisted in the British Army and was given a commission. He was assigned to Bletchley Park where he worked in military intelligence and, post-war, interrogated Nazi officers. The work had an enormous effect on him as a moral philosopher, causing him to affirm the reality of evil after having been in its presence, he claimed. He famously interrogated the SS officer Ernst Kaltenbrunner who was tried and executed at Nuremberg for his direct role in war crimes and crimes against humanity.

Like Feyerabend, the way in which Hampshire experienced war was affected by his formation as a philosopher. The difference between them lay in the fact that where Feyerabend took an 'aesthetic' view of 'strange' events, on whose waves he allowed himself to be carried, Hampshire believed it incumbent upon the free, acting agent to investigate his own psychological and social 'conditioning' as a prerequisite to making intentional moral choices.

He frequently told the story of how, towards the end of the war, he had to interrogate a French traitor (imprisoned by the Free French), who refused to cooperate unless he was allowed to live. Should Hampshire, knowing the man was condemned to die, promise him a reprieve, which he was in no position to give, or truthfully refuse it, thereby jeopardising the lives of Resistance fighters?

'If you're in a war,' said Hampshire, 'you can't start thinking, "Well I can't lie to a man who's going to be shot tomorrow and tell him that he isn't."'

But what the whole anecdote, and its incessant retelling, revealed was that Hampshire had, in fact, thought precisely what he said was unthinkable, and that whichever of the two decisions he finally took lay heavy on his conscience ever afterwards. Indicatively, too, it was especially loathsome to him because, although he did not say this in so many words, the traitor was almost a mirror image of himself – a cultivated young intellectual, looking like a film star, much influenced by elegant literary stylists – except that, in the traitor's case, his literary mentors were fascist.

HE **DRANK** FIFTY TO SEVENTY-TWO CUPS OF **COFFEE** PER DAY

Two Frenchmen preferred to **WRITE IN BED**

WRITING *is the* MOST IMPORTANT *part of* PHILOSOPHY

CHAPTER THIRTY-NINE

WRITING

When particularly INSPIRED, *he used to* STRIP *himself of his* TROUSERS

i   **AFTER THINKING**, writing is the most important part of philosophy: without it, we wouldn't know what philosophers thought. While thinking is largely a cerebral exercise, for some philosophers it is accompanied by physical activity. Aristotle, Kierkegaard, Nietzsche, Thoreau and Freud were vigorous 'think while walking' philosophers (*see* WALKING). By contrast two Frenchmen – René Descartes (*see* CONSCIOUSNESS ii) and Voltaire (*see* NICKNAMES vii) – preferred to write in bed.

...... ● ......

ii   **IN JANUARY 1650**, after a productive lifetime spent abed,* Descartes took on the job of tutoring Queen Christina of Sweden. It was a bitterly cold winter, and the queen announced she would like her lessons to commence no later than 5 a.m. in her unheated library. Neither the temperature nor the time appealed to Descartes. It wasn't just the temperature that was frosty: the queen objected to Descartes' mechanistic world-view, and he found her dull.

On the first of February Descartes caught a cold, which led to pneumonia. He died on 11 February. There was much speculation about the cause of Descartes' death – rumours of foul play and medical ineptitude. Some thought it was the sudden change of routine that did for the apostle of dualism.

...... ● ......

---

* Descartes did all his work from mid-morning, a habit he developed from his youth (being a sickly child, he was excused early-morning duties at school).

iii **VOLTAIRE AWAKENED** every day at around 3 a.m. and retired at 11 p.m., spending much of the day in bed. To keep himself alert while recumbent he drank, by one account, fifty to seventy-two cups of coffee per day. He was an extraordinarily productive writer. Illness – from which he suffered frequently – did not diminish his output. When unwell Voltaire would summon one of his amanuenses and dictate finished copy. He died, appropriately enough, in his sleep.

...... ● ......

iv **IMMANUEL KANT** was a prolific writer and a man of regular habits (his neighbours said you could set your clock by his daily walks). Kant (*see also* DUTY iii) rose every day at 5 a.m., even though he did not find it easy to stir from bed. It was the job of his manservant Martin Lampe, a retired soldier, to make sure that his master rose at the appointed hour. Upon rising he drank two cups of weak tea and meditated while smoking a pipe. He spent the next hour preparing for lectures, which ran from 7 a.m. to 11 a.m. He then spent two hours writing, before taking lunch in a restaurant where he enjoyed the company of ordinary folk. (His favourite for many years was Zornig in Junker Street. He changed that for Gerlach's, a billiard hall in the Kneiphoff.) Lunch was always followed by the famous walk by which clocks were set. He passed the afternoons with his English friend Joseph Green, a merchant. Upon returning home he would continue writing, ending the day with reading.

...... ● ......

v JOHN STUART MILL had a lifelong day job working for the British East India Company – the royal chartered joint-stock company that accounted for half the world's trade and which effectively was the British Empire in India. He began his career as a clerk, and rose to the rank of Examiner by the time of his retirement. The job provided steady employment, but the work was routine. Mill composed many of his philosophical works – *A System of Logic* (1843), *The Principles of Political Economy* (1848), *On Liberty* (1859), *Utilitarianism* (1863) – at his office desk. Doing his own work on company time was not unusual; doing it with no trousers on was. 'When particularly inspired, he used, before sitting down at his desk, not only to strip himself of his coat and waistcoat, but of his trousers; and so set to work, alternately striding up and down the room and writing at great speed.'

...... • ......

vi THE GERMAN IDEALIST PHILOSOPHER and playwright Friedrich Schiller built a small, one-room house on a hill near Jena in Thuringia, with a view of the Saale river valley and the mountains that rose from it. There, he wrote at night. On his desk he kept: strong coffee; chocolate; a bottle of champagne; a flask of old Rhenish wine and liberal supplies of smoking tobacco and snuff. His neighbours reported hearing him declaiming sentences at the night sky, and observing him pacing back and forth furiously in his eyrie.

Schiller was not the first philosopher (nor will he be the last) to fall under what the nineteenth-century British philosopher and historian Thomas Carlyle called 'the pernicious expedient of stimulants'. But the uniquely peculiar thing about Schiller's writing habits was his use of rotting apples. He loved the smell of them. His wife regularly filled his desk drawer with them. He claimed they made him think and write better.

- NOTES -

1. ADVICE

Page 10 **defaces Human Society:** Mary Pickering, *August Comte: Vol. 3: An Intellectual Biography* (2009).

2. AGEING

Page 14 **hardness of hearing:** Hippocrates, Aphorisms (*c*.400 BC).

Page 14 **when almost over:** Seneca, 'On Old Age' in *Moral Letters to Lucilius* (*c*.AD 65).

3. ANIMALS

Page 22 **upon the earth:** Genesis 1:26, King James Version.

4. BACKBITING

Page 30 **no intelligence whatever:** John W. Cook, *Wittgenstein, Empiricism, and Language* (1999).

Page 31 **corruption of a whole generation:** Arthur Schopenhauer, *Works*, Vol. 5 (1888).

Page 33 **you might go there:** Ray Monk, *Ludwig Wittgenstein: The Duty of Genius* (1991).

Page 33 **no talent for disentangling things:** Cook, *Wittgenstein, Empiricism, and Language.*

Page 33 **no one should be allowed to read them:** Ray Monk, *Bertrand Russell: The Ghost of Madness, 1921–1970* (2001).

Page 34 **but he remained unconvinced:** *Mind* 60 (no. 239), 1951.

Page 35 **statements which are absolutely empty:** Eugene Yue-Ching Ho, 'At 90, and Still Dynamic: Revisiting Sir Karl Popper and Attending His Birthday Party', *Intellectus* 23 (July–September 1992).

Page 36 **the pauperisation of French intellectual life:** Jason Burke, 'Has le philosophe been undone?', *Observer*, 8 April 2006. http://www.theguardian.com/world/2006/apr/09/books. france. Retrieved 27 November 2015.

5. BELIEF

Page 38 **and not the earth:** Martin Luther, *Table Talk* (1539).

Page 39   **expected better of reasonable persons:** W. V. O. Quine,
          Quiddities, An Intermittently Philosophical Dictionary
          (1987).

Page 42   **no ground whatever for supposing it true:** Bertrand Russell,
          Sceptical Essays (1928).

6. CHANCE

Page 45   **without a cause:** See Plutarch, Stoic. rep., 34, 1050A.

Page 46   **from any definite formula:** C. S. Peirce, *The Architecture of*
          Theories (1891).

Page 47   **a whole era to work out:** C. S. Peirce, *The Law of Mind*
          (1892).

7. CONSCIOUSNESS

Page 54   **British psychologist Stuart Sutherland:** Stuart Sutherland,
          'Consciousness', *Macmillan Dictionary of Psychology*
          (1989).

Page 57   **I refute it thus:** James Boswell: *Life of Samuel Johnson*
          (1791).

Page 60   **except as self-presence:** Jacques Derrida, 'Différance', in
          Peggy Kamiuf, ed. *A Derrida Reader* (1991).

Page 60   **neurons and the state neurons:** Igor Aleksander, 'Artificial
          Neuroconsciousness: An Update', *International Workshop*
          on Artificial Neural Networks, Vol. 930 of *Lecture Notes in*
          Computer Science (1995).

8. DAY JOBS

Page 68   **composed or written by him:** Steven Nadler, *Spinoza: A Life*
          (2001).

Page 70   **certainly the greatest American thinker ever:** Bertrand
          Russell, *Wisdom of the West* (1959).

9. DREAMS

Page 75 **by the soul during sleep:** Hippocrates, Vol. IV: *Nature of Man* (410–400 BC).

Page 78 **experienced during sleep:** Ben Springett, 'Dreams', Internet Encyclopedia of Philosophy. Retrieved 21 December 2014. http://www.iep.utm.edu/dreaming/#SH3b.

Page 79 **undreamed dreams comes from:** Gordon G. Globus, *Dream Life, Wake Life* (1987).

10. DRUGS

Page 82 **could be added to the wine:** A. P. Ruck, *Sacred Mushrooms of the Goddess* (2006).

Page 82 **alter their own consciousness:** David Hillman, *The Chemical Muse* (2008).

Page 84 **of a healthy person:** Sigmund Freud, 'Über Coca', *Zentralblatt für die gesamte Therapie* 2 (1884).

Page 89 **Sartre responded:** John Gerassi, *Talking with Sartre* (2009).

Page 90 **the better for it:** Paul Hoffman, 'The Man Who Loves Only Numbers', *Atlantic Monthly*, November (1987).

Page 91 **a goldmine of philosophical questions:** Douglas Husak, 'Four Points About Drug Decriminalization', *Criminal Justice Ethics*, Winter/Spring (2003).

11. DUTY

Page 106 **in the inevitable injustices:** Miriam Bankovsky, *Perfecting Justice in Rawls, Habermas and Honneth* (2012).

12. EXTRATRERRESTRIALS

Page 111 **that Jupiter is inhabited:** Michael J. Crowe, *The Extraterrestrial Life Debate, 1750–1900* (2012).

Page 117 **to witness its detection:** Martin Dominik and John Zarnecki, 'Extra-terrestrial Life', *Phil. Trans. R. Soc. A* 2011 369 499–507; DOI: 10.1098/rsta.2010.0236. Published 10 January 2011. https://royalsociety.org/further/extra-terrestrial-life/.

13. FOOD

Page 121 **from mortal wounds?:** Plutarch, *Morals* (first century BC).

Page 123 **food, furniture, etc.:** *Black's Law Dictionary*, 10th edn (2014).

Page 124 **gourmandise has become an art:** *Journal des Gourmans et des Belles* (1806).

Page 125 **and his tongue able:** Grimod de La Reynière, 'On Gourmands and Gourmandise' (1806).

Page 128 **in a way, more spicy:** *La Mettrie: Machine Man and Other Writings* (1996).

Page 130 **the bourgeois establishment:** 30 September 1973. http://www.rogerebert.com/reviews/la-grande-bouffe-1973. Retrieved 16 December 2015.

14. FREEDOM

Page 135 **but earlier useful and capable:** Translation by Edward Franklin Buchner in *The Educational Theory of Immanuel Kant* (1904).

15. FRIENDSHIP

Page 50 **Michel de Montaigne:** Montaigne, 'OF FRIENDSHIP', *Essays* (1580).

16. FUN

Page 158 **diversion, amusement, mirthful sport:** The *Online Etymology Dictionary,* http://www.etymonline.com/index.php?term=fun&allowed_in_frame=0. 25 March 2015.

Page 159 **unimaginable notions in prior history:** Brian Sutton-Smith, *The Ambiguity of Play* (1998).

Page 159 **for his own amusement:** John Morreall, *Comic Relief: A Comprehensive History of Humor* (2009). The wife of Amin's to whom Morreall refers is Kay Adroa. Her mutilated body was found in the boot of a car in 1974. Morreall further notes that when US soldiers were arrested following the publication of photographs which depicted them torturing prisoners or forcing them into degrading poses at Abu Ghraib prison, they explained that they were just 'having fun'.

Page 161 **such as eating or sexual behaviour:** Quoted by Sutton-Smith in *The Ambiguity of Play* (1998).

17. GOD

Page 167 **and this being we call God:** This brief summary quotes from Theodore Gracyk in 'St. Thomas Aquinas: The Existence of God can be proved in five ways' (2004). http://web.mnstate. edu/gracyk/courses/web%20publishing/aquinasFiveWays_ ArgumentAnalysis.htm. Retrieved 22 November 2015.

Page 170 **My God speaks to me through laws:** From a 1948 conversation quoted in William Hermanns, *Einstein and the Poet: In Search of the Cosmic Man* (1983).

Page 170 **a continual divine service:** Bernard Bosanquet and W. M. Bryant, 'Selections from Hegel's Lectures on Aesthetics', *The Journal of Speculative Philosophy* (1886).

Page 173 **refused to make them his own:** http://www.samharris.org/ blog/item/an-atheist-manifesto (2005). Retrieved 24 November 2015.

18. GOVERNING

Page 181 **for American women was 5 per cent:** Rose Eveleth, 'Soviet Russia Had a Better Record of Training Women in STEM Than America Does Today', *Smithsonian Magazine*, 12 December 2013.

19. GRIEF

Page 187 **human frailty will permit:** William Strachan on 26 August 1776, quoted in James Fieser, *Early Responses to Hume's Life and Reputation* (2003).

Page 189 **the very existence of sincerity:** Sarah Tooley, *Victoria, Queen of Britain* (1896).

Page 189 **time alone digests:** *Parerga and Paralipomena* (1851). Cronus is the Greek god of time.

Page 189　**whether grief is an expression of egoism:** *Philosophy Now*, December 2015/January 2016. https://philosophynow.org/issues/17/Is_Grief_Self-Regarding. Retrieved 15 December 2015.

Page 190　**the aporia of death:** 'Grief Revisited', *Philosophy Now*, December 2015/January 2016. https://philosophynow.org/issues/18/Grief_Revisited. Retrieved 15 December 2015.

20. HAIRCUTS

Page 193　**mistaken for a philosopher:** John R. Hale, *Lords of the Sea: The Epic Story of the Athenian Navy and the Birth of Democracy* (2009).

Page 195　**God is dead, but my hair is beautiful:** Celia Walden, 'Bernard-Henri Lévy: 'I have no problem with my virility'', *Daily Telegraph*, 26 June 2012. http://www.telegraph.co.uk/culture/books/9349823/Bernard-Henri-Levy-I-have-no-problem-with-my-virility.html. Retrieved 27 November 2015.

21. HAPPINESS

Page 200　**and masturbating in public:** Dio Chrysostom, *Discourses*, first century BC; Diogenes Laertius, *Lives and Opinions of Eminent Philosophers*, first half of the third century.

Page 201　**what is not present:** *Discourses* (AD 108).

Page 202　**it teaches us to attain happiness:** In his essay 'On wisdom' (*c.*1690).

22. HOPE

Page 206　**the tender age of seventeen:** *Essai sur la morale littéraire* and *Mémoire sur la morale utilitaire depuis Epicure jusqu'à l'école anglaise.*

Page 206　**hope is what carries us higher and farther:** Reprinted in *Choisies des grands écrivains*, ed. Ernest Renan (1895).

Page 206　**the wages of sin is death:** Romans 6:23, King James Version.

23. ILLNESS

Page 215 **clunky, difficult, abrasive:** Havi Carel, 'My 10-year death sentence', *Independent*, March 2007. Carel gives a more detailed account in *Illness: The Cry of the Flesh* (2008).

Page 216 **that I aim to cultivate:** Havi Carel, 'Living in the Shadow of Illness', *Royal Society of Arts Digital Journal*, Autumn 2008. http://www.thersa.org/fellowship/journal/archive/autumn-update-2008/features/living-in-the-shadow-of-illness. Retrieved 9 January 2015.

Page 218 **in experiencing Alzheimer's:** *Iris: The Life of Iris Murdoch*, 2002.

24. INSANITY

Page 221 **and all anti-Semites are abolished:** Quoted in Leonard Sax, 'What was the Cause of Nietzsche's Dementia?', *Journal of Medical Biography* 11 (2003).

25. INTUITION

Page 228 **without any grounds in reasoning:** A. G. Spirkin, *Fundamentals of Philosophy* (1990).

Page 229 **with which a man has ever been gifted:** John Maynard Keynes, 'Newton, the Man', lecture given posthumously by his brother Geoffrey Keynes at the Royal Society of London, 1946.

Page 229 **earlier intellectual experience:** Letter to H. L. Gordon, 3 May 1949; cited in Walter Isaacson, *Einstein: His Life and Universe* (2007).

Page 230 **surprised if I had been wrong:** 'What Life Means to Einstein: An Interview by George Sylvester Viereck', *Saturday Evening Post* (26 October 1929).

Page 231 **and why we do them:** Interview with M. K. Wisehart, 'A Close Look at the World's Greatest Thinker', *The American Magazine* (June 1930).

Page 231 **the 'open sesame' of yourself:** William Hermanns, *Einstein and the Poet: In Search of the Cosmic Man* (1983).

Page 232 **the brand-new automotive age:** Arthur Mitchell in the introduction to his 1911 translation of Bergson's *Creative Evolution* (1907).

28. MARTYRDOM

Page 256 **conducted elsewhere:** Michael A. B. Deakin, *Hypatia of Alexandria: Mathematician and Martyr* (2007).

Page 258 **a peaceful solution of the 'Jewish Question':** Lisa Silverman, *Becoming Austrians: Jews and Culture Between the World Wars* (2012).

Page 259 **sprang from his world-view:** Friedrich Stadler, 'Documentation: The Murder of Moritz Schlick', in Stadler (ed.), *The Vienna Circle. Studies in the Origins, Development, and Influence of Logical Empiricism* (2001).

29. MELANCHOLY

Page 262 **are clearly melancholics?:** The essay, 'On Melancholy', is attributed to Aristotle, but was more likely composed by one of Aristotle's followers.

Page 264 **about eating the apple:** Quoted by Jennifer Radden in *The Nature of Melancholy: From Aristotle to Kristeva* (2000).

Page 273 **essay titled 'Blackness Ever Blackening':** In Mosaic: The Science of Life (2014). http://mosaicscience.com/story/blackness-ever-blackening-my-lifetime-depression. Retrieved 23 December 2015.

30. NICKNAMES

Page 283 **barbed and satirical remarks:** Joakin Garff, *Søren Kierkegaard: A Biography*, 2004.

Page 285 **one woman student took her own life:** Karl Löwith, *Martin Heidegger and European Nihilism*, 1998.

Page 286 **dig more deeply than others:** François Dosse, *History of Structuralism: The Rising Sign, 1945–1966* (1997).

31. OBFUSCATION

Page 288 **seek to know of them:** J. G. Fichte, *Foundations of the Science of Knowledge* (1794).

Page 291 **until it is recognized:** Jacques Lacan, *Écrits* (1966).

32. RACISM

Page 299 **the white races:** Arthur Schopenhauer, *Parerga and Paralipomena*, Vol. II (1851).

Page 300 **philosophy professors are black:** Tina Fernandes Botts et al., 'What is the State of Blacks in Philosophy?', *Critical Philosophy of Race*, Vol. 2, Issue 2, 2014, pp. 224–42.

33. SEX

Page 306 **it hasn't injured him!:** Epicurus, *The Art of Happiness*, ed. George K. Strodach (2012).

Page 307 **that reason for learning:** Noel Malcolm, *Aspects of Hobbes* (2004).

Page 308 **the congruence of triangles:** Ray Monk, *Bertrand Russell: The Spirit of Solitude 1872–1921* (1996).

Page 309 **eight times a day:** Ray Monk, *Ludwig Wittgenstein: The Duty of Genius* (1990).

Page 309 **ruined by sex:** See David Papineau's review of Ben Roger's *A. J. Ayer: A Life* in the *Times Higher Education Supplement*, 19 November 1999. His *New York Times* obituary (29 June 1989) cited among his achievements 'countless lovers'.

34. SPORT

Page 312 **orgies of hatred:** George Orwell, 'The Sporting Spirit', *Tribune* (1945).

Page 314 **not wrong in their heads:** *The Works of Lucian of Samosata*, translated by H. W. and F. G. Fowler (1905).

Page 315 **and philosophy are many:** Bruce Rosenstein, 'Gordon Marino, Q&A on the Intersection of Boxing & Philosophy', 13 September 2013.

Page 316 **such as anger and fear:** Gordon Marino, 'Fellowship of

the Ring: Boxing, Courage & Philosophy' (2008). http://
oldarchive.godspy.com/life/Fellowship-of-the-Ring-Boxing-
Courage-and-Philosophy-by-Gordon-Marino.cfm.html.
Retrieved 23 February 2015.

Page 316   **in contemporary American sports:** William Morgan, *Why
Sports Morally Matter* (2006).

Page 318   **our education was much less important:** Benoit Peeters,
Derrida: A Biography (2013).

Page 318   **knew nothing of life:** Allan C. Hutchinson, 'If Derrida Had
Played Football', *German Law Journal*, 6.1 (2005).

Page 321   **Epicurus' Letter to Menoeceus:** Henry Winter, 'Football
philosopher Joey Barton targets managerial career after
football playing days come to an end', *Daily Telegraph*,
13 December 2015.

35. TRUTH

Page 324   **half a million dead Iraqis:** 4,489 US military were killed,
with 316 allied deaths. Source: Brown University Watson
Institute of International & Public Affairs, 'Allied
Combatants Killed in Iraq March 2003–April 2015'.
http://watson.brown.edu/costsofwar/costs/human/military.
Retrieved 10 December 2015.

Page 326   **beyond anyone's reproach:** This argument is made by
the Universalist Unitarian Doug Muder in an essay, 'The
Unreasonable Influence of Geometry', 2000. http://www.
gurus.org/dougdeb/Essays/Geometry/geometry.html.
Retrieved 2 January 2015.

37. WALKING

Page 342   **concave curves (undulations):** Aristotle, 'On The Gait of
Animals'.

Page 342   **anatomist of melancholy:** Robert Burton, *The Anatomy of
Melancholy* (1621).

Page 344   **In 'The Road is How':** Søren Kierkegaard, *Eighteen
Upbuilding Discourses* (1843–4).

Page 347   **then you are ready for a walk:** H. D. Thoreau, 'Walking',
1862.

Page 348 **the thought struck me:** Friedrich Nietzsche, *Ecce Homo* (written in 1888, published in 1908).

38. WAR

Page 352 **the artificial conflict:** Bertrand Russell, *Justice in War-Time* (1916).

Page 354 **attacking a British position:** Alexander Waugh, *The House of Wittgenstein: A Family at War* (2008).

Page 355 **returned by his students:** James Luther Adams, Professor Emeritus of Christian Ethics, Harvard Divinity School in a letter to the *New York Times*, 23 February 1988.

Page 358 **found a new audience:** The American philosopher and jurist David Luban reports that a search of the *Lexis* legal database 'reveals five law review references to Schmitt between 1980 and 1990; 114 between 1990 and 2000; and 420 since 2000, with almost twice as many in the last five years as the previous five'. David Luban, 'Carl Schmitt and the Critique of Lawfare', *Georgetown Public Law and Legal Theory Research Paper* No. 11–33, 2011.

Page 360 **thirty million were killed:** An account by David Glantz et al. is titled *Slaughterhouse: The Handbook of the Eastern Front* (2004).

Page 360 **false readings of Bäumler:** Eric Oberheim, *Feyerabend's Philosophy*, 2006.

Page 362 **his literary mentors were fascist:** Jane O'Grady, 'Stuart Hampshire', *Guardian*, 15 June 2004.

39. WRITING

Page 365 **at the appointed hour:** Manfred Kuehn, *Kant: A Biography* (2001).

Page 366 **writing at great speed:** Richard Reeves, *John Stuart Mill: Victorian Firebrand* (2008).

Page 366 **expedient of stimulants:** Thomas Carlyle, *The Life of Friedrich Schiller* (1825).

ONLINE SOURCES OF PRIMARY TEXTS

Internet Classics Archive. Greeks, Romans and some Oriental.
http://classics.mit.edu/Browse/

Project Gutenburg. 42,000 free ebooks, including thousands of philosophy texts.
http://www.gutenberg.org/ebooks/

Online Philosophical Texts. Large selection from Greeks to Russell.
http://www.philosophy-index.com/texts.php

Early Modern Philosophy. Easily searchable library, fifteenth–nineteenth centuries.
http://www.earlymoderntexts.com/

Akamac Etexts. Selection of texts from the eighteenth to the twentieth centuries.
http://www.cpm.ll.ehime- u.ac.jp/AkamacHomePage/Akamac_E-text_Links/Akamac_E- text_Links.htm

The Internet Classics Archive. Collection curated by MIT.
http://classics.mit.edu/

Liberty Library. Classic works on constitutional government from the Greeks to contemporary thinkers.
http://www.constitution.org/liberlib.htm

ONLINE PHILOSOPHY ENCYCLOPAEDIAS

Internet Encyclopedia of Philosophy. Peer-reviewed, unfunded.
Articles are written by experts in a style accessible to most readers.
http://www.iep.utm.edu/
Publisher's statement: 'The purpose of the *IEP* is to provide detailed,
scholarly information on key topics and philosophers in all areas
of philosophy. The Encyclopedia's articles are written with the
intention that most of the article can be understood by advanced
undergraduates majoring in philosophy and by other scholars who
are not working in the field covered by that article. The *IEP* articles
are written by experts but not for experts in analogy to the way the
Scientific American magazine is written by scientific experts but not
primarily for scientific experts.'

Stanford Encyclopedia of Philosophy. Peer-reviewed, grant-funded.
Articles are thorough and contain detailed technical information that
non-experts may find difficult.
http://plato.stanford.edu/
Publisher's statement: 'From its inception, the *SEP* was designed so
that each entry is maintained and kept up-to-date by an expert or
group of experts in the field. All entries and substantive updates are
refereed by the members of a distinguished Editorial Board before they
are made public. Consequently, our dynamic reference work maintains
academic standards while evolving and adapting in response to new
research. You can cite fixed editions that are created on a quarterly
basis and stored in our Archives (every entry contains a link to its
complete archival history, identifying the fixed edition the reader
should cite).'

BIBLIOGRAPHY OF SECONDARY WORKS CITED

Bankovsky, Miriam, *Perfecting Justice in Rawls, Habermas and Honneth*, London: Bloomsbury Academic, 2012.

Bayley, John, *Iris: The Life of Iris Murdoch*, London: Gerald Duckworth & Co., 2012.

Boswell, James, *Life of Samuel Johnson*, London: H. Baldwin for C. Dilly, 1791.

Cook, John W., *Wittgenstein, Empiricism, and Language*, Oxford: Oxford University Press, 1999.

Crowe, Michael J., *The Extraterrestrial Life Debate, 1750–1900*, Cambridge: Cambridge University Press, 1986.

Deakin, Michael A. B., *Hypatia of Alexandria: Mathematician and Martyr*, New York: Prometheus Books, 2007.

Dosse, François, *History of Structuralism: The Rising Sign, 1945–1966*, Minneapolis, MN: University of Minnesota Press, 1997.

Fieser, James, *Early Responses to Hume's Life and Reputation*, London: Continuum, 2003.

Garff, Joakin, *Søren Kierkegaard: A Biography*, Princeton, NJ: Princeton University Press, 2004.

Gerassi, John, *Talking with Sartre*, New Haven, CT: Yale University Press, 2009.

Globus, Gordon G., *Dream Life, Wake Life*, Albany, NY: SUNY Press, 1987.

Hale, John R., *Lords of the Sea: The Epic Story of the Athenian Navy and the Birth of Democracy*, London: J. P. Tarcher/Penguin Putnam, 2009.

Hermanns, William, *Einstein and the Poet: In Search of the Cosmic Man*, Wellesley, MA: Branden Press, 1983.

Hillman, David, *The Chemical Muse*, New York: Macmillan, 2008.

Kuehn, Manfred, *Kant: A Biography*, Cambridge: Cambridge University Press, 2001.

Löwith, Karl, *Martin Heidegger and European Nihilism*, New York: Columbia University Press, 1998.

Malcolm, Noel, *Aspects of Hobbes*, Oxford: Clarendon Press, 2004.

Mignon, Ernest, *Les Mots du Général*, Paris: Livre de Poche/Fayard, 1962.

Monk, Ray, *Bertrand Russell: The Ghost of Madness, 1921–1970*, New York: Free Press, 2001.

Monk, Ray, *Ludwig Wittgenstein: The Duty of Genius*, London: Jonathan Cape, 1991.

Nadler, Steven, *Spinoza: A Life*, Cambridge: Cambridge University Press, 2001.

Oberheim, Eric, *Feyerabend's Philosophy*, Berlin: Walter de Gruyter, 2006.

Pickering, Mary, *August Comte*: Vol. 3, *An Intellectual Biography*, Cambridge: Cambridge University Press, 2009.

Radden, Jennifer, *The Nature of Melancholy: From Aristotle to Kristeva*, Oxford: Oxford University Press, 2000.

Reeves, Richard, *John Stuart Mill: Victorian Firebrand*, London: Atlantic Books, 2008.

Ruck, A. P., *Sacred Mushrooms of the Goddess*, Berkeley, CA: Ronin Publishing, 2006.

Silverman, Lisa, *Becoming Austrians: Jews and Culture Between the World Wars*, New York: Oxford University Press, 2012.

Springett, Ben, 'Dreams', Internet Encyclopedia of Philosophy. Retrieved 21 December 2014. www.iep.utm.edu/dreaming/#SH3b.

Stadler, Friedrich, 'Documentation: The Murder of Moritz Schlick', in Stadler (ed.), *The Vienna Circle. Studies in the Origins, Development, and Influence of Logical Empiricism*, New York: Springer, 2001.

Tooley, Sarah, *Victoria, Queen of Britain*, New York: Dodd, Mead, 1897.

Waugh, Alexander, *The House of Wittgenstein: A Family at War*, New York: Doubleday, 2008.

Yue-Ching Ho, Eugene, 'At 90, and Still Dynamic: Revisiting Sir Karl Popper and Attending His Birthday Party', *Intellectus* 23 July–September 1992.

ACKNOWLEDGEMENTS

This book was conceived in the village of Limpley Stoke in Wiltshire and realized in Nashville, Tennessee. Several people deserve thanks for their assistance in ways big and small. I'm grateful to my agent Julian Alexander of Lucas Alexander Whitley for his wisdom and business acumen. This book is the brainchild of my longtime friend and collaborator Richard Milbank, nonfiction publisher at Head of Zeus. His broad learning, editorial skill, charm and wit are a constant delight. My thanks to Richard Collins for copy editing and Colleen Murphy for assistance with the apparatus.

In Nashville I have spent many happy hours discussing with W. T. Davidson several of the philosophical issues treated in this book. His innate sense of fair play, disposition to reflection and ready wit have been of enormous help to me while composing this text.

My greatest debt is to my partner, Colleen Murphy. Her willingness to adapt to my weird circadian rhythms, long periods of silence while writing and manic outbursts while not writing, is more than any scribbler could hope for.

Fiona Pitt-Kethley, Fiona Kelso, Kirk Parsons, Kate Ray, Havi Carel and Bharat Tandon provided useful information. Among the most useful things Bharat supplied were colourful accounts of Arsenal scores across a six-hour time difference.

GLOSSARY OF IDEAS
To be used in conjunction with the Index of Philosophers

ANALYTIC PHILOSOPHY The broad tendency in Anglophone philosophy that started with Gottlob Frege's work in grounding arithmetic in logic. It was taken up by Bertrand Russell and G. E. Moore, along with Ludwig Wittgenstein, to make a style of philosophy that reduced problems to their component parts, dismissing metaphysical approaches as meaningless.

ANXIETY Søren Kierkegaard characterized the position of humankind in the face of death as anxiety or dread. This theme was further elaborated by Martin Heidegger as **being-towards-death**.

A PRIORI A priori knowledge is derived before experience. Immanuel Kant said that the truths of geometry are given to us a priori.

ATOMISM The belief held by fifth-century BC philosophers Leucippus and Democritus that physical beings and things in the world are composed of atoms – particles of varying size – that give us and objects their physical presence.

AUTHENTICITY In Martin Heidegger's *Being and Time* (1927) the condition of *Dasein* or the human being coming to terms with its defining nature as **being-towards-death**. It is also used by Jean-Paul Sartre and the existentialists.

BEING-TOWARDS-DEATH In Martin Heidegger's philosophy, the defining condition of our existence, *Dasein*. Death is destiny and our lives are lived in the context of embracing that fact (or not, which would be inauthenticity).

CLASS In sociology and political theory, a term to denote the status of an individual. It can be determined by birth (nobility, common) or, in the sense used by Karl Marx, to describe a person's relationship to an economic power matrix; for instance, bourgeoisie (owners of capital) or working class (labourers).

COPERNICAN TURN In the *Critique of Pure Reason* (1781) Immanuel Kant argued that space, time and causal relations are to be attributed to the perceiving mind. This was to philosophy what Nicolaus Copernicus's declaration that the Earth revolves around the Sun (and not vice versa) was to astronomy, in that it upset the prevailing paradigm.

CRITICAL THEORY Its original meaning referred to a method of interpretation developed by members of the **Frankfurt School,** including Theodore Adorno, Max Horkheimer and Herbert Marcuse, which employed Marxist and Freudian ideas. Latterly it is used loosely to describe the activities of post-structuralists.

CYNICISM School of ancient Greek philosophy developed by Socrates' pupil Antisthenes in the late fifth century BC and then by Diogenes of Sinope. For Cynics the purpose of life was to live in virtue, in agreement with nature. Cynics rejected conventional desires for wealth, power, sex and fame, pursuing a simple life free from all possessions.

DASEIN Term used by the German philosopher Martin Heidegger to refer to the human condition of being. He defined it in his inaugural address as rector of Freiburg in 1933 as 'the power of the beginning of our spiritual-historical being (*Dasein*). This beginning is the setting out of Greek philosophy.'

DIALECTIC Term usually associated with G. W. F. Hegel, whose dialectical method involved the positing of a thesis, countered by an antithesis, yielding a synthesis.

DIALECTICAL MATERIALISM Term used by Joseph Dietzgen to describe a method of understanding reality through the combination of Feuerbach's materialism and Hegel's dialectic. It was the official philosophy of the Soviet Union and other communist states.

DUALISM The view that mind and body are separate (as opposed to **monism,** in which they are a unity). Plato was a dualist, as was René Descartes.

EMBODIMENT/EMBODIED SUBJECT Philosophical concern with the fact of the human subject being embodied. The problem of embodiment is central to the work of existentialists such as Søren Kierkegaard, Jean-Paul Sartre, Maurice Merleau-Ponty and, latterly, Julia Kristeva.

EMPIRICISM The position that knowledge derives from experience.

EPICUREANISM The Greek philosopher Epicurus advocated a life which avoided overindulgence and moderation. He avoided material interests, preferring to develop friendships and practise introspection.

ETERNAL RECURRENCE/ETERNAL RETURN A concept in the work of Friedrich Nietzsche, premised on the idea that each moment should be lived as if it will occur again and again in an endless circle.

EXISTENTIALISM European philosophical tendency (beginning with Søren Kierkegaard and descending through Martin Heidegger to Jean-Paul Sartre, Maurice Merleau-Ponty and others) to describe a concern with the ontological status of the subject after the death of God (although Kierkegaard was a Christian, as was the leading existentialist Gabriel Marcel).

FRANKFURT SCHOOL The Institute for Social Research – more popularly known as the Frankfurt School – is also a catch-all term to encompass the Marxist **critical theory** for which it became famous through the work of Max Horkheimer, Theodor Adorno, Erich Fromm and Herbert Marcuse. During the Second World War the school moved to Columbia University in New York.

GAME THEORY An attempt mathematically to describe subjects' behaviour in real-life games, like economics and politics, a sort of calculus of choices.

HEDONISM An ancient school of thought, promoted in the fifth and fourth centuries BC by Aristippus of Cyrene, which argues that pleasure is the most important intrinsic good. Pleasure is to be maximized while pain is to be avoided. Hedonists believe that persons have the right to pursue pleasure as they will, except when their actions violate the rights of others.

HERMENEUTICS Originally a term to describe the interpretation of biblical texts, it became in the hands of nineteenth-century German scholars like Friedrich Schleiermacher and Wilhelm Dilthey a tool for the analysis of larger 'texts', such as groups or societies. Hermeneutics was developed in the twentieth century by Martin Heidegger, Hans-Georg Gadamer and Paul Ricoeur. The hermeneutic circle refers to the analysis of texts by relating parts to the whole.

HISTORICISM The view that outcomes are historically determined.

This view was famously challenged by Karl Popper in *The Poverty of Historicism* (1957) and *The Open Society and Its Enemies* (1945). By believing in all-encompassing 'laws' of history, Plato, Hegel and Marx were the forerunners of **totalitarianism**.

INTENTIONALITY In the **phenomenology** of Edmund Husserl, the means by which objects of consciousness are constituted. Husserl's master Franz Brentano had reintroduced the term to modern philosophy, borrowing it from the **Scholastic** Anselm. But the term may also be traced back to Parmenides' fifth-century BC poem *On Nature*, and the discussion of the problem of what is.

INTERSUBJECTIVITY Refers to mechanisms or conditions under which our experience and perception of the world can be confirmed by and shared with others. It is a particularly significant theme in **phenomenology** and **existentialism**.

INTUITION A slightly fuzzy term often used to refer to the phenomenon of becoming immediately aware of something. It is specifically defined by Henri Bergson in *Creative Evolution* (1907): 'By intuition I mean instinct that has become disinterested, self-conscious, capable of reflecting upon its object and of enlarging it indefinitely.'

LINGUISTIC PHILOSOPHY A programme of thinking that identifies philosophical problems as ones that can be solved (or dissolved) by a proper understanding and application of language.

LOGICAL POSITIVISM Doctrine developed principally by Moritz Schlick and Rudolf Carnap (leaders of the Vienna Circle) which held metaphysics to be without meaning, and which judged a meaningful statement as one being verifiable using logical analysis.

LOGICISM School of mathematics which holds that the fundamental concepts of mathematics can be deduced from the laws of logic. This was the task of Bertrand Russell and A. N. Whitehead in *Principia Mathematica* (1910–13).

MATERIALISM The ontological position that everything that exists does so in material form, that it occupies space.

MONISM Literally 'oneness', from the Greek *monos* (single), monism signifies the notion of unity, as in the indivisibility of mind and body.

It is the opposite of **dualism,** where mind and body are conceived as separate.

NATALITY Term used by Hannah Arendt to describe the situation from which the subject proceeds towards its future, full of possibilities for freedom. It is posited to supplement the view of her teacher Martin Heidegger that we are characterized by **being-towards-death.**

NATURALISM The belief that all phenomena are ultimately accountable for by the methods used in the natural sciences.

NEOPLATONISM Neoplatonism is a term coined in the mid-nineteenth century to embrace a range of philosophies that were based on the thought of Plato, but which often sought to reconcile Plato's **dualism** with a religious worldview. The third-century Greek philosopher Plotinus was the first proponent of Neoplatonism.

NIHILISM A term first used by Ivan Turgenev in his novel *Fathers and Sons* (1862) to describe an attitude that denies all traditional values and moral truths. It is often used to describe the condition of believing in nothing. Friedrich Nietzsche is erroneously described as a nihilist, but he wanted to rediscover new values after the 'death of God', not to continue without any.

OTHER, THE In **phenomenology** (and particularly in the **existentialism** of Jean-Paul Sartre and Simone de Beauvoir) the Other is a necessary but threatening subject. On the one hand, by recognizing me, the Other confirms my existence and creates an intersubjective bond (*see* **intersubjectivity**). On the other hand, the gaze of the Other reduces me to the status of an object and denies my subjectivity.

PHENOMENOLOGY School of philosophy developed by Edmund Husserl that uses the method of eidetic reduction to eliminate preconceptions (bracketing them out) and so perceive the essences of phenomena under study. It is the dominant trend of twentieth-century thinking and it continues to inform post-structuralism.

POSITIVISM Term coined by Auguste Comte to describe the view that all phenomena can be understood by scientific method. Comte used his positivist method to study subjects that would now fall under the heading of sociology. It was on foundations laid by Comte that Émile Durkheim created sociology as an academic discipline.

PRE-SOCRATIC Term used by Eduard Zeller in his *Plato and the Other Companions of Sokrates* (1865) to refer to ancient Greek philosophers before Socrates.

REPRESSIVE TOLERANCE In his essay *Repressive Tolerance* (1965) Herbert Marcuse identified the mechanism which governs unfreedom as the 'ideology of tolerance, which, in reality, favours and fortifies the conservation of the status quo of inequality and discrimination'.

SCHOLASTICISM The medieval philosophy of the Church Fathers developed to define orthodoxy and to train theologians in the logical skills necessary for the defence of orthodoxy against heresy, and against the arguments of 'infidels'. The high point of Scholastic philosophy was the work of St Thomas Aquinas.

SOLIPSISM The position that only one's self and one's experiences exist. It is the opposite of **intersubjectivity**.

SOPHISM A style of teaching in ancient Greece by teachers who combined philosophy with rhetoric to instruct young politicians and the wealthy who sought wider influence. Unlike Socrates, sophists charged for their services. Plato has Socrates condemn them in his dialogues, the source of the modern use of the term as perjorative in relation to those – mainly politicians – who speak in riddles.

SPIRIT In the work of G. W. F. Hegel there are three types of spirit: subjective, objective and absolute. Subjective spirit is the physical and psychological existence of individual human beings. Objective spirit describes the structure of the communal world outside. Absolute spirit refers to knowledge and freedom accrued over time and expressed in religion, art and philosophy.

STOICISM School of thought founded by Zeno of Citium in the early third century BC. The Stoics held that virtue derives from maintaining a will that accords with nature. The good life is obtained by understanding the rules of nature and by being in harmony with it.

STRUCTURALISM A broad term used to describe a range of interdisciplinary activities that derive from the work of Ferdinand de Saussure, who argued that language was to be understood as a system with a particular structure, rather than a given set of words with fixed meanings. Gradually this methodology grew to include the study of everything – from historical movements to movies – that could be construed as a system whose signs could be identified and decoded. Early structuralists included Claude Lévi-Strauss and Roland Barthes, although Barthes soon became a post-structuralist.

TELEOLOGY The study of 'ends'; the belief that events and phenomena occur to some 'end' and therefore are explicable (and have meaning). The creationist position that God created the world in six days and put all life on it is a teleological one that is negated by evolutionary science. Aristotle's philosophy is based on the teleological premise that a prime mover is responsible for putting the world in motion. That view was superseded by Isaac Newton's discovery of gravity.

TOTALITARIANISM A system of government whereby the state has control of all institutions, public and private. The fascist (Germany, Italy, Spain) and communist (Soviet Union, China) examples of totalitarianism in the twentieth century were characterized by one-party rule and the use of military and police forces to keep order and punish deviation. Totalitarian regimes require adherence to dogma and discourage free thought, argument or disagreement. As a result they become intellectually weak. The discouragement of free thought leads to stagnation in science and philosophy.

TRANSCENDENTAL IDEALISM Immanuel Kant's doctrine that objects of perception do not just give themselves to consciousness, but that the subject plays an active role in perceiving them.

UTILITARIANISM Ethical theory proposed by Jeremy Bentham, James Mill and J. S. Mill, summarized by the latter thus: 'actions are right in proportion as they tend to promote happiness, wrong as they tend to promote the reverse of happiness'.

INDEX OF PHILOSOPHERS CITED

Averroes (1126–98). Andalusian polymath, Islamic theologian and promoter of secular thought: *278–9 (Nicknames)*

Ayer, A. J. (1910–89). British logical positivist: *35 (Backbiting), 309 (Sex), 332–3 (Truth)*

Bacon, Francis (1561–1626). English empiricist and founder of the scientific method: *207 (Hope)*

Bacon, Roger (*c*.1214–*c*.1292). English scholastic philosopher and advocate of the Aristotelian scientific method: *280 (Nicknames)*

Baxter, Richard (1615–91). English philosopher and Nonconformist pastor: *168 (God)*

Beauvoir, Simone de (1908–86). French existentialist and feminist: *12, 18 (Ageing), 286 (Nicknames)*

Bentham, Jeremy (1748–1832). British philosopher, founder of utilitarianism: *91 (Drugs), 276 (Nicknames)*

Bergson, Henri (1859–1941). French philosopher who put intuition above rationalism: *215 (Illness), 231–2 (Intuition)*

Berkeley, George (1685–1753). Anglo-Irish bishop who advocated idealism: *56–57 (Consciousness), 329 (Truth)*

Berlin, Isaiah (1909–97). Russo-British philosopher and social and political theorist: *132, 143–5 (Freedom)*

Bias of Priene (sixth century BC). Philosopher and legislator, one of the 'Seven Sages' of Greece: *234 (Justice)*

Bodin, Jean (1530–96). French philosopher who developed the theory of the divine right of kings: *136 (Freedom)*

Bonhoeffer, Dietrich (1906–45). German theologian executed for supporting a plot against Hitler: *356 (War)*

Boethius (*c*.480–524). Roman Neoplatonist, executed for 'treason': *336–7 (Vanity)*

Brillat-Savarin, Jean Anthelme (1755–1826). French lawyer and politician, father of the gastronomic essay: *126–8 (Food)*

Burke, Edmund (1729–97). Irish philosopher who is regarded as the father of modern conservative thinking: *136–7, 139 (Freedom)*

Burton, Robert (1577–1640). English rector and scholar known for his study of melancholy: *17 (Ageing), 269–72 (Melancholy), 342 (Walking)*

Carel, Havi (1970–). British 'continental' philosopher of medicine and illness: *215–17 (Illness)*

Carnap, Rudolf (1891–1970). German-American logical positivist: *35 (Backbiting), 257 (Martyrdom)*

Celer, Caninius (second century AD). Greek rhetorician, tutor to Marcus Aurelius: *65 (Day Jobs)*

Chrysippus (*c*.279–*c*.206 BC). Greek Stoic who developed a system of propositional logic: *16 (Ageing), 45 (Chance)*

Chrysostom, Dio (*c*. AD 40–*c*.115). Greek Stoic and Platonist: *192 (Haircuts), 200 (Happiness)*

Cicero, Marcus Tullius (106–43 BC). Roman philosopher and politician who promoted Greek philosophy: *16–17 (Ageing), 94–95 (Duty), 184–6 (Grief), 336 (Vanity)*

Clausewitz, Carl Philipp Gottfried von (1780–1831). Prussian theorist of war: *353–4, 359 (War)*

Cohen, Philippe (1953–2013). Algerian-born French journalist and essayist: *36 (Backbiting)*

Comte, Auguste (1798–1857). French philosopher and founder of the doctrine of positivism: *9–10 (Advice), 220, 222–3 (Insanity), 276 (Nicknames)*

Condorcet, Marquis de (1743–94). French philosopher, reformer and advocate of women's rights: *297–8 (Racism)*

Copernicus, Nicolaus (1473–1543). Polish mathematician and astronomer: *38, 40 (Belief), 110–11 (Extraterrestrials), 266 (Melancholy), 281 (Nicknames), 327–8 (Truth)*

Corvinus, Matthias (1443–90). King of Hungary, Croatia and Bohemia and Duke of Austria; a philosopher king: *176 (Governing)*

Crantor (mid-fourth century BC–276/5 BC). Greek Platonist *184, 186 (Grief)*

Crito of Alopece (*c*.469 BC–fourth century BC). Greek member of Socrates' inner circle: *254 (Martyrdom)*

Dawkins, Richard (1941–). British ethologist and evolutionary biologist who takes a gene-centred view of evolution: *42 (Belief), 172–3 (God)*

Democritus of Abdera (*c.*460–*c.*370 BC). Pre-Socratic philosopher and atomist, referred to as the 'father of modern science': *44 (Chance), 108 (Extraterrestrials), 246 (Laughing), 276 (Nicknames)*

Dennett, Daniel (1942–). American analytic philosopher: *51 (Chance), 78–79 (Dreams), 173 (God)*

Descartes, René (1596–1650). French philosopher and mathematician famous for his reductive method: *23–25 (Animals), 54–55, 58–59 (Consciousness), 67 (Day Jobs), 75 (Dreams), 228 (Intuition), 320–21 (Sport), 329 (Truth), 364 (Writing)*

Dewey, John (1859–1952). American pragmatist and founder of functional psychology: *209–10 (Hope)*

Diogenes Laertius (*c.* third century AD). Greek biographer of eminent philosophers: *108 (Extraterrestrials), 198–9 (Happiness), 277 (Nicknames)*

Diogenes of Sinope (*c.*412–323 BC). Greek founder of the philosophy of Cynicism: *15 (Ageing), 199–200 (Happiness)*

Einstein, Albert (1879–1955). German-American theoretical physicist who developed theories of relativity: *45 (Chance), 117 (Extraterrestrials), 170 (God), 229–31 (Intuition)*

Emerson, Ralph Waldo (1803–82). American essayist, poet and Transcendentalist: *152–4 (Friendship)*

Engels, Friedrich (1820–95). German philosopher and co-founder, with Karl Marx, of the theory of Marxism: *69–70 (Day Jobs), 141 (Freedom)*

Epictetus (*c.* AD 55–135). Greek Stoic philosopher: *201 (Happiness)*

Epicurus (341–270 BC). Greek founder of Epicureanism: *16 (Ageing), 108 (Extraterrestrials), 149 (Friendship), 198 (Happiness), 216 (Illness), 268 (Melancholy), 305 (Sex), 321 (Sport)*

Erdős, Paul (1913–96). Hungarian mathematician: *89 (Drugs)*

Euclid (mid-fourth century–mid-third century BC). Greek mathematician, father of geometry: *308 (Sex), 325–26 (Truth)*

Feuerbach, Ludwig Andreas (1804–72). German philosopher and anthropologist: *171 (God)*

Macer, Aninus (second century AD). Greek tutor to Marcus Aurelius: *65 (Day Jobs)*

Machiavelli, Niccolò di Bernardo dei (1469–1527). Italian Renaissance politician, diplomat and philosopher, often described as the founder of modern political science: *8 (Advice), 321 (Sport)*

Maimonides (1135–1204). Córdoban-born Sephardic Jewish philosopher, astronomer, physician and Torah scholar: *30 (Backbiting), 279–80 (Nicknames)*

Malcolm, Norman (1911–90). American analytic philosopher: *78 (Dreams)*

Marcel, Gabriel (1889–1973). French Christian existentialist: *208–10 (Hope)*

Marcuse, Herbert (1898–1979). German-American philosopher and political and social theorist; a member of the Frankfurt School: *141–2 (Freedom), 284 (Nicknames)*

Marx, Karl (1818–83). German-born thinker who studied capital–labour relations and created, with Engels, the revolutionary-critical philosophy that bears his name: *36 (Backbiting), 69–70 (Day Jobs), 132, 139–41 (Freedom), 176, 179, 181 (Governing), 228 (Intuition), 292 (Obfuscation)*

Merleau-Ponty, Maurice (1908–61). French phenomenologist and existentialist: *216–17 (Illness)*

Mettrie, Julien Offray de La (1709–51). French physician and materialist philosopher: *128–9 (Food)*

Mill, John Stuart (1806–1873). English empiricist philosopher, political economist, and influential theorist of liberty: *26 (Animals), 44 (Chance), 91 (Drugs), 139 (Freedom), 220, 225 (Insanity), 240 (Justice), 329 (Truth), 366 (Writing)*

Mises, Ludwig von (1881–1973). Austrian-American leader of the Austrian School of economic thought: *257 (Martyrdom)*

Monod, Jacques (1910–76). French molecular biologist: *47–49 (Chance)*

Montaigne, Michel Eyquem de (1533–92). French Renaissance philosopher, creator of the essay as a literary genre: *4 (Advice), 24–25 (Animals), 150–51 (Friendship), 268–70 (Melancholy), 329 (Truth), 337 (Vanity)*

Pythagoras of Samos (*c.*570–*c.*495 BC). Greek philosopher and mathematician: *15 (Ageing), 22 (Animals), 109 (Extraterrestrials), 121 (Food), 149 (Friendship)*

Quine, Willard Van Orman (1908–2000). American analytical philosopher and logician: *39 (Belief)*

Rawls, John (1921–2002). American moral and legal philosopher: *104–6 (Duty), 241–3 (Justice)*

Regan, Tom (1938–). American animal rights theorist: *26 (Animals)*

Rorty, Richard (1931–2007). American pragmatist who advocated a 'post-philosophical' culture: *333 (Truth)*

Rousseau, Jean-Jacques (1712–78). Genevan-born political philosopher, novelist and social contract theorist: *135, 137 (Freedom), 329 (Truth), 343–4 (Walking)*

Russell, Bertrand (1872–1970). British mathematician and a founder of analytic philosophy: *32–33 (Backbiting), 42 (Belief), 70 (Day Jobs), 161 (Fun), 203 (Happiness), 220 (Insanity), 232 (Intuition), 277 (Nicknames), 300 (Racism), 308–9 (Sex), 326 (Truth), 352 (War)*

Saint-Simon, Henri de (1760–1825). French political and economic theorist: *220, 222–3 (Insanity)*

Sartre, Jean-Paul (1905–80). French existentialist philosopher, novelist and dramatist: *35–36 (Backbiting), 87–89 (Drugs), 286 (Nicknames), 290 (Obfuscation), 309–10 (Sex), 329 (Truth)*

Schelling, F. W. J. (1775–1854). German idealist philosopher: *288 (Obfuscation)*

Schiller, Friedrich (1759–1805). German idealist philosopher and playwright: *366 (Writing)*

Schmitt, Carl (1888–1985). German legal and political philosopher, editor-in-chief of the Nazi legal review *Deutsche Juristen-Zeitung*: *357–8 (War)*

Schopenhauer, Arthur (1788–1860). German thinker who held that our world is governed by a metaphysical concept of will; a pessimist: *31–32 (Backbiting), 180 (Dreams), 189 (Grief), 249–50 (Laughing), 299 (Racism)*

Searle, John (1932–). American analytical philosopher of language and mind: *25 (Animals)*

Wilkins, John (1614–72). English Anglican clergyman, natural philosopher and a founder of the Royal Society: *111 (Extraterrestrials)*

Wittgenstein, Ludwig (1889–1951). Austrian-British analytic philosopher and author of the *Tractatus Logico-Philosophicus*: *30, 32–33 (Backbiting), 78 (Dreams), 220 (Insanity) 257 (Martrydom), 271 (Melancholy), 308 (Sex), 352 (War)*

Xenophon (*c*.430–354 BC). Greek historian and soldier, friend of Socrates: *2–3 (Advice), 15 (Ageing), 44–45, 49 (Chance), 352 (War)*

Zeno of Citium (*c*.334–262 BC). Greek founder of the Stoic school of philosophy: *16 (Ageing), 64 (Day Jobs)*

Zeno of Elea (490–430 BC). Pre–Socratic philosopher credited with inventing the dialectic: *149 (Friendship)*